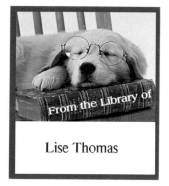

THE DOG WHO WOULD BE KING

Tales and Surprising Lessons from a Pet Psychologist

By John C. Wright, Ph.D.,
with Judi Wright Lashnits

Rodale Press, Inc.
Emmaus, Pennsylvania

Copyright © 1999 by John C. Wright and Judi Wright Lashnits

Illustrations copyright © 1999 by William Bramhall
Photographs copyright © 1999 by Mitch Mandel

All rights reserved. No part of this publication may be reproduced or transmitted in any form or by any means, electronic or mechanical, including photocopying, recording, or any other information storage and retrieval system, without the written permission of the publisher.

Printed in the United States of America on acid-free ∞ , recycled paper ♻

Interior and Cover Designer: Christina Gaugler
Layout Designer: Keith Biery
Cover Photographer: Mitch Mandel
Cover Author Photographer: Rod Reilly

Library of Congress Cataloging-in-Publication Data

Wright, John C., 1947–
   The dog who would be king : tales and surprising lessons from a pet psychologist / by John C. Wright with Judi Wright Lashnits.
      p.   cm.
   Includes index.
   ISBN 1–57954–002–3   hardcover
      1. Dogs—Behavior.   2. Dogs—Psychology.   3. Animal behavior therapy.
   4. Dogs—Anecdotes.   5. Wright, John C., 1947– .   6. Animal behavior
   therapists—United States—Biography.   I. Lashnits, Judi Wright.   II. Title.
   SF433.W75   1999
   636.7'089'689—dc21   98–39965

Distributed to the book trade by St. Martin's Press

2   4   6   8   10   9   7   5   3   1   hardcover

OUR PURPOSE

*"We inspire and enable people to improve
their lives and the world around them."*

For Zuk, my first and best canine companion
—J. C. W.

For Scout
—J. W. L.

Contents

Acknowledgments

I am grateful to the families and their pets whom I have come to know so well, and to my animal behaviorist colleagues whose knowledge and openness continue to make being in the profession a gratifying experience. Judi and I wish to thank our editor, Matthew Hoffman, and our agent, Jim Frenkel, for their guidance, encouragement, and good strokes. We'd also like to thank our families, especially Angie, Tom, Erin, and John for their patience, understanding, and enthusiasm.

Introduction

KNEELING JUST IN FRONT OF THE police department's holding pen, I braced myself for another lunge from the pit bull inside. In spite of my deliberately playful greeting—"Hi, fella, nice puppy!"—the agitated three-year-old male was clearly not interested in making friends. He threw himself at the fence, growling and biting at the metal barrier that separated us.

I suddenly remembered a conversation I had had months before with a Texas animal-control officer who had just built a special enclosure just for pit bulls. "Darn things can chew right through a chain-link fence," he told me. The pen that currently separated me from 45 pounds of snarling fury had not been built with enraged pit bulls in mind. I tried not to think about that as I got on with the testing.

"Go-o-o-od dog," I said. But the dog charged again. So much for the friendly approach. I took a deep breath and changed my tune. Still kneeling at the fence, I leaned forward a little and stared directly into the dog's eyes. I lowered my voice and growled, "Don't . . . you . . . look . . . at . . . me."

At such an approach from a stranger, considered by many animal behaviorists to be a very mild threat, friendly dogs typically become even more friendly and submissive: avoiding eye contact, wagging their tails, grinning, bowing, or rolling onto their backs. Aggressive dogs get irritated.

The pit bull went berserk. His lunges became more powerful and saliva dripped from his jaws as he frantically tore at the fence. His eyes were locked with mine, his teeth just a few inches from my neck. Again he snarled furiously. There was no question in my mind that he would tear me apart if he could get to me. Just a few days earlier, running with two other pit bulls, he had gone for the neck of a four-year-old boy.

I stood my ground as the dog pushed against the fence. This was definitely not a job I wanted to have to do many more times in my life. I wondered if his female companions in the adjoining pens would react to me with equal fury.

At long last, I got the signal from my colleague. I gratefully stood up and backed away from the cage for a moment before moving on to the next procedure in my role as the "stimulus person." I was collaborating with a behaviorist from a humane society in order to evaluate and videotape the three pit bulls. The results of our socialization and aggression assessment was to be used as evidence in the legal case against the owner.

The owner of those pit bulls was eventually found guilty and sentenced to five years in prison for involuntary manslaughter. It was one of the first convictions in the nation to result in an owner being incarcerated for irresponsible pet ownership.

That's about as bad as it can get. A child killed by a dog represents the ultimate failure of the human-animal bond. "Man's best friend" in the wrong circumstances has the potential to become a vicious killer, unable to discriminate between a human being and a target to be attacked.

At the opposite end of the spectrum are dogs leading the blind, warning people with epilepsy of impending seizures, conducting search-and-rescue missions, and helping developmentally challenged people improve their fine motor skills. There are dogs teaching prisoners about caring and responsibility, brightening the days of people in nursing homes, and aiding police and fire departments in crucial and often dangerous operations.

Between these two extremes are the millions of dogs who are companion animals in more than 50 million households throughout the country. None of them is perfect. But most dogs are loved despite one or two annoying habits that owners just put up with because Buster is so good with the kids or Duchess is a great pal to have on early-morning jogs.

Hundreds of thousands of owners, however, find that they just cannot tolerate something that their dogs do. Eventually, owners become desperate and the once-adored dogs are given away or left with the local humane society. The shelters are full of these healthy but unruly animals. Very likely, they could have been pleasant pets if only they had been given some basic care and attention. Even then, good manners on the leash or obedience to commands does not always translate into good behavior the rest of the time. It's just not that simple.

Nearly a third of the dogs that I have worked with have been to obedience school. Dropouts and graduates alike are referred to me by their trainers. These are the same animals that are biting their owners, howling in the backyard all day, tearing up the house, or urinating on the sofa. Or maybe they are incessantly licking a paw, going nuts when there's a thunderstorm, or biting the vet. And on and on.

Until pretty recently, people couldn't do much to help pets with tough behavioral problems like these because nobody really knew what to do. Even though dogs have been domesticated for at least 10,000 years, we are just beginning to understand what motivates them and how they learn. There have been so few scientific studies on the development of dog behavior that much of what is "known" is actually mere speculation. As animal behaviorists learn more about what normal dog behavior is, we will be better able to understand and correct tough behavioral problems, and so will owners.

A DECADE AGO, THE CONCEPT OF A "pet shrink" was drawing laughs on late-night TV. Today, many people have begun to use the resources of trained consultants who have devoted many years to learning about the behavior of companion animals. Unfortunately, by the time pet owners turn to such experts, they are usually desperate. Our services are often the last resort before they give up.

There are fewer than 50 certified applied animal behaviorists in North America, so the right kind of assistance is not easy to find. Even when owners locate a certified behaviorist—most of whom have doctorates in psychology or another behavioral science—they're not sure what to expect. Unlike trainers or obedience instructors, animal behaviorists don't work in the clinical confines of an office or training area. Instead, we prefer to see a dog in its own environment. We're more like detectives, looking for clues and piecing together pieces of a puzzle to figure out what will help each particular pooch get back to normal. We want to know which doors the dog avoids, which toys she guards, where she eats or hides, and what she jumps out from behind when she decides to bite her owners.

I don't get many clients who are concerned about training issues, like puppies chewing on shoes, digging holes in the backyard, or jumping up on people. These things can be learned from a number of excellent books or videos and by giving puppies a foundation in obedience and treating them decently. Generally, failure to learn good manners is not going to get dogs sent away forever.

In my practice, I concentrate on life-threatening issues, like aggression toward humans or other animals, excessive barking that is driving the neighbors crazy, or separation anxiety, which causes dogs to spend each day destroying valuable property or hurting themselves. When I say life-threatening, I mean the animal's life, because no one is going to put up with these kinds of problems until the dog "grows out of it," which he won't.

My phone calls sometimes go like this: "Dr. Wright, my dog graduated at the top of her obedience class, but she still lunges at the mailman every day." Or, "Hi, I have a dog, and he's going crazy and trashing the place when I leave for work. Can I bring him in?"

When I tell the caller that no he can't "bring him in" because I need to see the dog in his own environment, he is shocked. Few professionals work this way, but it's the way I feel I can work best with dogs.

It's sometimes hard for owners to comprehend that what ails their dog is not an obedience problem, but my experience has been that having obedience training doesn't guarantee that a dog won't have serious behavioral problems. I am not a dog trainer, whose mission is to teach dogs good manners via compliance with a number of specific commands. Nor am I a psychoanalyst with a specialty in misbehaving dogs. There is no such thing. What I do is help owners learn how to stop the problem behavior but not change the other things that make their dog terrific the rest of the time.

My callers, who are often referred to me by veterinarians or trainers, might ask, "What would you do that I haven't tried?" In other words, they don't want to pay for something that is obvious. Neither would I. If all those obvious things had worked, they wouldn't be calling me.

This line of questioning often leads to the "guarantee" query. Some discouraged owners want to know if results are guaranteed. "Or their money back," as the saying goes. The answer, of course, is no. It is never ethical to guarantee the outcome of this or any other treatment program in which animals are concerned, simply because living things will never be as predictable as a car or washing machine.

I explain that as long as they are willing and able to work with their pets, I will be available. By being available I mean for feedback and suggestions and to monitor the pet's progress until she is doing as well as she is going to do or until the problem is resolved and they no longer feel the need to check back with me.

I characterize results as a reduction of the unwanted behavior from week to week. An animal might respond immediately or, more often, during the second week of treatment. Sometimes, we won't get results until the third to fifth weeks. But as long as there are fewer incidents in the current week than in the week before, we know that the pet is learning something.

I have to know when to say to the client or concur when she says to me, "This approach isn't working. Let's try something else." At this point, I might turn once again to the professional literature or have an e-mail exchange with colleagues. We'll continue to try various procedures until we hit upon the right one for that particular pet. There is no one-size-fits-all treatment plan for dog behavioral problems.

I also have to consider how cooperative the owner is and how comfortable she is with change—even change for the better can be stressful. In some cases, we'll need to explore how owners feel about administering psychoactive drugs to their pets during the treatment program and possibly on a daily basis for a period of time thereafter.

In the past few years, a lot of media attention has been given to the use of drugs like Prozac, and there's been some misunderstanding about how these drugs work. Dog owners need to know that medication is not a crutch or solution by itself but a temporary tool to be used in conjunction with a behavioral program.

Very rarely have I found a hopeless case. If we've done everything possible to help the dog, and he is unable to change his behavior, I may say to the client, "We've both done everything we can to help Bingo. It's your decision whether or not you can now take what he has to give you and accept it as the way it's going to be."

In my 18 years of consulting, no one has ever had a problem with that. Very occasionally, a client has responded, "Well, the dog is still showing his teeth, and we just aren't comfortable having him around the kids. What are our options at this point? We can't give away a dangerous dog."

So I tell them that euthanasia is something they might want to consider. I have never advised anyone to put their dog to death. But I do discuss the risk that the dog may be posing to family members and the quality of life that the pet can look forward to—how he probably doesn't feel very good about biting people or constantly being "in the doghouse." But the final decision remains theirs. I can't make that decision for them.

When the first telephone call is a last resort, sometimes it comes too late—not for the pet, because you usually *can* teach an old dog new tricks—but for the owner. Some people are so emotionally exhausted, their patience worn so thin, that the prospect of spending six to eight weeks working every day with their pet, with possibly weeks of follow-up phone calls after that, is more than they can handle. And if they can't make that commitment up front, I can't even try to help them.

Once we discuss on the phone the amount of time and effort required on their part, and I am pretty clear about the nature of the problem, we talk about the probable outlook for controlling or managing the misbehavior. If the circumstances make the chances very poor, I tell the owner this and help her think about alternatives.

RECENTLY, A YOUNG WOMAN CALLED me because her dog was destroying her living room while she was gone all day. She had two pets: a well-behaved pit bull and the troublemaker, a ten-month-old wolf-dog hybrid. She lived, believe it or not, in an apartment and had no intention of moving out. In fact, she had just moved in.

Now right away, the question arises: What are the chances of my being able to help someone in this particular environment? Realistically, not very good. I told her that while there was probably a treatment program we could follow to desensitize the animal to being by himself, he would have no place to be safe during the training period. He had already destroyed a boarding cage, hurting his mouth in the process.

In addition, neither of her dogs had the opportunity to get much exercise during the day, which meant they were less relaxed than they should have been. And because the wolf-dog was either crated during the day or kept in an area with a courtyard view instead of facing the parking lot, he wasn't able to observe his owner's comings and goings. I explained that he was going nuts because he couldn't do his "job" of keeping track of where she was.

As we talked, the owner realized that the best course of action was to place the dog in a more suitable home, if she could find one where he wouldn't endanger human beings or other dogs as he matured. I told her the facts about wolf-dog hybrids—that their recent popularity had led to their being one of the problem "dog breeds" of the 1990s—and wished her well. Common sense might have told her that she had the wrong habitat for this particular pet.

On the other hand, some owners will take a situation with very little chance of success and insist on going ahead, no matter what. This was the case with a woman who phoned me about a German shepherd whose temperament sounded so extreme that I held out little hope for a satisfactory resolution.

If I hadn't made house calls, I wouldn't have believed the way she and her family were living—nor would I have had any hope of changing it. It is my philosophy that you can't separate the dog and the problem from the environment in which it occurs. The problem must be dealt with at home by the people who interact with the dog every day.

I discovered that their dog, King (whom you will meet in chapter 1), ruled the house with an iron paw. He bit each member of the family every day. He bit other people, too, so they really couldn't have visitors. They went out to dinner most evenings because he stole the food right off their table and would bite them when they tried to interfere. If they tried to get peace by locking King up, he destroyed the room. And so on. What were they going to do? I knew what most people would have done!

Here was a dog that was making his family's life miserable. They would have been more than justified in getting rid of him. But he was certainly not placeable with another family, and if they gave him to a shelter, he would, with good reason, be a candidate for euthanasia. The mere mention of the possibility of euthanasia sent the woman into torrents of tears. She clearly loved the dog, even though he was causing no end of problems for the family.

Their vet called and urged me to come up with some kind of program for these people. He confirmed that they seemed willing to suffer under this canine tyrant rather than give him up. So I reluctantly took the case, although my expectations were not very high. And I was pleasantly surprised. Although King was never able to accept obedience training, we ended up with a dog that no longer bit family members or visitors. It was, frankly, more than I had hoped for and due in no small measure to the family's unwavering determination to do what they had to do to keep their pet.

One of the things that helped in that case was getting the family to stop all physical punishment. Their only form of self-defense against King had been to take off a shoe and hold it above his head. If he kept biting, they would whack him on the nose with the shoe. It usually worked—until the next incident.

Almost invariably, punishment goes hand-in-hand with misbehavior. It is the rare owner that fails to reprimand—if not severely punish—a pet that jumps on Aunt Bessie for the umpteenth time. But some clients are afraid that I'll recommend hurting the dog in order to help him. They may have read or been advised to pin the dog to the ground, grab him by the scruff of the neck, shake him, or practice other forms of "tough love."

I have to admit that behaviorists were advocating this kind of thing a decade ago. Since then, research has taught us that household pets aren't wild animals and that humans will never pass for any member of the canine family tree. Yet this fact has not yet permeated the general population. Not a week goes by that I don't hear someone urging owners to act like "alpha animals" and growl at their dogs like their mothers did, and so forth.

A few of the owners you'll meet in this book had taken the advice of several trainers and hanged their dogs by their leashes until they passed out. And, of course, some people think this kind of inhumane treatment is perfectly okay, as long as it teaches the dog "who's boss."

At this point, I usually ask, "Well, when you hit the animal across the face or pin her to the ground, does it seem to work? Does it stop her from biting?" (Or defecating on the couch, or whatever.)

"Well . . . no, it actually gets worse," they admit. "But everybody told me . . ." or "The book said. . . ."

I always tell them, "I understand, but the more you meet aggression or misbehavior with aggression, the more of it you are going to get. So we don't use physical punishment in the treatment program."

And that makes them real curious. On the one hand, they wonder how I expect to correct the behavior without physical punishment. On the other hand, they are relieved that the animal—who is, after all, a member of the family—is not going to have to experience confrontation and pain.

So I float the concept that the way we change behavior is by inducing a mood that is happy, calm, or—in cases of aggression—incompatible with an angry or fearful mood. Once you do that, changing the behavior is easier. The idea is to get rid of the misbehavior, not to punish the pet. You just want the dog to stop what she is doing and do something else that you approve of.

When I go to clients' homes, I ask behavior-oriented questions: "What did the dog do? What did you do? What did the dog do in response to that? Tell me about the next instance of misbehavior. What did the dog do? What made him stop? Oh, he didn't stop—what did he do next?"

And so on. When you concentrate specifically on the animal's behavior and on people's responses, "animal behaviorist" begins to define itself.

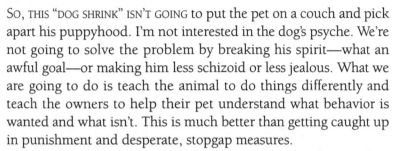

SO, THIS "DOG SHRINK" ISN'T GOING to put the pet on a couch and pick apart his puppyhood. I'm not interested in the dog's psyche. We're not going to solve the problem by breaking his spirit—what an awful goal—or making him less schizoid or less jealous. What we are going to do is teach the animal to do things differently and teach the owners to help their pet understand what behavior is wanted and what isn't. This is much better than getting caught up in punishment and desperate, stopgap measures.

Sometimes owners believe that their dog is doing "it"—whatever "it" is—out of spite or because he is lonely, mean, jealous, bored, or whatever. That's only natural. But it's what the pet does before, during, and after the misbehavior that they need to focus on. Was the misbehavior rewarding for the pet? Or was he punished and exiled? By asking people to focus on situations this way, I can help them figure out how we are going to go about solving the misbehavior.

And the problems, especially aggression, must be faced. They don't just go away. The bottom line is this: If a dog isn't raised as a companion and socialized properly to recognize people as things he should not bite, or if people don't get help when aggression crops up for no apparent reason, they are placing themselves and others at risk. The potential for serious injury is always there with an aggressive pet, even one who is "great" 90 percent of the time.

This is not a "how-to" book. As they say on the TV stunt shows, "Don't try this at home!" The course of treatment for each case in this book was custom-tailored for one particular animal in his own home, taking many circumstances into account. Owners have occasionally found that being "creative" instead of following instructions can either be dangerous or cause the problems to resurface.

I remember one man I worked with to try to solve his dog's thunderstorm phobia. I put together a program and explained to him that the course of treatment would involve a very gradual de-sensitization to scary noises, using, among other tools, a recording of a storm.

After following the procedures for a while, the owner decided that although the dog was becoming more relaxed, the program wasn't working fast enough. So he stopped the program and went on vacation for a week.

When he came back, he decided—without consulting me—to resume the program right where he left off. What a mistake! The dog, who had actually been making good progress in the beginning, was terrified by the sudden onslaught of noise. He immediately streaked for the bathtub and hid there, a quivering mass of fur. By the time the owner, more frantic than ever, checked back with me, the dog had been needlessly stressed. We had to start the program all over, and the "cure" took twice as long as it would have had the owner been able to get with the program and stay with it.

What you'll take away from this book is the knowledge that you can go home at night without fear (people whose dogs tear up the house in their absence especially dread quitting time); that you don't have to give up your pet or shut him in a cage all day; and that you and your spouse don't have to take turns missing work to stay home with the dog when thunderstorms are forecast. Most of all, you'll learn that there is almost always hope, that your beloved pet is not a bad dog but simply a dog who's doing something that isn't good. It's always the behavior that we need to change, not the pet's personality.

I recently opened a note from a client. Inside was a photo of a now-grinning pooch who, several months earlier, had been dangerously aggressive. The owner had drawn a balloon over the dog's head and penned the following:

Hi, Dr. Wright. I'm doing just fine now!

Your friend, Ginger."

This is the kind of result to aim for, one that makes everyone, including me, feel great. My practice and this book are a tribute to those dog owners who cared enough to give their companions one more chance and to the dogs and puppies who made it all worthwhile.

Chapter One

The Dog Who
Would Be King

My friendly knock was greeted by an ominous, throaty growl. This was not the "doorbell bark" of the average pet. This was the growl of a dog with an agenda.

I get your message, buddy, I thought uneasily, and I really, really hope you're on a leash. I heard footsteps approaching, but no one was telling this dog to lie down or be quiet.

Unfortunately.

But that's why I was here. The dog was in charge instead of the owners, and I was supposed to turn that around. I hoped my uneasiness wouldn't show. After all, I was the professional "dog shrink" these desperate people were counting on to help their angry canine. I couldn't let them see that the beast scared me before I ever laid eyes on him.

Although my animal behavior practice at the time was fairly new, I had dealt with aggression many times. Usually, when I made a house call, the dog in question was leashed, crated, or in another room. Or the aggression problem wasn't linked to the dog being overly protective—it didn't go berserk when people came to the door.

So it had always been my habit to say hello to the client, shake hands, and sit down to start the session. I had never been attacked—so far. I hoped my luck hadn't run out on the doorstep of this modest bungalow in suburban South Carolina.

When the door to the Farley house opened, I came face-to-face with what turned out to be the most controlling dog I'd ever encountered. The young male German shepherd stationed himself just inside the door, barking, growling, and staring boldly into my eyes. His trio of owners stood placidly off to one side in the small entrance hall, and I quickly noticed two things that made my growing feeling of alarm even worse.

The first was that Janet Farley, her husband, Tom, and her brother-in-law Carl all sported a number of wounds in various degrees of healing on their wrists and ankles. The second was that nobody had a hand, much less a leash, on the dog.

"This is King," Janet stated without preamble. "Come on in before he gets you." The two men standing behind her chuckled nervously. King kept growling.

I moved my briefcase from my side and positioned it between me and King. Canceling the planned handshakes—almost certain red-flag attack signals—I greeted my clients with as much enthusiasm as I could muster and stepped slowly and carefully into the malevolent canine's kingdom.

King's body language told me everything. After years of studying dog behavior, I didn't need a textbook to recognize the classic signals of an animal who was about to lose control. If I didn't stoop or squat down immediately to defuse my threatening position at the door, I was fairly certain King would attack. So down on my heels I went.

Dogs can do a bunch of things with their bodies to tell you to back off before it's too late. And King was doing just about all of them. For starters, his tail was held high, swishing slowly back and forth.

Lots of dog bites are accompanied by tearful kids exclaiming, "He was wagging his tail!" It's important to know what a dangerous dog looks like, and there's a key difference between a warning swish and the typical exuberant wag. If people don't want to get nailed, they'll respect a dog's communicative displays.

King's ears were rotated toward me. His mouth was puckered with his lips brought forward—the opposite of the typical smile face of the calm canine. His weight was on his front feet, and he continued to stare challengingly into my eyes as he revved up his throaty growl. His nose was pointed directly toward me, so it appeared that his erect tail was growing out of the top of his forehead. All of these signals told me that King was in a highly aroused state and that my best move was to stay low and still.

As I squatted down and continued to smile—a decidedly strained smile at this point—deliberately at the owners, King approached me. I made a concerted effort not to look at him. If you move your gaze toward a dog who is staring at you, the animal will become even more aroused and potentially dangerous.

I usually demonstrate this point to help owners become more familiar with what their dog is trying to tell them. If the dog is 10 to 15 feet away and staring and the owner has control over him, I'll say, "Has he always stared at people like this?"

And they'll usually shrug and say, "We don't know; we never noticed."

At which point, I'll say, "Watch what happens when I stare back." As I'm talking to them and smiling, I'll move just my head toward the dog and direct my gaze at him. The dog almost always increases his barking or growling and arousal level.

When I take my eyes away from the dog and look back toward the owners, the dog will quiet and relax to some extent. I do this demonstration to show how eye contact with an aggressive dog is very provocative. It is one of the worst things a person can do, especially in a situation like the one I found myself in with King.

But since King was about to tear me to shreds and was not under anyone's control at all, I thought it prudent to forgo the demonstration and explain this point to the Farleys at a later time. As I continued to look away from King, smiling nonthreateningly at the owners to show him I meant no harm, King did something no unfriendly dog before or since has ever done to me: He walked right up, still growling, and set his chin on my shoulder.

I froze. He put his nose in my ear, with his mouth about an inch from my jugular vein. Now, I could actually *feel* his low, terrifying growl.

I had had enough.

Very quietly, I said to the Farleys, "Would you mind getting your dog away from me?"

The three of them looked at each other for a while. Then Janet replied in a dubious tone, "I'll try."

And with that, I knew this was something I would never do again. If I got out of this alive, I would never fail to instruct each and every client that the aggressive dog must be under restraint before I would take one step into the lion's den.

I was lucky this time. Janet was able to put a leash on King, and I gingerly made my way to the living room sofa and took a seat at one end. With a big coffee table in front, King had very little access to me, and I began to regain my composure. I set my briefcase against my legs. The leashed King came up and sniffed my knee, then sat down some feet away. He never took his eyes off me.

I took a deep breath. Feeling a little like a priest at an exorcism, I said, "Shall we begin?"

From our initial conversation over the phone, I had already tentatively diagnosed King as a head-of-household dog. These dogs take total responsibility for running the family. When a visitor comes to the door, they position themselves between the residents and the visitor, as King did, and attack if they feel it's necessary. It was King's self-appointed job to protect his people.

But he also needed to control them. Head-of-household dogs want to be in charge of the type and level of activity that goes on in the house. They generally don't like people moving too quickly, and they'll run over and bite their owners' feet to stop them. Everything must be done on their terms. King, I was told, would bite anyone who didn't do what he wanted.

King's veterinarian had referred the owners to me when King attacked him. He thought it was a hopeless case and handed them my card when the owners rejected his suggestion to destroy the young dog.

To determine whether or not King was really a control freak, it was necessary for me to find out if he was aggressive to strangers and the family in a variety of situations. This was the diagnostic phase: Describing what the dog does is at least as important as tracing the development of the problem.

"Would you tell me about a typical day with King?" I asked.

With King glaring from a distance and Tom and Carl occasionally adding details, Janet sat next to me on the sofa and matter-of-factly described their lives as subjects ruled by a canine king.

At 7:00 A.M., King awakens and goes to the sliding glass door in the kitchen. He scratches on the door until Janet gets up and lets him out. Nothing undesirable about that, I thought, as we began the session.

"But if I keep him waiting, he just chomps on my arm and brings me over to the door," she said. She glanced down at her left wrist, covered with scabs. "That's where I got most of these."

Okay. So King wasn't Lassie. I took out my pen and started taking notes. Figuring that most pets go out two or three times a day, I asked Janet how often she let King out.

"Whenever he wants to," she said, stroking her wrist gingerly. Seven or eight times a day was all she was willing to admit to, but I had a feeling it might have been more.

While King was outside, Janet would take treats from a box and line them up along the edge of the counter on either side of the sink. This routine came to light when I asked her if she had King sit or do anything for her when she brought him back into the house.

"No," she said. "King doesn't obey any commands at all."

"But do you try to reward him for things that you want him to learn to do?" I asked.

"Oh, yes, we reward him all the time!"

"How do you do that?"

"Well," she replied, "I line up these snacks on both sides of the sink, and all day King will go and get them."

"I see," I said. Then I thought for a minute. Her routine didn't really constitute rewarding King for something he was doing right, but it certainly did reward him. Every now and then—often enough for King to make the connection—he would bite his owners, jump up and put his paws on the sink, and take a biscuit. Here was the ultimate head-of-household dog: He was even in charge of rewarding himself for biting people!

But Janet never made that connection. In fact, she frequently reinforced King's aggression by giving him food. "Sometimes," she said, "I feed King a tidbit in order to keep his mind off doing bad things," which was sort of the right idea, but her execution was off. There's a difference between feeding a dog treats to put him in a mood not compatible with aggression and giving him treats because he was aggressive.

King had essentially learned, *If I bark, growl, or bite, I'll get something to eat. Cool!* And so he would do bad things to get his treats, thereby earning himself a reward for misbehaving. The Farleys, however, hadn't thought of it this way.

During the day, King would get bored and want to play. The way he started playing was to nip someone's ankle or hand. The owner would draw back, which elicited more nipping because a dog will try to bite that which is moving. When people got frustrated enough, they would strike out.

Great, King thought. *This is a play session.* The more excited he got, the more likely he was to bite, sometimes severely. Nor could he be controlled on a leash. Tom, I learned, had taken to hitting King on the nose with the handle of the leash. Eventually, the leash itself started to stand for something that predicted the aggressive play.

While many dogs will accept a pull on a choke collar and react obediently, King would bite his handler on the arm, which would stop the pulling or punishing. King made this connection, too. Biting would stop the uncomfortable behavior. The sight of the leash, rather than calming him, actually made him more excited. His owners couldn't start to train him because he would bite.

Strangely enough, the Farleys were totally devoted to King. He was aptly named: Here was a real king of the castle, and his human family treated him royally, with a respect born out of love and fear. Any hint from the veterinarian or me that King's behavior might be intractable or that the ultimate issue of human safety might make euthanasia an option led Janet into heartfelt rivers of tears.

"He's a real mean dog," she admitted when I brought up the subject on the telephone. "But we still like him." I never take it upon myself to recommend to an owner that a physically healthy animal be put down, but it is an alternative that responsible people must be made aware of, especially in the occasional sad case of a dog who won't respond to the best efforts to control aggression.

So we had already ruled out euthanasia in this case. These folks were in it for the long haul, which increased the pressure on me to figure out what was up with King and to make sure he could change. I admired their unflagging devotion and hoped I could somehow make King less dominant and their lives more pleasant—as well as safer—since they were determined to keep him.

"How is King around his food bowl?" I asked. "Does he seem to guard his food or growl at you when he's eating?"

"No, he's fine," replied Tom.

Good, I thought, making a note. Finally, one area where King didn't need correcting.

"It's *our* food bowl that's the problem," Tom added. "Can't even eat a meal at home anymore."

I looked up from my note-taking. The three nodding heads told me he was not making a joke.

"Are you serious?"

"You bet," he answered sheepishly. "Dog's got us trained."

It seemed that when the family sat down to dinner, King would get up on a chair or put his chin on someone's legs and stare up at them, much as he had done to me at the door with his chin on my shoulder. He had done this as a puppy, and everyone thought it was cute. Naturally, they had had a rule that no one would feed the puppy at the table, but of course, every once in a while someone did anyway.

Now, if King didn't get some action, he would jump up and scratch them, putting his front feet across their laps, until someone fed him something from the table. If he didn't get food, he would playfully bite them. Then he would jump down, go to the next person, and do the same thing until he was fed.

They all agreed that it wasn't cute anymore.

One night, according to Janet, King reached up and grabbed the barbecued chicken the family was about to enjoy. He ran around the house with it, and they chased him. But they weren't able to get it back. King thought they were playing, and they all knew how playing always ended up.

So nowadays, they just stood at the kitchen counter and ate their takeout or went to town for dinner. Things were easier that way.

"Well, King is certainly very assertive," I said lamely as I finished writing about that part. Assertive, my foot. Dogs like him were the reason people bought goldfish as pets.

"Let's move on," I said. I was beginning to feel very sorry for these people. But despite the horror stories, a picture was emerging of a dog I thought I could help.

"What about bedtime?" I asked, since no one had complained about King's behavior during the night. "No special problems?"

"Oh, boy," Carl piped up, slapping his knee. "That's a good one."

My heart sank. I suggested he tell me about it.

The family almost always spent a quiet evening at home by themselves; because of King, people didn't visit much. So they would play cards, talk, or watch TV—anything that didn't require them to move around too fast because King didn't like that and would nip their ankles.

When Janet went upstairs to prepare for bed, King would follow her, jump up on the bed, and wait for her to get in. Then Tom would go upstairs. King would jump down and lie in the bathroom while Tom got ready. Then King would get back into bed when Tom got in. In King's mind, he was doing his duty by putting his family to bed.

Part of his job, as King saw it, was protecting his immediate family. If by chance Carl were to poke his head in to say good night, King would jump down from the bed and stand guard at the bedroom door, growling until he went away. The poor fellow was not permitted to enter the room.

Nor were Tom and Janet allowed to leave. Once King had put them to bed, they were virtually prisoners in their bedroom. King made sure they stayed put. In fact, one of the reasons they finally called me was a disturbing bedtime incident.

Tom tried to come downstairs at midnight to get a glass of milk. King was lying at the foot of the stairs, where he stationed himself after everyone was asleep. Getting him to move was out of the question, and King growled so menacingly that Tom was afraid to step over him. He went back upstairs without his milk.

The next day, the family discussed the fact that if there were ever to be a fire in the night, they would be trapped upstairs be-cause King would never let them pass. They were willing to put up with a lot more than most dog owners, but they weren't going to put their very lives in jeopardy. That's when they decided to ask for help.

Some people call me with alarm the first time their dog looks at them cross-eyed. Yet after months of living with King, it took the thought that he might kill them for these folks to dial the canine equivalent of 911.

I asked about the obvious possibility of shutting King out of the bedroom at night and keeping him away from the steps. Janet shook her head.

"We can't afford it," she said, motioning for me to follow her into the family room, which adjoined the kitchen.

"This is the last place we tried to shut a door on King."

From the kitchen side, the door was okay. But the family room side of the hollow door was splintered and wrecked all along the bottom 10 to 12 inches. I also noticed that the carpeting around the door was scratched threadbare.

"You can't shut King in," Tom said as we looked at the damage.

"Or out," his wife added.

"And he sure doesn't like his leash," Carl said.

I looked at King, who was now pacing back and forth in the family room like a caged tiger, still eyeing me suspiciously. I hastily told the Farleys I'd appreciate it very much if they would leave the leash on until the session was finished and I was out the door. Or better yet, out of town, I thought to myself as I eyed the unhappy canine.

THAT WAS ABOUT IT. THEY COULDN'T think of any other major problems right now. Since they had amply demonstrated that King was running things, my next task was to get a handle on why he was acting this way.

I suspected that King's litany went something like this: *I'm taking responsibility for my people. You have to play by my rules—or else.*

King basically had control of when and how he played, when he went outside, where he stayed, how he got a treat, and how the family moved about, socialized, ate, slept, and so on. It was a horrendous situation.

"You've had dogs before?"

"Yes, sir," Janet said. "Good dogs. Not biters. And we treated them all exactly like King."

"But none of them acted like this one," added Carl. "He's just plain mean—born a bad apple."

Was King born mean? I hoped not. Temperament problems are difficult if not impossible to reverse. They're also not usually the problem.

In order to do a good diagnosis, I had to put on my pet-detective hat. I needed to backtrack to find out what happened during the onset of these misbehaviors. That would help me understand what caused them and why they lasted so long. Would we be able to quickly squelch one or two bad habits, or were King's problems so pervasive and entrenched that resolving them would require a total reversal of King's handling and routine?

Interestingly, the family had previously raised four German shepherds. I had to consider them to be fairly savvy about the breed and its behavior. This is an important point because many people will argue that a dog wouldn't turn out badly if it weren't the owner's fault. Others believe that the genes determine the behavior. It's the old argument of environment versus heredity.

Certainly, good breeding (good genes) makes a difference, which is why breeders are able to produce desirable physical traits and behavior. However, in some cases, the same mild rough treatment is likely to cause one puppy to "go off," and a similar (but genetically different) puppy to inhibit her aggression. Thus, both genes and rearing contribute to the likelihood of biting.

In this case, if I took the Farleys at their word, they raised all their shepherds the same way, played the same games, and provided the same environment. But this time, they came out with a totally different kind of dog than the good-natured bunch that had come before.

My belief is that in many cases, not including those involving deliberate abuse, well-meaning owners unintentionally contribute to the onset of aggressive behavior problems and, in some cases, may actually cause it if the animal has those underlying tendencies.

Parents might spank a child, for example, and end up with a well-behaved kid who knows what the rules are. Or they might spank a sibling for the same transgressions but find that this child tends to hit back or use physical aggression on the playground. The difference in the outcome most likely lies within the differences among individual children. And it is the same with other mammals.

So what happened to little King, a puppy brought home from a backyard breeder at about six weeks of age? I wanted to find out in what situations King first started biting. I wished I could turn back the clock and make sure King stayed in the litter until he was seven to eight weeks old. These are weeks of rough-and-tumble play among puppies, when they learn from their littermates and their mother, if she's around, that hard nips from sharp little teeth are met with hard nips back.

In my early research, I compared puppies who were hand-raised by people from birth with those who were raised with their littermates and their mothers. One of the most striking differences I found was in play-fighting and aggression. The human-raised puppies—handled by people but not exposed to play with their siblings or their mothers—tended to show more aggression. They sometimes bit too hard because, when they played with people instead of other dogs, nobody was biting them back.

Within the first eight weeks, pups develop an inhibited, or gentle, bite with their littermates. This allows them to play and play-fight without hurting each other. Usually by around six weeks, they are starting to get the hang of it, but it's not until seven to eight weeks that they'll have learned pretty much what they can and can't get away with in play. By about eight weeks of age, behavior patterns and interactions with littermates become more consistent and predictable.

When a puppy is taken out of the litter at five to six weeks of age, he is being asked to learn to inhibit his bite among human family members. But it's up to the people to teach him how to do that. This is when the trouble usually begins, because people don't realize that's their job, much less how to do it.

Here's what probably happened with King. He nipped his owner, and it hurt. So his owner whacked him on the nose or smacked him across the mouth. Over time, King began to get hand-shy. When he saw hands, he became overly aroused and excited. This may have caused him to either bite his owner first or to mouth the hand before it could hit him. And this, of course, led his owner to hit him again.

This is apparently what started to happen in the Farley family. Tom and his brother would play tug-of-war with King, using a little towel or an old T-shirt. As one of the Farleys was pulling with the right hand, for some unfathomable reason, he would try to smack King on the head with the left. Or he'd shift the towel from the right to the left hand, and when King wasn't paying attention, he'd get whacked with the other hand.

I see lots of toys in pet shops designed for tug-of-war games. I realize this is an old traditional form of play between dogs and their owners, and it can be fun for all involved, but my advice to dog owners is to instead consider engaging their canine buddies in games of catch the ball, fetch the stick, or jump for the Frisbee. For puppies who show early aggressive tendencies, teaching them rough games that encourage aggression, like tug-of-war or any kind of wrestling, can be asking for big trouble.

A recent study did show that tug-of-war isn't more likely to produce aggression than other types of play. But in my experience, a significant number of cases where dogs bite their owners have tug-of-war as part of the play scenario. So if a dog begins to get aggressive toward anyone during tug-of-war games—even if the bite is accidental—I recommend discontinuing the contest and substituting a less confrontational form of play.

In the Farley family, tug-of-war usually ended with the owner winning. It became clear to me that it was important to the Farley men that King not get the better of them. They characterized just about every situation with King as a contest that "I win" or "King wins." Sometimes, when King had too good of a hold on the towel, Tom would give it a powerful tug and little King would go tumbling against the wall. Tom would win.

But as King got stronger and his reflexes improved, he was able to hold on a little bit better. That's when the nips started. As King would chew his way farther up the towel, he'd eventually get to somebody's hands. After a few months, King was getting pretty adept at nailing a hand before the owner could move it. He was learning that the only way to stop getting hit on the head or thrown across the room was to bite first.

Tug-of-war was more than just a game for this family. For example, sometimes King would get up on the sofa, and the only way to get him off was to offer to play with him. Enticing him with tug-of-war, the men would drag King off the couch with the towel. King eventually learned that any time he got up on the sofa and the people had a towel, it was time to play. During play, he bit and they hit.

King started to interpret all kinds of physical reprimands—hitting, slapping, and even the word *no*—as predicting play. He was willing to put up with the pain of being hit because he interpreted it as play, as long as he could bite back.

That's why physically punishing this dog wasn't an answer. Trainers used to recommend tackling and pinning a dog to the ground in order to stop aggression. This never worked very well, and it isn't recommended anymore. To do it with an unaltered male whose sex hormones, called androgens, are beginning to kick in is even less advisable, and it certainly wasn't going to work with King.

Of course, many dog owners wouldn't think of hitting a puppy under any circumstances. And it seems logical for nonhitters to conclude that it was understandable that King turned mean; he was being abused. But when I questioned the Farleys, I discovered that these were the same games they had played with their other shepherd puppies, and none of them became biters.

This is where the genes part comes in, and I can only theorize that King probably had a different genotype or genetic milieu than the previous dogs. He was more genetically prepared to respond to this kind of treatment in an aggressive fashion. King is a prime example of how each dog or cat must be treated as an individual, because even within the same breed there are often puzzling differences that emerge.

I am not always able to figure out why an animal started doing something he shouldn't. Fortunately, it isn't usually essential to know the why in order to help the pet and his owners because sometimes the root of the problem is impossible to ferret out.

Janet didn't play tug-of-war with King, but he bit her anyway. And she learned that if she brought her hand up in order to hit King, he got extremely excited and would lunge at her hand or dart back and forth biting her ankles, depending on which was most available.

"But I found one way to stop him," she told me. She bent over and took off a worn brown loafer. "I used to have to whomp him on the nose," she reported, "but now he goes and lies down when I raise it up here." She whipped her arm up over her head, waving the shoe in the air.

I wasn't surprised that King had learned to back off at the sight of the shoe. A dog's nose, where the olfactory nerves form a pathway to the brain, is very sensitive. Even so, this was unacceptable. It was abusive to King. And who wants a biting dog— one who can only be stopped by whacking him across the nose with a shoe?

Although the veterinarian had expressed the fear that King would be impossible to rehabilitate and should be euthanized, I left the Farley home that day believing that there was some hope, especially in light of their determination to keep King. I believed that King was not born mean but that most of his problems came from two sources: His distorted concept of play, going back to his early separation from the litter, and the Farleys' misguided attempts to win control over him through inappropriate games.

First, in consultation with the veterinarian, we decided to have King neutered, which can help lower non-fear-related aggressive tendencies in young males. After the surgery, I asked the vet to administer a female hormone to further calm King while he learned his new, more appropriate behaviors. We planned to reduce the dose over time as King's behavior improved, since the long-term use of hormones can lead to unpleasant side effects. (Today, safer drugs have replaced hormones for this type of problem.)

Now King was in better shape to learn some new habits. But it wouldn't be easy. To start with, I had the family stop all physical punishment. No hitting, tug-of-war, or any of the things that King used to escalate into play, aggression, biting, or threats. I felt that if we could remove the pleasurable consequences of doing these things—the fact that King always got what he wanted—we could stop the bad behavior. This wasn't a dog who could be forced into doing something by the jerk of a leash; that would cause him to latch right onto the person's arm or leg. So we had to do something called submissiveness training.

When King showed any kind of submissive behavior, the Farleys were to praise him and pay attention to him. They had to learn a little dog body language for this exercise to work. I taught them the kinds of activities that would cause King to demonstrate a subordinate relationship to his human family.

The Farleys needed to watch for submissive signals from King, such as laying his ears back against his head. If they saw any, I told them that they were to pay attention to King and praise him. We started by praising King with a soft, low "Go-o-od bo-oy." I asked the family not to look directly at him for the first few days. Eye contact was arousing to King, and we wanted to de-arouse him, especially during these early learning sessions. If he were less aroused, he'd be more likely to absorb what we were trying to teach him.

Very gradually, from week to week, the Farleys would have to continue to praise King whenever he did something submissive and ignore him when he nipped or tried to escalate an encounter into aggressive play.

Initially, this praise-the-good, ignore-the-bad strategy led to more bites, not an unusual outcome when a dog is first learning new behaviors. But when King found that he wasn't getting positive consequences—food or play—he began to stop misbehaving. He learned that his aggressive play didn't get him what he wanted. Only being submissive paid off.

At mealtimes, for example, he was encouraged to sit. No matter how much he carried on—yipping or putting his head under their elbows—he was ignored until the end of the meal. Then the family decided whether or not they wanted to give him a treat. Eventually, King learned that he didn't have to bother the Farleys while they were eating because he would get something when they were finished.

After a couple of months, the Farleys took King to an obedience trainer to see if he could learn some basic commands beyond "Sit." I explained to the trainer that this was not a dog he could jerk with a choke collar if he valued his life. The trainer had pretty good results, probably because he was not on King's turf during the exercises and King was willing to cut him some slack.

Upstairs, King was put on the leash at bedtime and made to sit while Carl stood in the doorway and talked to Tom and Janet. King's initial protests were ignored. When King was able to accept this intrusion calmly, Carl gradually made his way into the room, progressing a few steps a night until King no longer objected. At the same time, King learned to let people pass on the stairs without biting or growling, and he received a reward when Tom reached the kitchen unscathed.

Similarly, King was leashed when people came to the door. He was sent outside for time-outs if he became overly aroused or aggressive. Since he was not being fed anymore when he was in an excited state, he learned that being calm led to praise, a treat, and entry back into the house.

Because King was earning all these treats, being fed a new

high-protein dog food (protein was believed at the time to increase levels of a neurotransmitter in the brain that has calming effects), and taking hormones that, as a side effect, increased his appetite, he gained more than a few pounds and got a bit lazier. This was okay because with a little less energy, he tended to lie around more and had less interest in controlling or biting people.

Unfortunately, Janet projected magical powers onto the new dog food. She credited it with most of the behavior changes and refused to cut back or replace it as King grew rounder. There was no way the vet and I could convince her otherwise, even when we talked about the potential physical problems an overstuffed shepherd might encounter. King continued to have a weight problem, but at least he wasn't biting people.

THIS WAS A VERY LENGTHY CASE, about four months from start to finish. Most of the problems I deal with are resolved, or well on their way to significant improvement, within six weeks. But considering what we were up against, I was amazed at our success. All three family members had been retrained along with King. They went right to work with determination and reminded each other that they weren't supposed to do certain things and that they needed to do other things. We consulted regularly by phone.

After four months of constant effort, King was safer to be around and had relinquished his stranglehold on the household. The Farleys began to have people over to visit again. They ate at the dinner table, said good night to one another wherever they pleased, and walked downstairs for a midnight snack—activities that most people take for granted, to be sure, but in a household where a dog was King, simply a small miracle.

Chapter Two

The Dog Who Didn't Know How to Play

HE'S JUST A JUNKYARD DOG," Jill Slattery said, shaking her head wearily as we watched the skinny yellow puppy jet around the living room of her simple home. "Maybe I should have just left him there."

I saw the tears welling in her eyes. It wouldn't be the first time a client had been driven to despair by a pet's misbehavior, but I sensed a heavier burden on Jill's shoulders. There was no way I could help if we started out with this kind of defeatist attitude.

"I think it's great that you rescued this puppy," I told her. "It's a really big change for him, but I bet we can help him adjust pretty well." She answered with a wan smile.

"You seem pretty discouraged," I ventured.

"It's just that I wanted everything to be so perfect for Shawn, my son. And now this dog isn't exactly turning out to be Benji." She brushed at her face and laughed a little.

I could see that Jill had a great deal invested in the scrawny mutt who was now chewing on a small sneaker. "No!" she yelled, grabbing the shoe. The dog, Rusty, scampered away.

"I'd like to hear a little bit about what's been going on with your son, and we'll see if we can help Rusty become a better companion for him," I said.

Jill nodded her assent as she looked after the departing pup. "I don't even think he knows that his name is Rusty," she said. "All we ever call him is 'no' and sometimes 'stop that!'"

"Well, he wouldn't be the first dog named 'no,'" I assured her. "I've met quite a few. Now, what's up with Shawn?"

For the next half-hour, Jill told me a sad tale of being a single mom with a lonely eight-year-old boy, who had just been let down by his father for the umpteenth time. The two of them had recently moved and Shawn was trying to make friends at school, but it wasn't easy being the new kid. Then Shawn had come home with the news that there was a puppy wandering around the junkyard next to the local strip mall and asked if he could bring him home and take care of him.

"I thought it would be good for him to have something to love that would love him back," Jill explained, "so I said yes, as long as he took care of it. But that dog is just wild. We've put up with it for almost a month, and I'm about ready to get rid of him. I really don't want Shawn to have to lose anything else, so that's why I called you."

It was a tall order. Had I met Jill four weeks earlier, I would have advised her to get a more appropriate pet for a child—an animal that would be fun to interact with, but lower-maintenance, like a cat or guinea pig. I would have told her not to expect her son to be able to assume the total care of a dog. He was simply too young for that responsibility. And I sure wouldn't have told her to see if she could find a solitary puppy in a junkyard.

Despite wanting to reassure her, I had some rather serious reservations about the puppy's ability to adjust. Never mind that Rusty's general health was likely to be compromised. A dog who grows up in a junkyard without positive human contact or the presence of his mother and littermates is apt to have a very difficult time interacting with people later on.

Puppies figure out how to act around people and other animals most easily before 12 to 14 weeks of age. Rusty had been rescued when he was only 5 to 6 weeks old. There was no telling how much time he had spent with his mother and littermates, whose whereabouts were unknown. From the looks of him, he'd been alone and scrounging from garbage cans for a while. Role models had been sadly lacking for this little survivor.

One of Jill's complaints was that when Rusty came inside from his "pit stop," he was pure energy. "I think I've let him use up his excess energy, but when we get in the house, he's all hyper," she said. "He zooms around and barks and goes crazy."

"I'm afraid puppies aren't very good at regulating their own energy levels," I told her. "Rusty doesn't know how to occupy himself to blow off steam yet. I'm afraid you're going to have to increase the exercise until he seems worn out when he comes in."

"I guess Shawn could take on some of this," she decided.

"That should be the fun part," I pointed out. "It's a good time for them to start building a relationship where they can look forward to being with one another. Let them run and walk until the puppy is calm, and then bring him in. I bet you'll see the difference in his behavior."

After taking a thorough behavioral history, I told Jill that it would be up to her and Shawn to make Rusty fit into their family. All I could do was offer some suggestions, but when I left, the ball would be in their court. I made sure that Jill knew she could call with questions and asked her to keep me posted on Rusty's progress.

I didn't realize how little the pair knew about dogs until Jill went on to tell me about an incident in which Rusty growled and nipped her for no reason at all.

"That doesn't sound good," I frowned. "What were you doing at the time?"

"I was trying to plant some flowers in the garden, just digging in the ground. Luckily, I had my gloves on when he attacked my hands."

"Okay, I see." I leaned back in my chair. "Did Rusty bow and have his rear end up in the air quite a bit before he went for you?"

"I don't know," Jill said. "But I didn't do anything to him." It hadn't occurred to her that the dog was just playing. Pouncing on her hands and biting them with a ferocious growl was the pup's equivalent of a kid playing the bad guy in a game of cops and robbers. But Jill didn't know the rules of the game. Nor did she want any part of it if it involved puncture wounds to her hands. Who could blame her?

When a puppy starts a play-fight with another puppy and bites too hard, chances are the other puppy will bite it back pretty hard. He soon learns that if he bites gently, he will be bitten back gently.

"That pup really nips hard," Jill complained, rubbing her hand. "He nips me whenever I yell at him."

"What do you do with your hands when you're yelling at him?"

She jumped up, pointed her finger at an imaginary dog, and moved her hand up and down in time to the familiar refrain, "No, no, no, no, no!"

It was possible that Rusty bit Jill's hand to get the pointing to stop. One of the things he would have learned if he had been in the litter instead of picking his way through acres of dented hubcaps was to inhibit his bite. I believe this is the most important social skill puppies teach each other. If they are taken away from the litter when they're young, the new owner has to do the teaching.

If the pup hasn't had the chance to experience this and is brought home prematurely, chances are he's going to bite his owner. That's what happened to Jill. When you're getting bitten, your first reflex is to strike out, or yell no and slap the dog, or, if you've read certain books, pin him to the ground or hold his mouth shut and say, "No bite." This is what Jill did, but Rusty hadn't read that book and bit her even harder.

Fifteen years ago, some animal behaviorists who had studied wolf behavior thought that pinning the dog to the ground was a sound idea. They figured the dog could relate to this way of keeping him in line. Many dog bites later, we've learned that they were largely mistaken. With puppies, holding them down may not be such a terrible thing if it's done in a playful sort of way when they're being a bit rambunctious. With a maturing or adult dog, it can have disastrous consequences.

We now know that there are better ways to teach a dog to be compliant than through force and confrontation. People-dog relationships are not like wolf-wolf relationships. It's best to start out with a relationship where there's a mutual respect for each other's roles: The dog will try to please you and be compliant, and you will praise the dog for doing so.

You don't want to go to extremes physically and force a puppy—or a grown dog, for that matter—to do things that he doesn't want to do. Let him get used to one room at a time. Get him on a regular feeding schedule, probably three times a day in the beginning. Make sure you keep track of when he's getting overly excited, which will probably be pretty often at first.

He will need to go outside frequently, and you need to go with him. When he sniffs the ground and does his business, praise him. Then go play with him in a different location. There are many good books on basic house training and puppy care (see page 251 for a list of my favorites), and you should take the time to read up before you get the puppy—and before you start making easily avoidable mistakes like allowing him to mouth your fingers.

It's never a good idea for puppies to use people's hands as playthings, even when they have a gentle bite and it doesn't hurt yet. The key word here is "yet." When dogs get older and stronger, even a "gentle" bite is capable of doing real damage. When dogs learn that fingers, hands, wrists, and arms are not toys, they will concentrate on developing other favorite playthings.

Our friend Rusty had already discovered a favorite toy, and it was attached to little Shawn's foot. His big sneakers with the shoelaces dragging enticingly were too much for Rusty to resist. He would jump on Shawn and latch on to his foot, much as he bit Jill's gloves in the garden. And of course, Shawn would scream bloody murder. All of which served to excite Rusty even more, and much barking and nipping usually ensued.

Then, when Shawn removed his shoes and left them lying around the family room, as he did every day, Rusty felt free to chew on his "toy," which of course was marked with his own scent. Jill admitted that this problem was still unsolved. "I've given up asking Shawn to put away his clothes. So how can I keep Rusty away from Shawn's sneakers?"

I told her to put a dab of petroleum jelly on the toe of the shoe, or, if that wasn't effective, to try a squirt of shaving cream, which is easier to remove. Both of these substances are nontoxic and have a flavor and consistency that most dogs find unpleasant. Then Jill needed to find at least three different kinds of toys the dog would like and keep forbidden things off the floor. After all, Rusty didn't have a clue that Shawn's shoe was not a toy, since it was always sitting there invitingly.

Some dogs like tennis balls or squeaky rubber things or chew ropes. I suggested that Jill keep a stick or Frisbee handy outside the door. Puppies need toys as much as kids do, and they should learn that it's good to pick up and play—as roughly as they want—with these toys and not with hands. Hands are for stroking, petting, and for making your dog feel good, not for chewing.

Having too many toys available seems to get some puppies too aroused. They either go helter-skelter from one toy to another or gradually lose interest in playing with anything at all. (This may sound familiar to the parents of toddlers suffering from toy overload.) The idea, I told Jill, is to make the three toys different in function, looks, size, or texture so that they are distinctive and remain interesting. If she couldn't resist buying more, I said, she should keep them in the closet for a month and then swap them with the old toys.

"What do you suggest I start with?" Jill asked.

"Rusty could start out with a soft teddy bear he can carry around, a large rubber ball, and a Buster Cube," I offered.

"A what?"

"Oh, a Buster Cube is a hard, octagon-shaped toy with a hole in the middle that you can put doggy treats in. The puppy pushes it around with his nose until something falls out." I might have suggested giving Rusty some items already in the house (an old sock, tennis balls, and so on), but since the family was already struggling with Rusty attacking the shoes, I thought it best to buy some strictly dog toys.

Jill agreed to take a trip to the pet store. As for the sneaker problem, she found that the shaving cream worked pretty well. During the next couple of weeks, I gave Jill some additional play strategies for Shawn to use when he wanted to divert Rusty's attention away from the shoes. For example, I recommended that Shawn stand still when Rusty attacked his shoes (dogs are excited by moving objects) and flip the new rubber ball across his line of sight. This caused Rusty to redirect his chase and chew on something more acceptable. It didn't take very long to break Rusty's shoe habit, and Shawn no longer needed to cover them with goop. A little at a time, Shawn and Rusty learned to play together and enjoy each other more.

RUSTY EVENTUALLY GOT USED TO being a civilized dog, but it was a long struggle. I'm not sure that Jill would have taken him on if she had known she would have to be a surrogate parent until Rusty (and Shawn) learned the ropes. She could have used some help. Strange as it may sound, she might have done better rescuing two dogs.

Dogs have a lot to teach each other, which is why some people choose to get a couple of puppies. They can occupy each other's time and generally pal around together. Older dogs, however, are another story, as Annie and Clark Baker found out when they decided to get married. Merging two households that include dogs is a little trickier than bringing two puppies home to one family. In this case, the newlyweds very quickly discovered that the honeymoon was over.

The two dogs couldn't have been more different, and they were already set in their ways. Annie owned a dog named Sheriff, an intense black Labrador who was a former drug-sniffer and trained attack dog. He sported a pronged collar and an in-your-face, assertive attitude. Clark's dog was a fun-loving, laid-back golden retriever named Radar. Radar had always been queen of the castle until Annie and Sheriff moved in, but things changed once the households merged. Sheriff decided that he was going to show Radar who was boss in this new house, even if Radar did already live there.

One day Sheriff growled, grabbed Radar, and shook her. Radar didn't want to fight, but she wasn't going to take that on her own turf, so she growled back. And that was only the beginning. By the time I was called, the two dogs were being kept in separate rooms most of the time, and there was definitely tension in the air—and not only between the dogs.

There was Annie, an attorney, gripping her macho dog on one side of the coffee table, and Clark, a journalist, holding his mellow dog on the other. Their personalities sort of matched those of their dogs, it seemed to me. That happens all the time. So, there I was in the chair, looking at both of them, and they were looking at me. Soon they were interrupting each other with all of these horror stories and, in between accusations, asking me what to do.

One of the things they should have done to start with was to introduce the dogs on neutral territory. This is really a common-sense thing to do, but you have to be looking at the meeting from a dog's point of view to think of it. Meeting on neutral ground—in a park, for example—sidesteps the problem of territorial aggression, in which one dog feels obligated to defend his turf from an intruder. On neutral ground, the dogs start off as equal, so neither has to defend or intrude into a territory. This is their best shot at becoming friends.

I always advise couples that are introducing two dogs to take them to a park several times. Then, when it's time to move in together, they should take the resident dog for a walk and let the new dog explore the house and be sitting there quietly when the resident dog comes back. This can be done in the backyard when there's not enough room for comfort in the house.

You can pretty much tell from the start if two dogs are going to get along. They should be able to spend time together without starting a fight. The main thing is to make them feel like they're both welcome and they're good dogs, and that the sight and presence of the other dog predicts good things to come: *I'm going to get a treat because I'm a good girl when that dog's around. She's okay!*

It was too late for that in this situation. Neither dog could be praised as good right now. What made all this worse was that Sheriff was very possessive of toys, especially tennis balls. There were a lot of tennis balls floating around, as both owners were avid players. If poor Radar even got close to a ball, Sheriff would threaten to go into attack mode.

Those balls definitely had to go. Then I had to explain to the owners how to help the dogs establish their respective roles in the household and to hand out the perks accordingly. Even though Sheriff was only three years old, and Radar was six and the resident dog, Sheriff was clearly going to rule the roost. It's natural for dogs to assume dominant or subordinate roles, depending on their personalities. It's up to the owners to make sure that the dogs feel good in their respective roles and that they don't get taken advantage of. We set down some rules whereby Sheriff would get important resources first, and more of them. Radar would get things, too, but maybe not in Sheriff's presence or in the best locations.

The dogs were to be kept separate when there was the possibility of turf battles. For example, they shouldn't go down narrow hallways at the same time, and they definitely shouldn't be fed right next to each other. As for the owners, they were to take control of their dogs and make sure that they played by the rules. I wrote down these instructions, including the reminder, "You are both dominant to both dogs." Sometimes, that fact gets lost in the shuffle.

The dogs' roles in the family gradually stabilized. Sheriff was going out first and coming in first, sleeping in the choicest location (on the foot of the bed), and picking fewer fights. Radar was receiving lots of praise for not rushing out the door first and not mixing things up with her former rival. Eventually, a peaceful coexistence was reached.

This was one situation in which properly introducing a dog to a new household, if it had been done more slowly and with a little more knowledge of dog behavior, would have helped ensure that the dogs had a more successful meeting—and also helped the marriage get off to a less rocky start. Unfortunately, in these days of blended families and merging households, the various companion animals are sometimes temporarily forgotten.

MOST PEOPLE WELCOME NEW DOGS into their homes as puppies. And few of them are chosen from the local junkyard, although my wife's dog, a sweet terrier named Peanut, was found on the railroad tracks. It's wonderful to rescue an abandoned dog. But in general, taking in strays is probably not the best way to get the puppy of your dreams, although you couldn't convince my wife of that.

People often ask me where they should get a puppy and what they should look for. They think that because I'm an animal behaviorist, I am going to send them to the fanciest breeder around, someone who uses a pedigree file to determine the pup's genetic health and a fine-tuned battery of tests to make sure that she's exceptional in all ways. Well, that's one way to go about it, but it's certainly not the only way—or necessarily the best way.

If you don't get a dog from a top breeder or pick one up from your local scrap-metal dealer, where should you go? Well, it depends on what you are looking for. If you have your heart set on a certain breed, and you've done the research necessary to convince yourself that this is the right breed for your temperament, the rest of your family, your environment, and your pocketbook, you can find reputable breeders in your area. These are perhaps best located through word-of-mouth from someone whose pooch you admire. Or you can look in the newspaper, find some ads, and hire someone who knows about puppies to go with you. That's what a friend of mine, Ted Proski, did when his beloved German shepherd died suddenly. "You have to help me find a good dog," he said. "My wife and I want to do this right away, but she's too broken up to go with us."

Although most of my cases begin after a dog has developed behavior problems, I also work to head off calamities by helping people pick the right dog for their families, prepare a dog for the arrival of a new baby, or introduce an older pet to a new home. I wasn't familiar with the particular breeders Ted had located, but I had done a lot of research with shepherds and could help him identify a good dog. As we drove to see different breeders around Atlanta, we talked about some of the things to consider when choosing a new puppy.

The first thing I want to see is the mother and father. I particularly want to see if either parent shows signs of aggression or shyness. Neither trait would make me feel comfortable taking a puppy from the litter, no matter how cute. I want to watch how the parents greet visitors to the kennel (interested, but not paranoid) and how relaxed they seem around the people handling their offspring (calm).

Ted's first ad led us to a small brick house with a privacy fence surrounding it. The yard was overrun with weeds, and as we stepped from the car, we were assaulted with a most unpleasant smell. It was not a good sign. There were no parents around to look at. The puppies were being reared in a makeshift fenced-in area that was originally designed to be a turnaround for the driveway. Ted and I looked at each other. We knew it wasn't the kind of rearing situation from which we wanted to take a dog. We got out of there quickly.

On to the second place. This breeder lived in a nicer section of town. He had the shepherds in a big garage attached to the house. Half of the garage had been made into a pen, and the other half was open for the eight or nine puppies to run around.

The parents were present, but I didn't much care for what I saw. The female was fairly pleasant, but the male barked and growled at us. "Yeah, Honcho has bitten a couple of people," the breeder told us. "He's a real good watchdog." He swept his arm toward the puppies lying about or wrestling on the garage floor. "Any of these pups will be a great protection dog."

Ted and I looked at each other again. Ted and his wife wanted a companion animal, not a guard dog. We thanked him and said we'd like to keep looking.

One more breeder to go. Ted shook his head as we drove to our third and final destination, several miles out of town on a country road. "I sure hope this one is better," he said as we came to a long dirt driveway with a gate. "I want to have some good news to take home to Bonnie."

A sign on the gate said, "Please close the gate." That was good, responsible. I was grasping at straws now. But Ted and I needn't have worried. We drove up to a long, ranch-style home. There was a neat row of kennels in the back. Each kennel had its own run, and there was a large, fenced-in yard where a bunch of puppies were playing. Best of all, the front and side doors of the house were open to allow free access to the dogs. Bingo, I said to myself.

A couple of big black-and-tan German shepherds greeted us as we got out of the car. They were not terribly interested in us, but they were friendly enough and didn't bark. We walked forward and they were willing to greet us. They didn't really care much about us because they were German shepherds and that's the way they ought to be. These were the parents.

The breeders, Mr. and Mrs. Novak, invited us in. We went into the living room and there were four or five two-month-old puppies. They really looked good, all fluffy and romping around. While Ted focused on the pups, I checked the kennels out back.

"We breed for temperament," Mrs. Novak told me, walking briskly to the rear of the property. That was the magic word. Only dogs that displayed positive traits like friendliness and submissiveness, rather than aggressiveness, were chosen to be bred. Mrs. Novak pointed out that the kennels housed dogs from litters three years ago, two years ago, and one year ago. That was great, too. The Novaks kept the best dogs from past litters to breed for strength and conformation as well as temperament.

Everything we saw and heard was positive. But then Ted took me aside and said, "They all look good. How am I going to pick the right one?"

This is the same dilemma my wife and I found ourselves in when we decided to add a standard poodle to our menagerie a couple of years ago. We already had Peanut and two shelter cats, Domino and Turk, but we felt we could accommodate one more pet. We heard of a good breeder through some contacts at the university where I teach, so we went to pick out a puppy.

The breeder lived a little bit out in the country. She had horses and a trampoline and eight adorable poodles running around a pleasant outdoor pen.

The parents seemed well-adjusted, so we went to look at the puppies. We were interested in those that showed no tendency toward the extremes of behavior: aggression on the one hand or shyness or fearfulness on the other. What we wanted was a pup who would notice us, approach us without fear, make some eye contact, and not struggle to get away if we picked him up. They were all black, so we weren't swayed by cute markings or colors that matched our living room drapes. That is how some people pick a puppy. Trust me.

We noticed that the dogs were all very stable and they weren't reactive, meaning they didn't go bananas when we arrived. We were looking for a puppy who was in good health, robust, and playful. He would be neither cowering in the corner nor beating his littermates to a pulp. The middle of the spectrum was key, as it should be for any potential owner sizing up a litter.

We were looking for a female, simply because we didn't want to have to deal with the slightly higher risk of aggressive behavior that comes with male dogs. At any rate, whichever pup we chose, we knew we would have it neutered, so the sex didn't really matter all that much.

After playing with the pups and watching them interact for a few minutes, we rejected several because they seemed to have more interest in the nearest shrub than they did in us. Eventually, we narrowed it down to two pups.

Now for the scientific, how-to-pick-a-puppy test: Are you ready? Angie, my wife, picked up one of the pups, who looked up at her and licked her chin.

"This is the puppy," she said, and RooRoo joined our family. It was as simple and unscientifically subjective as that. Because in the end, picking out a companion for the next 10 to 15 years has to be a decision made in the heart.

I related all this to Ted, and he seemed to brighten. "What I'm going to do is go home and get Bonnie and let her pick him out," he said. And that's what he did. Bonnie used the lick test, too, and picked a nice, friendly puppy who turned out to be a great dog.

Breeders and animal behaviorists use a number of tests to evaluate a pup's personality and compatibility with people. But the most important thing for owners is to start out loving the puppy. After that, you can begin molding him to be more or less assertive, or more exploratory, or less curious, within the parameters of his personality.

National breed clubs can provide listings of reputable local breeders and information packets containing questions that you should ask the breeder. But if you couldn't care less about pedigree,

I recommend adopting a puppy from a local animal shelter or humane society. If you haven't done that lately, you'll be amazed at the changes that have taken place at the pound.

At today's adoption facilities, prospective owners are usually asked to fill out an application form. You'll be asked how long your last pet lived with you and why it no longer does; whether you have a fenced-in yard; and whether you're willing to pledge to have the dog neutered (often at a reduced cost through the rescue center).

You should be prepared to ante up from $35 to $75. But even with the adoption fee, the shelter dog is a bargain compared to the $300 to $500 you will pay if you get your pet from a breeder or pet store.

Speaking of pet stores, I think they can be the worst places to buy a puppy. Many pet stores are supplied by horrible puppy mills that breed sickly dogs in inhumane conditions. The humane societies have worked hard to shut down these puppy mills, but legislation tightening up controls on the industry is still necessary.

When you're getting your dog from a shelter, it's important to interact with him for a bit before making the final decision. If the first thing he does is jump up and start grabbing your fingers, he could be a little too aggressive. Conversely, if he runs and hides in a corner, he may be too timid. What you're looking for is a dog who is friendly and confident and enjoys your company but does fine on his own, too. And, of course, the "lick test" is a hard one to beat!

When Angie and I got our next dog, we used a similar method to make the choice. Only this time we didn't go to a breeder. Charlie, a chocolate Labrador-mix, caught us off-guard when we wandered into the local PetsMart superstore. We had no intention of adding another animal to our menagerie of two cats and two dogs. But knowing full well that a pet shouldn't be acquired on impulse didn't stop us. All it took was one pleading look from the big brown eyes of the sweet brown dog, and we were goners.

I said earlier that purchasing a dog from a pet store wouldn't be my first choice. PetsMart is different. Each of its stores sets aside a space for showcasing adoptable animals brought in from local rescue groups, humane societies, and shelters. This approach makes a lot of sense to me. I applaud their efforts and hope other companies will follow suit in the years to come.

We didn't adopt Charlie that first day. We agreed that we didn't need another dog, and we left her behind. I think we both went home crying.

But the next weekend, we were at the store again, and there was Charlie, right where we had left her. She licked Angie, just as RooRoo had done at the breeder's. But this time, something else happened. Charlie licked me, too! That was the only puppy test I needed. Unlike RooRoo, with her mile-long pedigree and her parents on the premises, Charlie came to us as a totally unknown entity, like most dogs who are adopted from shelters. But she has turned out to be a great dog, and we're glad we took the risk.

We've had some close calls since then—there's always another puppy in PetsMart's Adoption Center who would make a great companion. But we are well aware of our weakness. We've made a rule that we can't go near that adoption area again. We go in, buy food, treats, and toys, and leave. That's it.

WE'RE NOT THE ONLY ONES WHO can't be trusted around pets who need homes. Jennifer and Sam Harris, a couple I worked with, found themselves in quite a pickle when they ventured into the adoption area of their local pet store.

The Harrises had recently lost their dog. Chase, a mixed breed, had been much loved, and they were severely shaken by the tragedy—Sam especially, because he blamed himself for letting Chase run loose in the neighborhood. Although they lived in a gated community, Chase had wandered past the guardhouse and found his way into the busy street, where he was hit by a car.

Sam approached me shortly after the accident and asked if I'd help them get a new dog. He and Jennifer had talked about various breeds, and after much discussion, they decided on a Brittany spaniel. I took them to a professional breeder, who showed them some gorgeous puppies who were well-tempered, true to the breed, and of good hunting stock. I advised them in advance not to consider the runt of the litter, if there was one, or the overly boisterous types that jumped on everyone. They agreed—or so I thought.

After playing with all the puppies, they chose—what else?—the boisterous runt. They loved this little guy because he constantly pounced on their shoes and tried to eat the shoelaces, and they liked the spunky way in which he did it. I didn't try to dissuade them. After all, a Brittany should have quite a bit of spirit. It was best that they were secure in their choice, and I knew that all the pups in the litter were likely to be good ones.

"Thanks for walking us through this," Jennifer said as we left the breeder's. "It's going to be hard without Chase, but it will be nice to have a new dog around." I assured them that I would be on call for any advice they needed in helping the pup adjust to his new environment. They went home several hundred dollars poorer, but eager to prepare the way for the new puppy, which they planned on naming Topper.

After a few days, Topper started to settle in and settle down, and everyone was happy. But one evening, Sam and Jennifer called me from the pet store, where they had gone to buy toys and supplies for their pedigreed friend. Could I come over right away and help them out? I assumed they were having trouble selecting just the right toys and needed my advice. An easy one, for once.

When I got to the store, they were nowhere to be seen. I didn't find them in the toy section. I had no reason to suspect they'd be in the adoption area, but sure enough, there they were, staring into one of the cages, a package of squeaky dog toys and an aqua blue collar forgotten in a small shopping cart beside them.

"What's up, guys?" I asked warily.

They turned to look at me. "You're not going to believe this," said Sam. "It's got to be fate," Jennifer added. I sighed and looked in the cage. An adorable, scruffy brown-and-white mutt smiled back at me, her head tilted to one side.

"Cute," I said. "They're all cute. I don't get it."

They pointed to the card attached to the side of the cage. It said the dog was six to eight months old and had been abandoned at the shelter. Her name was Chase.

"Wow," I said. "Now I get it."

Well, the upshot was that Sam and Jennifer had fallen in love with this dog even though they had a new puppy at home and they felt that having two dogs was out of the question. And they wanted me to tell them what to do. So much for helping them choose between a rubber ball and a rawhide hamburger.

"Look, I can't make this kind of decision for you," I said. "This one you're going to have to think about and then live with it."

"We understand," said Sam, looking glumly at the floor. I looked in the cage once more. Two bright brown eyes looked back hopefully.

"We don't really know anything about this girl, do we?" I said, trying to get a rational conversation going.

"No, just like you and Angie didn't know anything about Charlie." Touché.

A few days went by. Then Sam and Jennifer called to say they had a new dog.

"We couldn't bear to call her Chase," Jennifer explained, "so we changed her name to Lucky."

"Very fitting," I replied. And the other dog? Sam was able to find him a new home with one of his good friends, who was also a hunter. Topper, it appeared, would soon be joyfully chasing rabbits through the Georgia countryside.

UNFORTUNATELY, THE STORY DIDN'T end there. A few weeks after bringing Lucky home, Jennifer and Sam discovered that she had heartworms, a potentially fatal condition. They were devastated.

"We're going to take care of this puppy," Sam told me on the phone. "I let one dog die, and I'm not going to lose another one." The treatment would involve, among other things, restricting Lucky's activity until the danger was past. I wished them well and encouraged them to call anytime.

Shortly thereafter, a local television news station contacted me to do a profile piece, and I mentioned my friends' predicament. "Can we film their story?" the producer asked. I said I would check, and a few days later, there was little Lucky, the star of the six o'clock news. But what I remember more vividly is the image of Sam, a pretty tough customer and a macho guy, sitting on the floor of the living room with his legs apart, enclosing a scruffy little dog in a blanket so she couldn't run about. After the TV cameras were gone, Sam was still there, petting and talking to Lucky. He and Jennifer took turns doing that until the heartworms were gone. When the crisis was finally over, I don't believe the dog was the only one healed.

You would think that with all they had been through, Jennifer and Sam would have put all their energies into caring for, and enjoying, Lucky. But it wasn't long before they called on me again.

"It's about Lucky," Sam told me. "She's a one-person dog." That one person wasn't Sam, it turned out, and he was somewhat miffed. Lucky, he explained, had become very attached to Jennifer. She followed her constantly and totally ignored the man who had noticed her in the first place. "After all the time I spent nursing her back to health!" he groused. "Don't you think I should get a dog of my own?"

I could see he was determined to do just that, and nothing I said was likely to change his mind. So, after discussing the situation, I suggested they take Lucky along when they went to pick another dog. That way, they could discover right away if there were likely to be problems bringing the two dogs together later on. I also gave my usual advice not to pick a dog that seemed overly aggressive or overly shy.

After a few near misses, they finally settled on a little black dog—the only one Lucky didn't bark at. Why would she bark at this pathetic, quivering little dog who literally had to be pulled from her cage? Despite my plea not to take the most timid creature, Sam and Jennifer did just that. They felt that this dog, at least, wouldn't give Lucky any trouble, and they'd be able to give her the love she so obviously needed.

Their vet examined the dog, which they named Comet, and declared her free of heartworms. But he noticed a number of scars on her legs, which he suspected had been caused by barbed wire used to confine or tie her. Comet surely needed a good home, Sam and Jennifer agreed. At first I was concerned that Comet would be too timid to make a good pet, but I needn't have been. Once Sam and Jennifer brought her home and started showering her with attention, Comet's personality began to change.

Within days, Comet rapidly gained confidence. She didn't cower as she had at first, and she seemed very much at home in her new surroundings. These changes should have been a blessing—and they were, for Comet. For Lucky, however, Comet's newfound confidence and her place at the center of the family's affections were more than a little threatening.

Very quickly, Lucky, who previously had been the little princess, accustomed to the couple's undivided attention, began challenging the newcomer. Comet was about twice as big as Lucky, so she wasn't a pushover. I had told the Harrises that same-sex dogs tend to be competitive, but they hadn't really remembered that tidbit when Comet stole their hearts. Besides, Lucky had approved this dog!

Sam and Jennifer wanted to intervene and maintain the status quo. After all, Lucky was there first. But I urged them to let the two dogs sort out for themselves which was to be dominant and then take steps to reinforce their respective roles. In the meantime, they would simply have to cope with dominance wars as the two dogs established their relationship.

When dogs vie for position (and not all dogs do), they make a lot of noise: growling, snapping, and occasionally delivering an inhibited bite. This is normal, I told the Harrises, but in no cases should they allow the jockeying for position to escalate into real aggression, in which dogs aren't just signaling their roles but are biting. If that happened, I would have to step in and help sort things out before they did real damage.

Fortunately, in this case, the dogs worked things out for themselves fairly quickly, with Comet coming out on top. To keep the peace, I told the Harrises, they had to recognize Comet's status by giving her a little more attention, for example, and greeting and feeding her first. Once the roles were clearly established, the dogs' competitiveness would naturally diminish.

After a few months, as things became pretty routine, Sam reassessed the situation and gave me another call. Believe it or not, he wanted another dog! Comet was great, he explained, but she was just too independent. Sam was still longing for that dog who would be devoted to him. Man's best friend, and all that.

I knew I couldn't change the personality of either dog, and I sure couldn't change Sam. He obviously wanted me to say that it was okay to get another dog. I asked if they could handle the demands of a three-dog family, and the answer was an emphatic yes.

"If you can do it, so can we," Sam said. He knew our three dogs were a handful, but definitely worth the hassle. Now, what kind of dog would be best?

"Why don't you go with a male this time?" I offered. Female dogs can usually get away with things in the presence of a male that another female would not tolerate, like being pushy, getting more treats, and so on, the same sorts of problems we'd encountered with Lucky and Comet.

"Try to find one that's pretty submissive," I suggested, "but leave the dogs at home. This time *you* pick the new one." It was important for Sam and the pet-to-be to really connect this time. He couldn't keep going back for more indefinitely.

So Sam and Jennifer went back to the pet adoption area at PetsMart. This time it wasn't the dogs in the cages that attracted their attention, but a cuddly German shepherd-mix who was curled up contentedly, almost catlike, on a volunteer's lap. Sam looked in Zorro's friendly brown eyes and, after a few words with the volunteer, decided to take him home. That was how he finally got his one-man dog. Zorro fit into the family beautifully, never really challenging the other two dogs for a place in the hierarchy.

By this time, the Harrises had become known as an easy mark by the adoption people. Despite the fact that they already had three dogs of their own, they were asked if they'd consider being foster parents for dogs in transition—dogs that had been in the kennel for a long time and needed to be moved out to make room for new arrivals.

"That's really hard," I warned them. Interactions and relationships among four dogs would be even more complex and potentially problematic than among three. Besides, as soon as their pets had adjusted to the newcomer, he'd be on his way out and another would take his place, bringing along an entirely different set of needs and demands. They pretended to listen, but I knew they were hooked. Right away, they took in a cute basset-mix named Candy. Predictably, Jennifer called a few weeks later.

"Don't tell me you can't bear to give her up," I said.

"No, but you were right," Jennifer confessed. "It's been rough on all the dogs, and now it's going to be really hard to let Candy go. She's being adopted by a great family. We just called to tell you that we're not going to foster any more dogs, or adopt anymore either."

"So you're all done for a while, huh?"

They were. What they really wanted now was to quit acquiring and start having fun. They wanted to know if their three dogs could meet with our three for a puppy play date. So we went to a park and had a grand old time—Charlie, RooRoo, Peanut, Lucky, Comet, and Zorro.

In the end, it didn't really matter how the dogs were acquired. Among this romping, bowing, pawing, chasing, panting bunch, one dog was found wandering, one was purchased from a breeder, and four were adopted. But all became much-loved members of their respective households, without any serious behavior problems following them home. Knock on wood.

What it boils down to is this: Nobody really needs a dog or any other pet. But more than 50 million American households decide to get one anyway. To those who are able to use research and common sense to decide what is right for them, and then bite the bullet, take that leap of faith, and bring home that puppy or dog from the breeder or shelter or railroad tracks or junkyard, I applaud you. After that, you just have to figure out how to make that dog the best friend that he was meant to be.

Chapter Three

The Dog Who Needed an Interpreter

"Why is he doing this to me?" Shirley Barnett demanded as she opened the door of her small row home on the outskirts of Atlanta.

"Hi, Shirley," I said. "I'm sure we can . . ."

"Sherlock's been a great dog," the 26-year-old social worker continued, leading me into a small front parlor. "But lately, he's been acting nasty for no reason whatsoever." Sherlock, a one-and-a-half-year-old male basset hound, sniffed at my socks, his ears dragging across the carpet, while a smaller basset followed closely behind.

I had taken a pretty detailed history over the phone, and I knew that Sherlock had been nipping pretty frequently—nothing serious, but cause for any owner to get help before things got worse. I looked down at my notes.

Dog has bitten owner in the car and in the house. Bites guy next door—lunged when scolded. Mother's visit—more incidents.

"So, Sherlock bit your mother on the stomach?"

"Oh, my God, that was awful," Shirley said. "Talk about alienating your parents! He didn't really hurt her, but my mom threatened not to visit me again until I got him to stop this stuff." She cautiously patted Sherlock on the head as Watson, the smaller basset, plopped down at her feet.

Sherlock looked friendly enough, but I knew from 15 years of house calls that looks can be deceiving. Sometimes the animal puts on his best doggy manners when the animal behaviorist makes a call. That's why having the client tell me about the animal's misdeeds is the best way to get the picture. Even if the owner doesn't understand what is going on or have a clue what to do about it, she can usually pretty accurately describe the behavioral problem.

As we sat together in the parlor, Shirley told me in more detail what had been going wrong. "Sherlock will get up on the couch, and he might have a dog bone or a toy or something," she said. "He'll be chewing or eating away, and sometimes I'll come over. That's when he starts growling."

"Whoa, let's back up a little, okay?" I said. "Shirley, have you ever heard that some dogs feel threatened if people come around them while they're eating or chewing on something?"

"Of course, I've heard that," she said, giving me a look. "But Sherlock isn't that kind of dog." She shook her head firmly. "He's not like that at all. He's so sweet most of the time. Something else must be wrong with him."

I sat back to reflect for a moment. Here was a dog displaying clear signs of protecting his food or play toy, but his owner, who seemed to be quite intelligent, was in deep denial. I had to find out why.

"Shirley, it's possible there's something wrong, but I'm kind of curious as to why you are so sure that Sherlock isn't just protecting his food or toy. Why isn't that a likely scenario? Is it just too obvious?" I privately wondered if the complex situations of her own social-work clients had blinded her to the simple nature of the situation on her own turf.

"Of course," she replied. "What dog is all of a sudden ready to growl and bite after he looks right at you and wags his tail? If he looked threatened, I wouldn't go up to him. But he seems all ready to play, and then he nails me."

"I see," I replied. Now we were getting somewhere. "What exactly do you mean by 'wags his tail?' "

Shirley gave me another look. "You know, a dog moves his tail back and forth to show he's happy and friendly and all that." I noticed her tone had changed to one a teacher might use with a slow first-grader. She peered at me to see if I understood the concept of a dog wagging his tail.

"Yeah, gotcha," I said quickly, before a crisis of confidence could develop. "But I need to know more about Sherlock's tail when it's wagging. Does he hold it high or low? Is it really wagging, or is it more like swishing back and forth?"

After a few minutes of discussion, I was able to convince Shirley that Sherlock wasn't wagging his tail in happy anticipation of playtime, as she thought. He was swishing it and staring at her, his way of telling her not to come any closer. From Sherlock's point of view, he gave her fair warning. She ignored it, so he did what he had to do. It wasn't his fault if humans didn't understand him.

Shirley wasn't the only one confused about canine communication. One of my students and I conducted a study at Mercer University in Macon, where I teach psychology, to test students' understanding of dog body language. I had an artist draw slides of a German shepherd in various postures, from submissive and friendly to assertive and slightly aggressive. In the drawings, the ears, eyes, mouth, and tail were decidedly different. My intent was to find out if people could recognize and interpret the differences.

I was not surprised to find that the students did indeed see the differences. But the majority said they would be more likely to approach the dog with the aggressive posture than the "friendly" dog.

It's easy to misinterpret the signs a dog is displaying. But a dog looking at you with intense interest, muscles taut and tail held high, swishing back and forth, is not being friendly. He's probably trying to control your activity or debating whether or not to take a piece out of your hide.

A truly friendly dog, on the other hand, will display a smiley mouth and avoid prolonged eye contact. His hindquarters might move from side to side, propelled by a rapidly wagging low tail as he makes his approach toward you. A friendly dog may actually bow to you by lifting his rear end and stretching his legs out in front of him, inviting play. Or he may roll onto his back in a more passive friendly manner.

Then there are the verbal cues. Barking can be harmless or a warning. But overall, give me a barking dog any day over a silent, staring one or one who has an ominous growl to offer you. Those guys mean business.

One of the things Shirley tried when Sherlock started growling was squirting him with a squirt gun. Many of my clients have tried squirt guns before they called me, usually with little success. Either the squirt had no effect or the problem got even worse. Yet squirt guns continue to be popular tools in the hands of cat and dog owners trying to control their pets. I don't recommend them because they're usually not effective, or they may be too effective and can freak out certain overstressed animals.

Anytime you get into a situation when a dog is growling at you, and you add just about any kind of stimulation, especially the kind that's likely to anger him even more, he is likely to get more aggressive. I explained this to Shirley, and she replied that she had employed yet another method to stop Sherlock from growling. This one was even worse.

"I stick my hand in his mouth so he'll stop growling," she explained. I looked at her incredulously. After hundreds of house calls, it still amazes me to hear how some people let good common sense fly out the window when it comes to their beloved pets.

"Shirley, let me count your fingers," I said, shaking my head.

"Please don't do that again. Let's see if we can't find some better strategies for coping with Sherlock."

I explained that she needed to become the leader in the relationship, and Sherlock had to be the follower. This was not to be accomplished by squirting him, putting her hand in his mouth, hitting him, yelling at him, staring him down, or pinning him to the ground.

Experts once believed that people needed to confront dogs with canine aggression signals in order to become dominant to them. We now know this isn't the case. In fact, for dogs who are already aggressive, this behavior sets up a confrontation, and a dog can inflict severe damage in the blink of an eye.

"Well, if that doesn't work, what does?" Shirley asked.

"We've found that you can get a lot more compliance out of your dog if you don't threaten him but if you manipulate him into doing 'good' things, then praise and reward him as though they were his idea," I replied.

"Okay, like how?" she asked.

I asked Shirley to think about what made her dog happy. Even the most difficult dog usually has a toy, activity, or phrase that makes his ears perk up and his tail start wagging, not swishing. I asked her to make a list, with the most favored phrases or sights at the top and the less favored but still happy items at the bottom. The idea is that a dog will do something—even give up something lower on the list—to get something higher up.

So we sat down and came up with a list of things that made Sherlock stop what he was doing and look up or smile in anticipation. The list included the sight of his leash, a shaking doggy-treat box, his squeaky mouse, chow time, and the phrases "Let's go for a walk," "Wanna go outside?" "Where's your red ball?" and "Get your bowl."

Shirley was to use this list as a guide whenever Sherlock showed signs of becoming aggressive or noncompliant. The concept behind this is pretty simple. A dog can't be all tensed up, staring, and growling at the same time he is smiling, wagging his body back and forth, and anticipating a good time. Shirley could use one or more of the items on the list to change Sherlock's mood and, therefore, his behavior, for which she would then praise and reward him. Eventually, he would learn that the way to get what he wanted (praise, rewards) was to behave in a certain way. That certain way was made possible by the sight of his favorite toy or talk about his dinner. It's the very essence of the old saying, "You can catch more flies with honey than with vinegar."

Shirley found she could use the ball and mouse together, since Sherlock would give up one to get the other—a very different scenario from his usual growling and swishing his tail when she came to take something from him. When she made a game of it and acted as if she had the best toy, Sherlock would drop the one he was playing with, and Shirley would toss him the ball or mouse she had been holding.

I told her not to tease him with a toy but to use his favorite words and toys to elicit a happy, playful mood. As time went by, Shirley discovered that when nothing else did the trick, she could rely on the old favorite "Outside!" to get his attention. Their bouts of play became a daily habit, and their relationship gradually improved. During our weekly phone follow-ups, Shirley told me that Sherlock occasionally would get into a confrontational mood, and she would occasionally respond in kind until she remembered what worked. Eventually, she tossed the squirt gun in the trash can and saved a lot of fingers as well.

THERE IS NO ONE POINT AT WHICH you are done with behavior modification. It's an ongoing process. Sometimes one or the other of you will slip up; that's just human and canine nature. But the slipups are made tolerable by the stable relationship you and your dog will develop—a relationship that's reaffirmed daily through actions and a variety of nonverbal cues. Your dog lying contentedly by your side, gazing adoringly into your eyes—this speaks volumes!

I recently had another client who was in big trouble because he misinterpreted his dog's behavior. The dog was simply continuing to do certain things that she had been rewarded for doing when she was a puppy. Now that she was older, her owners thought she was bad.

"I don't know why she has to be so rough or why she's always hanging on us," Joe Berenson complained as we stood on his patio watching his one-and-a-half-year-old Akita, Kippy, chew on a rawhide bone. "She begs us to pet her, follows us from room to room, and leans against us every chance she gets," he went on. "And she growls when we roughhouse with her."

"Okay," I said, jotting down some notes, "How long has she been doing these various things?" It didn't take him long to answer.

"Oh, she's been doing them all her life." He grinned ruefully. "We used to think it was cute, the way she'd put her chin on our laps, but now it's like she's demanding attention. And when we put our fingers in her mouth like we used to, she nips pretty hard."

I put down my pen. "So is your dog doing exactly what you trained her to do from puppyhood? She doesn't know these things are not cute anymore?"

He nodded his head. "I guess you're right," he said. But he didn't understand why roughhousing with a puppy was a problem. Everyone does that, don't they?

I explained that some dogs seem to be more inclined to continue assertive behavior as they mature and that he had picked one of them. If we had met when Kippy was a puppy, I would have recommended that he and his wife take on a stronger leadership role from the beginning.

"Right now, she does pretty much what she wants," he complained.

"Hasn't she always, Joe?" He nodded. That was just my point.

Joe needed some education on the signals animals give. He also needed to focus on what signals he was sending back to his dog. And the signals he and his wife, Beth, had always sent to Kippy were, "That's so cute, do it again!" Then Kippy got older, and the message the Berensons wanted to send was, "Hey, cut that out!" It must have been extremely confusing for Kippy, who liked everything just the way it had always been, thank you.

It's important to think about what you are training or conditioning a dog to do, right from the beginning. Remember, your dog does not enter your life as a clean slate. He's already done a lot of communicating by the time he gets to your home. His experience with his mother and littermates will shape his response to people and other animals in the weeks to come and, barring a traumatic experience, for the rest of his life.

Imagine a litter of puppies, about a month old. Even though they are all twins, they are in the process of becoming individuals. They are walking around, stepping out of the whelping box, going back in, and so on. This one likes to explore; this other one wants to stay with Mom; this one over here is afraid of strangers. They're all different, and they're all in the process of learning how to behave. They depend on body language—their own as well as that of their littermates—to figure out what's going to happen next. *If I walk up to you, are you going to be friendly, are we going to play, or are you going to do something that will hurt me?*

Puppies start to make associations between the way their littermates look and what is going to happen next. They are egocentric in this sense: They can only view the world in terms of what will happen to them. They view people the same way. *Gee, I see you're leaning forward and making eye contact. I've seen that before in this pup over here. I know you're not a dog, but I just need to keep track of when you look that way so I'll know what's going to happen next.*

Communication is a two-way street, which is why it's so important for people to be able to decode dog body language and social signals.

Speaking of eye contact, I think it's the single most important motivator of behavior in dogs. It's also very individual. That's why I ended up telling the Berensons to instruct visitors in their home not to even look at, much less touch, their Akita.

"Our neighbor, Ted, just loved to play with Kippy," Beth told me. Kippy loved to roughhouse, and so did Ted. But since Kippy had confrontational tendencies, she often got carried away and got a little too rough. Ted remembered something he had read about how to show a dog who's boss. But Kippy hadn't read the book. And she wasn't used to being challenged.

"He thought he should grab her by the jowls, look her right in the eye, and shake her," recalled Beth. "It seemed to make sense at the time."

"Did he yell 'No!' too?" I asked.

"Oh, yes, he sure did."

I didn't even need to ask her what happened next. I knew it would involve snarling and growling and lunging and biting. Anytime you set up a confrontation with a dog like an Akita, you are asking for trouble.

In Kippy's case, the Berensons had set the stage for future problems when they allowed her to manipulate them. Kippy learned early on how to get what she wanted by displaying cute puppy behaviors like staring up at them with soulful eyes or putting her chin on Joe's thigh.

The Berensons didn't know it, but this particular behavior is well-known to animal behaviorists. It's called, strangely enough, the chin rest, and it's a move puppies perform with each other. The chin-rester is generally the dog who is being assertive or controlling of the other dog. If the other dog accepts it, then you have the beginning of a relationship in which one dog is dominant and the other subordinate. The Berensons, you'll recall, accepted, praised, and rewarded Kippy for this behavior. In essence, they were encouraging her to be in charge.

Kippy's next move was to put her head on their feet so they couldn't get up and move around. Or she'd mouth their hands and arms and encourage them to move in one direction or another. Once again, they would laugh, pet her, give her a treat, and, of course, do what she wanted. As she got bigger, Kippy began using these moves to demand rather than ask for things. She would lie in the halls at home so no one could get by. When people stepped over her rather than making her move, Kippy knew she had the upper hand. It was a small step from that to aggression. Kippy didn't even have to fight for her dominant status in that household. She was rewarded for it from the time she was a puppy.

Now I'm not blaming the owners or the roughhousing neighbor for the dog's problems. There is no point in assessing blame in most cases of animal misbehavior, especially when the owners are taking steps to try to change the situation by calling me rather than kicking the dog out of the door.

At any rate, Kippy was definitely prepared to act in a dominant role, and, unfortunately, the human beings in her life played out the scenario beautifully. With another dog, the chin-resting and constant gazes might have meant nothing more than "Hello." But with Kippy, they were warning signs. It took a program of mood manipulation, submissiveness training, and a lot of praise for nonassertive behavior to restore the balance of power in that household.

When owners ignore assertive, demanding behavior and praise submissive behavior, dogs get a new perspective on how to be good dogs. Removing temptations like hands and feet, giving time-outs, and learning to change the dog's mood helped the Berensons establish a new relationship with their pet. The new signals Kippy was getting enabled her to become a more friendly animal, and eventually, visitors were even permitted to look at the proud Akita without their gaze being taken as a gauntlet thrown down.

This is not to say that eye contact with a dog is bad. In most cases, if you happen to lock eyes with your own dog, it's not going to provoke World War III. My three dogs are a case in point. With Charlie, the chocolate Lab, all you have to do is glance at her from across the room and instantly, she's beside you, ready for action. On the other hand, I can sit and look at RooRoo, the standard poodle, for a minute, neither of us averting our gaze, and we just go on sitting there and that's that. Peanut, the mixed terrier, is somewhere in the middle. She can establish eye contact and wait half a minute, then will usually walk over and give your hand a nudge, as if to say, *I'm here, what's up? Now pet me already!* With Peanut, an ignored nose nudge leads quickly to, *Oh, never mind.* She lies back down again and groans. Not exactly a dominance challenge.

So eye contact with each of them produces a very different pattern of behavior. The more you pay attention to what your dog responds to in terms of eye contact, the more you'll understand what he is trying to tell you, and the better relationship you're likely to have.

I SEE A LOT OF PEOPLE LIKE Shirley and the Berensons, who don't understand dog communication and whose dogs can't figure out what people want from them. We think we're being friendly, and they think we're being threatening. Or they're trying to give us fair warning before they nail us, and we think they're inviting us to pet them. Misunderstandings like these are what lead to house calls from animal behavior therapists or even trips to the emergency room. We know that dogs don't regard people as other canines, but they use the same rules because they are genetically prepared to work that way.

When you try to teach a young dog to shake hands, you pick up his little paw and say "Shake." Lo and behold, he shakes. It's a nice activity, and if the dog is fairly submissive to you, he will readily raise his paw.

This isn't because you're such a good teacher but because when dogs are puppies they learn that raising their paws and getting access to Mom standing over them is the best way to get some nourishment. They associate picking up their paws with things that feel good, and it's a nice subordinate gesture that transfers into adult life. The rules the puppy learns in the early weeks of life help him adopt certain roles in relation to other dogs and to people.

The first role is the subordinate role I just mentioned. A dog can be passively submissive to a person or another dog, for example, by rolling onto her back. Or she can be actively submissive, in which she approaches a person or another dog in an indirect, side-to-side sort of way. If you speak to an actively passive dog, she may look away, crouch down, or roll over into a passive, submissive posture.

In a submissive posture, the ears are rotated back against the head, and the dog avoids eye contact. It's pretty interesting to watch a submissive pup approach a dog he doesn't know. He may pretend to be sniffing the ground rather than risk a direct approach and a possible confrontation.

We go through pretty much the same kind of thing when we approach someone, even someone we know, and dogs probably have the same kinds of feelings. When I see a person from a distance, I smile, but then I look down and avoid eye contact while I'm approaching. As I get near, we look up and greet each other. Dogs do this, too.

Think how uncomfortable you would be if the person you were approaching stared at you the entire time. Well, assertive dogs use this technique, although probably not consciously, and other dogs perceive it as a threat. The other dogs, unless they're assertive themselves, will avoid eye contact if they know what's good for them. They will also display other submissive signals and behaviors if they are prone to subordinate status. So will a prudent person if the dog is unfamiliar to them or is known to be aggressive.

Animal behaviorists have spent quite a bit of time studying how dogs greet each other. We often find ourselves in the middle of a bunch of bounding little guys and girls who joyfully run up and throw themselves at us, literally. Wham, right into a leg! They don't know how to greet politely yet, much less how to stop. Eventually, they start to pay attention to what other dogs do in greeting. *Aha! We come up and we stand, and then we sniff things like ears and rear ends.* At the same time, they figure out what their littermates are going to do by the signals they're giving.

They learn there are right and wrong ways to greet, whether they're approaching a puppy or a person. They approach, circle, stand, and sniff—either head-to-head or head-to-groin. The chemical attractants in urine, called pheromones, give an indication of whom they are sniffing.

Who are you? Do I know you? Have I smelled you before? Are you a male or a female? Did you leave your smell on that fire hydrant back there? And so on. Studies have shown that by 24 weeks of age, a puppy can identify not only his own litter by the smell of urine but the identity of individual pups as well.

Unfortunately, dogs can get the same information from people, which is why their noses poke into such embarrassing places. It's important for owners to teach a young dog that this kind of communication is okay for dogs, but not permitted with people. But if we understand that dogs are simply gathering information, we might be less likely to swat them with the newspaper for being rude.

Most of the time, when two dogs greet, the one who initiates the sniff is the more assertive and is likely to wind up in the dominant role. The one who allows the sniff is on his way to being the underdog. Many times, both dogs are subordinate and there are no problems if both allow the sniffing. But if they both want to be top dog, there may be a fight.

When I talk to pet owners or animal-control officers, I explain that when they see a dog they don't know in the distance, the dog will expect them to follow canine rules of greeting. They don't have to get down on all fours and sniff. The appropriate way to greet a strange dog is to avoid eye contact, squat down so you're on the dog's level, and let him come to you and sniff. Contrary to what most people have been taught, the dog does not have to sniff your hand. In fact, if you stick out your hand, particularly by raising it over the dog's head, the dog very well may view that as a threat and respond accordingly.

You have odors everywhere, including on your knees and shoulders. If you keep your hands in front of you, between your legs, the dog can come up and, as you're glancing away, sniff your knee. Chances are he will start to wag his tail, and then you may want to stroke or pet him underneath the chin. You will have greeted the dog in a way he can understand and won't feel threatened by. You've set the stage for a good relationship.

Some other submissive signals dogs use are a smiling face or grin and a tail that is down and wagging. Sometimes the dog's whole rear end moves back and forth. This, of course, is a very good sign. The looser the muscle tone, the less likely it is that the dog is prepared to bite. When a dog lies down and rolls over onto his back as you or another dog approaches, that's about the ultimate submissive signal. *I'm totally defenseless, but since I'm being so honest, I know you're not going to hurt me.*

Sometimes you'll see a dog yawning or licking her lips. She may be carrying her weight a little more toward the rear, or she may be standing off to the side. These are signs that she's a little bit conflicted. She may be willing to do something in a subordinate role, but she's not sure she wants to.

When I give workshops to animal-control officers, I try to help them learn about dog communication signals so that they can avoid personal injury when they have to deal with dog fights. I tell them that if they see dogs staring at one another, that is the time to move in quickly, but cautiously, and draw the dogs' attention away from each other. This will make it easier to separate them.

As owners, we usually follow our instincts when our pets go into battle with another dog; that is, we yell bloody murder. And your dog is very likely to misunderstand. You yell, "No, Brutus! Stop! Get off! No! Bad dog! Come here!" But Brutus hears, "Go Brutus! Yes! Hold him down! I'm coming in!" And then he wonders why he's relegated to the doghouse to lick his wounds when it's all over. Since he might not understand your signals, you'd sure as heck better learn to understand his.

Chances are, before the fight, one or both dogs were doing things like staring and appearing rigid and stiff, with their weight distributed toward the fronts of their bodies. Their ears would have been rotated forward and tails held straight up or out and swishing slowly back and forth. The lips would have been pushed forward, just the opposite of a smile face. The dogs would have been facing each other straight on or standing next to each other. There may have been low, throaty growls or snarls. The dogs might have barked or been silent, intent on their target. Never assume that a dog who is not barking is a happy camper, especially if the body language tells you otherwise.

Of course, body language can be tricky, depending on the breed. A Doberman is sometimes hard to read because its tail is docked. Beagles are tough to read, too. In the studies I've done with beagles, I'd have to say that the tail is simply always up. If it's up, that means they're aroused. I think beagles are a bit aroused a lot of the time.

Does that mean beagles are always ready to rumble? No. There is no communication value to a tail being held aloft unless there is another animal or person in the picture. Only then does the tail position become a social signal. If the dog is looking at a worm on the sidewalk and his tail is high and waving, that is not communicative behavior. But when he turns and looks straight at you, his tail seems to be growing out of his head, his ears are rotated forward, his body is tense, and he growls, that's when his tail position takes on relevance.

I remember one time when I was participating in a voluntary flea dip, in which people would bring in their pets for a dousing. I handled a bunch of them with no problem, but then there was one big Rottweiler. The owner handed me his leash. I was purposely not looking at the dog, but I could see out of the corner of my eye that he was looking at me. He was actually staring at me. Tail up, muscles tense, and ears forward. Did I whisper in his ear, pet him, and then force him into a prone position and hold him down while the medicine was applied? Not on your life. I handed the leash back to the owner and said politely, "Would you mind handling Tiny yourself today? I don't think he likes me."

"Sure thing," he said brightly, with a condescending smile. I didn't care. I play by the rules, too.

Fear consists of an entirely different set of communicative signals. It's not really a role, the way dominant and subordinate are, but it is an emotional state that is pretty easy to recognize.

A frightened dog will tuck his tail between his legs and turn his body away from the person or animal. There may be a whimper or whine. The ears will be back against the head, and, of course, there will be no eye contact, at least at first. A fearful dog will often bite as well.

Sometimes a frightened dog will try to bluff those around him into thinking he is the most macho thing going, but his signals give him away. To illustrate this point, I sometimes show a video of a dog and cat in the waiting room of a veterinarian's office. Everyone knows that dogs hate cats and torment them and so forth, right? Well, if you have a dog and cat and you've been around them for any length of time, you know it's usually the opposite. In my tape, the dog, a big shepherd-mix type, probably feels he has a job to do: Show the cat who's boss.

I'm a dog, and I've read those books, too, and this cat better watch out. So he starts making a fuss, and, of course, the cat hisses back at him and swipes at him with her paw. The dog is barking up a storm, but his tail is tucked and his ears are back. *I guess I have to get this cat, it's my job and all, but I really don't want to. She's pretty scary. Maybe she'll be my friend.* Eventually, the cat jumps on her owner's lap, turns her back, and starts licking her paw to get that icky taste of dog off. The dog goes up to his owner, a 10-year-old kid who's reading a comic book, and licks his hand. *Wasn't I good? Wasn't I tough? What do I get for that?* And the kid, who couldn't care less, tells him to sit down and be quiet. And it's all over.

So instead of just looking at the barking and chasing behavior of the dog, you have to look at the components, the whole constellation of behavior signals, to read the dog's emotional state.

Yet another set of communication behaviors that we see in dogs is play. Play signals are really not signals that convey information in and of themselves. But they indicate something about the behavior that will follow. When a dog wants to play, he may make a huge play-bow to another dog or a person. We see this in the litter and later on at home when your dog wants you to throw a ball for him. The legs are extended in front, the rear end is up in the air, and the tail is wagging. You may see an expectant look on his face.

With these larger-than-life gestures, a submissive dog may approach a more assertive dog and in effect announce, *We both know I'm subordinate to you, but if we play, you promise not to bite me or pin me to the ground and do nasty things to me, right?* And the dominant dog shows his agreement by bowing back or pawing at the first dog's face as they did in play with their littermates. And then they play and all the signals they display and the behavior they show is exaggerated. Big smile faces. Meta-communication.

Sometimes roles are reversed during play. The dogs have an understanding. The subordinate one can pin the more dominant dog against a wall and escape with his hide still intact. But the dominant one can call it all off by turning his back and walking away or giving a little nip to the other dog, signaling, *Okay, enough of this. I'm boss again.*

What does all this mean to the owner? Well, dogs are going to give humans the same signals they give other canines. If the dog turns his back as if to say "Enough," and the human doesn't get the message, the dog may give that very same nip to emphasize that he's ending the play session. That can be frightening and dangerous.

Dogs need to play and to end play, and we want to efficiently and effectively fulfill their needs. Owners should be aware of what signals their dogs are sending when they want to play and when they want to stop.

A colleague of mine, doing research with wolves, noted that two wolves would consistently move next to each other and then freeze for a few moments before beginning to play. After much studying, he finally concluded that one wolf was rolling its eyes to indicate it was time to play. Dogs usually give much more obvious signals. They paw the air, or they paw a hand or knee. They'll bring a toy, bark or howl, run in circles, jump up, or whack you with their hips.

On the other hand, sometimes a dog will give a play-bow and then bite you! There are dog con artists out there. Or sometimes play develops into play-fighting, which can develop into real fighting. So just because you see a play-bow, don't say to a visitor, "Oh, don't worry, he's just playing," Many facial bites in youngsters under 10 years old are in the context of play. Don't just assume a dog will never bite, even your own.

We need to know communication behaviors because they help us interpret what the dog's emotional and motivational state is. They help us interpret what he's likely to do next, and they allow us to use some of these behaviors ourselves, like smiling, looking away, staring, greeting properly, and playing.

My point is that we can avoid getting into bad relationships with our dogs if we just remember that we need to respond in ways they understand, which are the ways they learned from their mothers and littermates.

If an owner totally ignores his dog's language and thinks of his pet as an unfathomable thing or just an empty vessel, that's when animal behaviorists—or the emergency room nurse—are likely to hear that the dog did crazy things for no reason or that the bite or scratch or attack was completely unprovoked. When I hear this, I can make an educated guess that the dog and his owner weren't communicating, and they're not going to have a mutually satisfying relationship. Unless things change, the behavior problem is probably going to get worse, not better.

Luckily, that doesn't have to happen. When we humans educate ourselves about dog language and communication, we will be more effective in teaching our dogs to do what we want them to. And it sure is better to be on speaking terms with a companion animal than on the outs.

Chapter Four

The Dog Who Kept His Master Out of the Bedroom

ORVIS WAS A GORGEOUS, SILKY springer spaniel who could have been plucked from the robust hunting scenes that decorated the library walls of his family's tasteful brick home in the heart of Atlanta. Orvis and his owners had a bad case of the notorious malady, "a failure to communicate." And for this trio, that meant Orvis was in charge.

After bluntly stating on the phone that he was fed up, Orvis's owner, Ashley Bancroft, confided that the dog was "negatively impacting" his marriage.

"Trying to ruin our private life, if you catch my drift," he hinted darkly.

"Uh, I see," I said. Ashley declined to elaborate on the telephone but said I'd understand when I got there.

Before he hung up, he told me that his wife, Lauren, was upset because Orvis had apparently failed to recognize her the day before and had stopped just short of a snarling attack. Two men working on the house hadn't been so lucky. Orvis had bitten both of them as well as a four-year-old boy. Could I come at once? It sounded as though I needed to. So I cleared my calendar and headed over.

As I lifted the heavy, pineapple-shaped brass knocker, I noticed the boarded-up window next to the front door. A few remaining shards of glass lay at my feet. Lauren, dark-haired and clad in a peach suit, opened the door. She glanced at the window as she offered me a manicured hand.

"Orvis did this yesterday, trying to attack a friend of ours," she said without preamble. "The glazier will be here this afternoon to fix the window," she said, "if he's brave enough." She withdrew her hand. "Please come in, Dr. Wright. We're so glad you're here."

To my relief, Orvis was shut in the laundry room, barking at the unknown intruder. I shook hands with Ashley, an energetic corporate-exec type who had joined us in the living room and announced briskly that he was ready to get down to business if I was.

"This dog is out of control," Ashley said. "He thinks he's running the place, and if he bites another plumber, I'm going to have lawsuits coming at me. What am I going to do with him?"

"Well, let's get a handle on what's going on with Orvis," I said. "Does Orvis seem to try to control your movements?"

"Control?" Mr. Bancroft said. "Only if you consider forcing me out of my own bedroom trying to control me. I haven't slept with my own wife for six weeks thanks to that dog!"

"Now, Ashley . . ."

"Well, Lauren, let's call a spade a spade here," Ashley fumed, shaking his head. "Are we or are we not sleeping in separate bedrooms because of Orvis?" His wife nodded her head miserably. I decided to forge ahead.

"Some dogs see it as their job to guard certain family members at night," I told them. "What exactly does Orvis do?" I looked at each of them, my pencil poised over the diagnosis form. They both started talking at once. By the time they finished half an hour later, I understood pretty well what was going on in this exquisite show-place. Essentially, two high-powered executives were being held hostage by a springer spaniel.

They had started out with Orvis just like most people do when they get a dog, making decisions from a human point of view, naturally. They picked a convenient (for them) room for him to sleep in, the utility room. They provided a wonderful (to them) cedar-chip, scotch-plaid dog bed ordered from an expensive mail-order house. For a time, Orvis was comfortable in his new digs, and everyone was happy.

But problems began to surface. Whenever Orvis would mis-behave, he'd be shut in the utility room for a time-out. He began to associate his bedroom with being punished. So he looked for a new place to sleep.

When he evaluated the master bedroom, Orvis found it very much to his liking. It had the added advantage of providing a great vantage point from which to stand guard over the family—his per-ceived duty.

This would have been fine, except Orvis decided that once the Bancrofts entered the bedroom to get ready for bed, no one else was allowed in. This wasn't a problem when they both retired to the bedroom at the same time. But when one of them tried to come to bed later, Orvis felt it was his duty to guard the sleeping one and treat the other as an intruder. He would block the doorway and growl, stare, or lunge threateningly until he or she stepped away.

So Ashley had taken to sleeping in a guest room. "It was safer that way," he said. "And don't think I'm being cowardly," he added. He removed his glasses. "Five stitches," he announced, drawing my attention to a wound on his upper cheek. "I made the mistake of petting the dog when he was waking up on the couch."

I took down all their complaints, then tried to summarize in my mind the types of aggression this dog had exhibited to his family.

"Don't you want to meet Orvis, Dr. Wright?" Lauren asked.

"I don't want to overly excite him right now," I said. Even less did I want to have to make a detour to the emergency room on the way to my next appointment. "I may want to say hello to him later, but I think I understand Orvis pretty well from your description of what's been going on."

Okay. Orvis was showing a combination of dominance aggression toward both of the Bancrofts and possessive aggression, especially when he was occupying a particular area of the house—which to Orvis was an important resource. He would also guard a chair, couch, or chaise in the bedroom. If they approached him while he "protected" these resources, he would lunge. There was also protective territorial aggression, in which he would lash out at those who didn't have his permission to be close to him and his family.

Each of these different kinds of aggression was characterized by a tendency to control, assert, and act out, rather than avoid.

"He's always been a little hyper," Lauren said. "But now he just won't let anyone come in the house. We have to lock him up."

"Look, we've got a pretty good security system here," Ashley said. "I don't mind if the dog barks at a stranger, but we sure don't need him to be ripping people apart."

"I understand."

Orvis's aggression wasn't limited to the house. When Lauren was with him, he would act protectively in other places as well—in the car, for example, or at the vet's office. This also suggested protective territorial aggression, in which the dog exhibits aggression toward anyone who gets too close to *his* car, owner, or another family pet. It's as if the dog takes responsibility for determining who will have access to which people and what desirable things.

What to do? The two-year-old Orvis was already neutered. What he needed was some experience in being subordinate to the people in the house, and they needed some direction in how to be effective leaders.

"It's much easier to be in charge at the office," Lauren remarked. "And not nearly as dangerous," Ashley added, gingerly touching his cheek.

"Okay, let's do some brainstorming," I said. "I need you to come up with a list of items, words, or expressions that hold some pleasant meaning for Orvis. Put the things he likes best at the top of the list and things he likes less well at the bottom. We're going to use the items on this list to elicit a change of mood that will head off some of these behaviors before Orvis gets too carried away."

I advised them to start somewhere around the middle of the list when Orvis began showing signs of impending misbehavior.

"Why?"

"Because if that doesn't work, you can go to the next higher item and you haven't run out of options. The idea is to create a happy, compliant mood with items, objects, or activities he likes and short-circuit the dangerous moods. A dog can't be happy and angry at the same time."

The Bancrofts had told me that Orvis would typically stiffen up when he was about to do something aggressive. When they saw this in the future, I told them, they were to use one of the items on the list to put him in a happy mood.

"That sounds awfully simple," Ashley said suspiciously.

"It's not complicated," I agreed, "but there's a lot of research behind the process." It's a classical, or Pavlovian, conditioning procedure, and it's only part of the answer. "Do you want to start making the list now, or do you want to work on it together later?"

"No, let's do it," Ashley said. "Let's see . . . his walk is a big one, so 'Go for walk?' should be on there. And then there's 'Go get your ball.'"

"Don't forget 'Where's Daddy's slipper?'" Lauren added. "There's 'Popcorn time!' and 'Go-o-od Orvis' and 'Here's your leash.'"

With that effort well under way, I turned to another aspect of the treatment plan. An important way to put the owners into a leadership position is to make the dog do something for them before he gets what he wants. Fortunately, Orvis was willing to obey a variety of commands, so the Bancrofts could use this tool to its fullest. In the future, they were to make Orvis sit before he was fed. He had to stay before he was taken outside for a walk. He had to lie down before he was permitted to jump on the couch.

Animal behaviorists have aptly described this concept as "nothing in life is free." By making Orvis work for his pleasures, he would learn to be subordinate to both owners. In addition, I told them, it was important to praise him for being subordinate.

This approach works much better than forcing a dog to do something, which is sometimes impossible anyway, and then praising him. In aggressive dogs, coercion followed by praise rarely works, and even if it does, it can be dangerous. It sets up a power struggle in which the dog struggles against the people, the people struggle against the dog, and you have a snowball effect, causing the aggression to escalate.

Orvis tended to be at his most intransigent in certain areas. I felt it made sense to make those areas off-limits. If Orvis was no longer permitted in the bedroom at night, I explained, he would automatically experience fewer instances of controlling-type aggression.

The Bancrofts looked at each other and rolled their eyes.

"We've already tried that," Ashley said. "It didn't work. That's why we called you."

"What did you try?" I asked, trying to ignore his patronizing tone. People don't call animal behaviorists until they've tried everything in the book. Even when they're on the right track, they usually give up in frustration because they've been looking for an easy fix.

"Two different things," Lauren said. "Closing the bedroom door and shutting him in the laundry room. But Orvis cried and barked all night," she said. "No one got any sleep."

That made sense. "You were preventing him from doing his duty," I said. "He must have been frantic."

Unfortunately, there was no easy way to solve this part of the problem. "The good news is, I'm going to ask you to move back into the master bedroom together."

"And the bad news?" Ashley asked.

"Well, you're very likely going to lose a few more nights' sleep before things begin to turn around. May I suggest that you think about starting the retraining on a weekend, when you don't have to face your business day in the morning?"

I knew they'd be more likely to persevere if the stresses surrounding them were minimized. I asked the Bancrofts if they would consider buying a baby gate to put across their open door at night. This would allow Orvis to still keep tabs on them, but he would not be allowed in the bedroom to growl and lunge at them.

The Bancrofts took my advice. They put a nice braided rug on the hardwood floor in the hallway where Orvis could lie down and still see into the room. Of course, he carried on for the first three or four days. Then he started to comply. After a while he learned that this was a comfortable place to sleep, and he began using it more often.

After the first week, he would start the evening lying on the carpet, then move to other locations during the night. This helped change the dynamics of what had been an unhealthy relationship. Orvis no longer felt he had to protect his owners all the time. He was less likely to be in a confrontational mode and a rotten mood, and the Bancrofts began to assume the leadership role.

The idea was that the Bancrofts had to take responsibility for the household, letting Orvis off the hook. I literally wrote that in their treatment program. If they could manage a staff of employees at work and a stream of service people at home, they should be able to take charge of their dog. Once they understood the concept, the specifics were pretty easy.

For example, when Orvis started to act up when people came over, the Bancrofts were to put him in the utility room until he calmed down and the people were going about their business. Then Orvis would be brought out to see what was going on. Since he was no longer sleeping in the utility room, it was an appropriate time-out area. To make it attractive rather than scary, the Bancrofts occasionally put some treats in the room, or they would spend a few minutes a day sitting there with him—sometimes with the door open and sometimes with it closed.

Eventually, when people came to the door, Orvis would bark and give them the once-over. Then he would retire to the utility room on his own. It was almost as if he didn't really want the re-sponsibility of running everything once he had a taste of the subordinate role. *Not my job,* seemed to be his general feeling. So, with the unofficial chairman of the board stepping down, the Bancroft household was back in business.

THE BANCROFTS MADE A BAD CALL when they decided to relinquish their roles as leaders to their dog. It didn't do them or Orvis any good to let him be so dominant that he drove them out of their bedroom or, eventually, out of their minds.

I think all dogs should be submissive to all people. I once had a shepherd named Zuk, for example, who needed only a glance or a word from me to show compliance. He would lie patiently outside my office while I taught class, and he submitted politely to all sorts of students and professors petting him or speaking to him. He never tried to take the upper hand, even though he was big enough to have swallowed them with one gulp had he so chosen.

Sometimes, when I would tell people, "I have a submissive dog," they would tell me how sorry they were to hear that. But by submissive, I don't mean somehow weak. There was no prouder animal than Zuk. He just knew and played by the rules. And he was always treated firmly, but with kindness and affection. I know it wouldn't have been so easy to do that if he were tearing up the house or snarling in my face. But then I'd need to ask myself how he came to be doing that sort of thing in the first place. It goes back to the dog's role in my life.

Owners must decide how they are going to treat their dog. Is he going to be a real member of the family? Some people say they want a pet, but they treat the dog as a possession, like a camera or a computer. This doesn't work. You can't decide to put a dog on a shelf, as it were, and still expect him to behave like a pet. Nor can you beat the heck out of him and expect him to be your best friend.

I had a phone call recently from an owner whose one-year-old cockapoo was getting snappy and aggressive. The young woman didn't want an appointment, just some free advice, which I was happy to offer. Before she hung up she said, "My friends tell me I'm supposed to beat him. Now you're saying I'm not supposed to?"

I explained that I've been treating dog misbehavior since 1980, and in all that time, I've never told a client to do anything to cause a dog pain. But I've helped quite a few animals get back on the right track, so there must be another way.

I'm still surprised by the number of people out there who think that the appropriate way to stop aggression or anything else the dog is doing that they don't like is to slap him upside the head. One owner, whom we'll discuss in a bit, routinely hit her dog with a fly swatter. Another found it logical to stick a piece of wood in his dog's jaws every time he tried to bite. I can't count the number of people who rub their dogs' noses into messes or hit or otherwise hurt them. The most surprising part is that they don't seem to realize that they are doing anything wrong.

I call this the authoritarian approach to discipline. The dog is being tightly controlled, and the emphasis is on being coercive, threatening, commanding, and punishing. In these situations, owners will give the dogs orders, punish them by yelling "No!" and gradually move up the ladder of coercion. They'll say things like, "Get your butt over here or you're going to get shut in the basement," and then do it when the dog doesn't respond. The orders may be very arbitrary, and the enforcement often includes physical punishment and pain.

Sometimes an ill-informed trainer meets a misguided owner and the results are disastrous, even if the methods aren't causing pain. I remember a family that owned two beautiful huskies. I observed the dogs in their backyard through a window and was amazed at how wolflike they were. The male would walk up to the female, and she would get up and walk away with her tail tucked. There were a lot of vocalizations and wrestling as well. And then the dogs would look up, and those blue eyes would knife right through you. The male in particular seemed to be quite in charge of things.

These were not the kinds of dogs I would advise an owner to grab hold of, shut their mouths, and blow on their noses, but that's just what their old-school obedience trainer taught them to do. It didn't take long for the dogs to associate hands with things that didn't feel good and react accordingly. Their owners readily admitted that they had chained the dogs in the backyard for the first month they owned them and had incorrectly used a shock collar. They thought the male's aggression was sort of cool as long as it wasn't directed at them. But of course, it would be after that kind of treatment.

There are other stories. A very fearful dog I treated had been hung by his collar by a trainer, who would wait until the dog stopped struggling and then praise him for his compliance. She thought this bizarre method was the right way to get the dog under her control. In fact, it seems to me it could just as easily have killed him. In any event, that was one messed-up pooch, and we had to start by trying to restore his trust in humans.

Fortunately, bad-apple trainers are few and far between, and many are very skilled at teaching dogs basic good manners.

Obedience training is generally a good idea. It allows you to have verbal control over your dog, which is important for safety reasons if you live near busy streets or your dog will be meeting new people. It also makes dogs more pleasant to be around. But I advise owners to rely on their common sense and the recommendations of people they trust when it's time to choose a trainer. Don't just go blindly along.

It always makes me a bit uneasy when certain breeds take on sudden popularity. How many people just had to have a Jack Russell terrier when *Frasier* became a hit? Suddenly, Jack Russells were the "in" dog. The same thing happened when Disney's *101 Dalmations* hit the big screen. Unfortunately, many people, caught up in the excitement of the moment, hadn't really thought through what they were doing. Which is why animal shelters across the country were flooded with Dalmations about six months after the movie came out.

THIS IS NOT TO SAY THAT A DOG acquired for status can't be loved and treated properly. But what about an animal that is treated almost like a toy? The owners may mean well and not realize at first that for the dog who wants his own way—and don't they all?—this kind of role can't endure. I'm thinking specifically of one little dog who weighed less than my overstuffed briefcase and stood all of 10 inches at the shoulder. And he had a family of five, Phil and Sue Ettinger and their three kids, quaking in their boots.

The Lhasa apso is described by the American Kennel Club as being gay and assertive. But Seng Key, named for the little lion-dog of Tibet, had spurned the gay part in favor of assertive.

"Unfortunately, he runs the place," Phil told me over the telephone. "It's ridiculous."

Now, a dog the size of a well-fed kitty faces challenges unimagined by the likes of German shepherds and their hefty cousins. When you're little and fluffy, people tend to want to put bows in your hair, pick you up, and cuddle you. Seng Key didn't want any part of this lapdog business, and he let his people know in no uncertain terms.

Anyone in the family who tried to touch or brush Seng Key was treated to a snapping, biting, growling bundle of flying fur.

Despite belonging to a breed that can be wary of strangers, Seng Key was actually better with visitors as long as they didn't try to do anything with him.

But for the Ettingers, it was hard to tiptoe around this ornamental, unpredictable little dog and still call him a pet. They deserved better.

Seng Key would lie down and roll over when he felt like it, but no one could pick him up when he didn't want to be, which was most of the time. He had bitten everyone in the family and never failed to draw blood. I wondered if the dog was just showing defensive behavior, considering that there were three young kids in the house.

But there was more to it, as I learned when I met the family at their vine-covered village colonial home. The dog's idea of fun, Phil complained, was trying to con them into going for a toy he wasn't paying much attention to, then attack when they reached for it.

Furthermore, Sue added, Seng Key had a strange obsession with toilet paper. He would unroll it and drag it all over the house.

"Aha," I said.

"Is that important?"

"Well, it's another piece of the puzzle," I told her. "It's one of the things many dogs that are into control do. You'd be surprised how many cases like this involve a paper fetish of some sort, and we have yet to figure out why. It's also hard to resolve. Keeping the bathroom door shut seems to be the best defense."

I've run into quite a few dogs with dominance problems who focused on toilet paper, and it's always been a mystery to me. For some unknown reason, the dogs will string it out all over the house, hold a little piece in their mouths, or run away from you if you look like you're too interested in it. Newspaper runs a lukewarm second to these paper nuts.

Tangles of toilet paper weren't the only problem in the Ettinger home. There were more serious reasons that the family was troubled. It was nearly impossible for Seng Key to be handled by the vet, groomer, or other canine professionals because he would snap or bite.

I didn't want to become another victim, but I needn't have worried. As we settled on the living room sofa, Seng Key bounced into the room, took one look at the three adults and three children, and prudently scampered away. He then busied himself unrolling the toilet paper in the powder room.

I explained to the Ettingers that they needed to give Seng Key some space and not to expect him to act like a stuffed animal that they could cuddle at will. In general, they needed to respect his dignity as a companion animal. The youngsters didn't do things like pull his tail or knowingly tease him, Phil told me, but they all wanted to love him, not just from afar. After he described some of the most recent kid-dog disasters, I thought a little talk with the children might be in order. With the parents' permission, I asked the giggling trio to sit down on the couch and knelt in front of them.

"You know, if you don't touch Seng Key when he's waking up, he probably won't bite you," I said. "How would you like to be sound asleep and have somebody grab you or throw a toy at you?"

"Johnny does that all the time," said the pigtailed six-year-old.

"I do not!" he screeched in reply.

I explained that even the sweetest dog may attack the nearest object if he is startled and confused by being wakened suddenly. A much better habit would be to speak softly to the dog as he awoke and not to attempt to pet him for a minute or two until he showed some interest in being friendly.

"How many of you think of Seng Key as one of your toys?" I asked.

The littlest one's hand shot up proudly. "He looks just like one of my stuffed animals," he said.

The other two looked at each other.

"You try to dress him up like a baby," the older child said accusingly.

Poor Seng Key—smothered by love! I talked to the kids about the difference between the dog and the collections of stuffed animals on their beds. The youngsters grudgingly agreed to try to restrain themselves a bit more.

Seng Key needed more than just his space in order to become a happier dog and a good companion animal for his family. Neutering, the temporary use of an appropriate drug, behavior modification, and omission training were all necessary to set him on the right track. In omission training, the owners were to praise good behavior and ignore controlling behavior. In other words, the little dog would be praised for any behavior that wasn't aggressive.

Since Seng Key was behaving as if he were dominant to each member of the family, they all had to participate in changing his behavior. I asked each of them to give the dog a command, such as "Sit," "Lie down," or "Off." If he obeyed, he was to be given a treat, a verbal reward, or a few strokes. If he didn't obey, he was to be ignored and given another chance a minute later. This way, he could learn the pleasant consequences of doing what he was told and avoid social isolation, which he found unpleasant. (This process works only if the dog is already obedient to commands and wants something from the owner.)

Seng Key's aggression toward strangers was definitely a problem. The easy way out would have been to let the vet worry about handling him—an occupational hazard, after all. But the family preferred the do-it-yourself approach and was willing to put in the work necessary to change the dog's behavior.

To wrap up our initial meeting, we brought in Seng Key so the Ettingers could practice their new approach. I instructed Phil to hold the brush in front of Seng Key while saying, "Good brush," which he was actually able to do with a straight face. Seng Key looked up warily. Phil flipped over a dog treat and Seng Key snarfed it up. *Hey, this is something new!*

Next, I showed Phil how to put the treat and the brush in the same hand. When Seng Key came closer to investigate, Phil could flip the food to him and pass the brush over his head or underneath him, just touching him briefly. Phil repeated, "Good brush," which helped Seng Key associate the words with the treat. Soon he would readily accept a brushing when it was accompanied by treats.

The same method worked for getting him used to hands and stroking. Even the kids practiced this, under their parents' supervision. In less than six weeks, they were all petting, and, when necessary, picking up Seng Key without unpleasant results. Only the parents were to brush him, a risky undertaking that we decided the children should not attempt.

As long as they didn't force him to do anything or tease him with food, Seng Key's behavioral problems gradually began to lessen. In some ways, though, Seng Key was a tough case. Phil called a few weeks into the program to report that progress had been made on several fronts, with the exception of one. The tiny tyrant was too possessive of his favorite toy, a rubber hamburger. He had picked it up in his mouth and deliberately offered it to one of the kids. When the child tried to take it, he growled and bit her. What should they do?

"Throw away the toy," I said. "It's much simpler than trying to desensitize the dog to this one item." Admitting defeat? Maybe, but my hunch was that Seng Key wouldn't have the same emotional investment in other toys. Before giving him a toy, I added, they should make him obey a command, such as "Come," perhaps followed by "Sit." When he obeyed, he could be given the toy. And with some prompting, Seng Key eventually learned to play peacefully with his toys by himself, leaving less energy for bites and snarls. No more con jobs from this half-pint.

REFLECTING BACK ON THIS CASE, I can see that the Ettingers could have used some guidance before picking a cute Lhasa apso for a pet. While these dogs can make perfect companions, a family with three young children might have been better off with a calmer, kid-tolerant breed, such as a well-bred Labrador or golden retriever, or a rough-and-tumble mixed breed better suited to the exuberant affections of youngsters. When choosing a dog, people often make the mistake of equating little and cute with less work and easier to handle. But, as the Ettingers discovered the hard way, it isn't necessarily so.

Most people want pets they can bond with and still keep under control. It's striking the appropriate balance that is sometimes difficult. One reason people often have for not forging that bond is the possibility of spoiling. This is a real concern that raises some valid questions about how much of a pal we really should permit our dogs to be. Should we pull out all the stops and treat him like one of the kids? Or should we be cautious about losing all control of the animal—and ending up with the equivalent of a spoiled brat?

Two colleagues and I were so intrigued by this question that we did a study on it. I worked with Victoria Voith, D.V.M., Ph.D., and Peggy Danneman, D.V.M., then at the Veterinary Hospital of the University of Pennsylvania in Philadelphia, to devise a questionnaire, which we administered to people waiting to see the vets. Nine of the questions related to treating the dog "like a person." We asked people if they let the dog sleep on their bed, get up on furniture, eat from the table, or share their snacks. We wanted to know if they took their dogs along on errands, included them in vacations, celebrated their birthdays, and confided in them. And we asked point-blank if they considered the dog a family member. (Ninety-eight percent answered yes to this question.) We also asked whether or not the dog had formal obedience training and if the dog ever engaged in a behavior that the owner considered a problem. The results showed that dogs whose owners interacted with them in an anthropomorphic manner, which means treating them as though they were humans, or did not provide obedience training were no more likely to engage in problem behaviors than were dogs not viewed in this way.

This is not to say that treating a dog like a child or a peer will result in a well-behaved dog. I remember one client, Millie Gates, who spent a great deal of time reasoning with her dog, almost mirroring the way she treated one of her kids. She may have been helping the child, but the dog, a three-year-old male beagle named Jingo, was very confused and therefore pretty undisciplined.

Her approach was to suggest to Jingo that he behave in a certain way and to explain to him why he wasn't supposed to behave in other ways. Not surprisingly, Jingo's response was often, *Hey, I want to keep it my way!* And he would go back to what he was doing because he hadn't really learned anything.

You can't teach a dog by lecturing him about consequences. You have to show him consequences and teach him what to do instead. Millie was a wonderful mother but a pretty lousy dog trainer. It's not uncommon for people to wind up with an unruly dog because they try reasoning with him to do what's right. It just isn't going to happen.

Sometimes people form a needy, codependent type of relationship with their dogs. This might sound ridiculous, but as long as we're treating dogs like pals and confiding things to them and throwing them birthday parties, is it such a stretch to consider that emotionally unhealthy relationships might occasionally develop?

I had to wonder if this was the case with an elderly couple I visited one autumn day. Bess and Dan Parker were the proud parents of a one-and-a-half-year-old miniature poodle, cute as a button. In fact, that was his name, Buttons. The little guy was sitting on the back of the couch when I walked into their ranch-style home. When Buttons jumped down from the couch and then up on the dining room table, I surmised that he probably had free rein of the house.

The problem, I discovered, was that Buttons would occasionally bite Bess. He did not bite Dan, a lanky old guy whose only words to me were "Hey" and "Take care," and who seemed totally uninvolved with the dog. There's a saying that you always hurt the one you love. Well, Buttons must have loved Bess a lot, because whenever he saw her coming, he would start yapping and sometimes snap or give her a nip.

Poor Bess. She gave Buttons a lot of attention for his misbehavior—so much attention that he probably figured she liked his aggressive style of play and would do it again. Sometimes Bess, at her wit's end, would go after him with a fly swatter. That didn't make Buttons behave better, but boy, was it ever exciting. Dan, in the meantime, would just shake his head as the two of them tangled in a mix of fly swatter and flying fur and go do some chores in the barn. It wasn't a bad idea.

I told Bess that she needed to establish rules in which Buttons would have to do something for her before she did anything for him. We set about trying to get him to sit. It was really tough for Bess. She wanted so badly to give Buttons anything he wanted, and she felt so sorry for him, having to do all this sitting just to get a little biscuit. Even her command to sit sounded more like a request. I had to teach her not to say, "Sit Buttons, sit Buttons, now sit! Buttons! That's a good boy. Sit down, all the way," and so forth. She had never learned how to give a simple one- or two-word command.

It was one of those situations where I just wished I could have waved a magic wand and the two of them would get along. We worked on it. It was only marginally successful, probably because Bess didn't seem very interested in following my suggestions. She told me later that she didn't really mind too much that Buttons hadn't changed.

🐾 🐾

LOOKING BACK ON IT, I THINK Bess was lonely. Dan seemed to spend a lot of time out in the barn doing chores. I think she called me because she wanted to have someone come over to the house and talk about Buttons; solving the problem wasn't really the goal. In fact, I think she enjoyed giving attention to Buttons when he misbehaved, and also the attention he gave her, even if it was nipping. Though it wasn't necessarily a healthy thing, it was something they did as a daily routine. I wasn't happy with the situation, but it wasn't going to kill her.

I wish that I could have felt the same way about Lydia Blackburn and her two pit bulls. Lydia was in complete denial about her pets' problems. The two dogs, male and female, had rap sheets a mile long. They were constantly fighting. They snarled and threatened people, and everyone in the neighborhood knew to give them a wide berth.

I know pit bulls have a bad reputation, and many have been used as fighting dogs and guard dogs. They have been the drug dealer's dog of choice for years, offering protection in exchange for the chance to bite the heads off chickens, or whatever these unfortunate dogs kept for "business reasons" do for fun.

In fact, pit bulls can be lovable, gentle dogs if they are treated kindly. But I was worried about Lydia and her pets, Mutt and Mica. I didn't like all the snarling, fighting, and threatening, especially in a breed that has been known to grab on and not let go until the object stops moving, and sometimes not even then. I was just a tad nervous that Lydia was calling because one of the dogs had nipped her on the forehead. I was more than a tad alarmed when she told me that both dogs slept in her bed when her husband was away, and that's where the attack had taken place.

"All I did was move my leg a little under the covers, and Mica jumped up and bit me," Lydia said as we discussed the attack. "I grabbed her by the collar and dragged her downstairs to the bathroom and shut her in. I was furious."

I tried to imagine this soft-voiced, mild young woman being furious but failed. It was a miracle that the dog hadn't nailed her again on the way down the stairs. Then she told me something pretty unbelievable. Four hours after the attack, she felt so guilty about banishing the dog—who spent the time crying piteously in the bathroom—that she brought her upstairs and let her back into the bed. She slept the rest of the night with the dog's head on the pillow next to hers.

My heart was pounding just thinking about it. She was a lucky girl in my opinion.

"You're quite the risk-taker," I said lightly.

She looked surprised. "Oh, well, not really. I mean I just felt so guilty about what I had done, dragging her into the bathroom and everything. Besides, I know she didn't mean it. It must have been something I did." She trailed off into a stream of excuses for her dog's unprovoked attack. In the future, she would just have to be sure not to move a muscle when she was in bed with the dogs so that they wouldn't have a reason to bite her.

Sure, that's the ticket.

Here were two companion animals who were spoiled. The spoiling had nothing to do with taking them on vacation or giving them a choice of ice cream or pudding for dessert. It was about allowing them to get away with vicious, even life-threatening behavior, not correcting it, and then blaming yourself.

Luckily, I was able to convince Lydia of the seriousness of her problem. We worked out quite an extensive program, beginning with the reminder that she should never place herself at the risk of being bitten, no matter what led to the attack. I taught her how to elicit happier moods in her dogs so they were less likely to bite. More important, I taught her to recognize when the dogs were calm enough to be around people and showed her ways to establish her own leadership role within the family.

Lydia was eventually able to come to a better understanding of what she should expect from her dogs and how to get it. That's real important. Even though you can call an expert when your dog is having behavioral problems, ultimately that's not enough. It's the people in the dog's life that determine whether he'll be a joy or a menace. They hold the key to every gratifying success—or frustrating failure—in their own hands.

Chapter Five

The Dog Whose Owner
Jumped Out the Window

I WILL DO ANYTHING TO HELP MY DOG. Just name it, and I'll do it."
Patricia Wharton looked me in the eye and repeated firmly, "Anything."

I can't count the number of times desperate owners have said
exactly the same thing when we met to discuss a tough behavioral
problem. It's wonderful to know that they're dedicated and ready
to go to any lengths to help their pets.

The trouble is, a lot of people don't really mean it.

Oh, they *think* they mean it, until they hear what's involved.
Then they're not so sure. A plan to solve behavioral problems
sounds like a lot of work, or it's too disruptive of their lifestyle,

inconvenient, or boring. They often ask if we can't try something a little less . . . whatever. And so we go to plan B, which probably won't work quite as well and won't even take less time. As it turns out, they didn't really mean that they would do anything, they meant anything within reason.

But once in a while, somebody surprises you. And there was something about the look on Patricia's face that made me think she might be one of those people. Little did I know that she would turn out to be one of the most amazing owners I've ever come across. An animal behaviorist's dream.

But that first day, sitting in her tiny ground-floor garden apartment, I gave her my standard encouraging response, "Of course you would do anything to help Wizard. She's worth it, aren't you, girl?" I reached down and patted the panting yellow Labrador sprawled at my feet. The dog was ten-and-a-half years old, but she still had a lot of living to do. If only she could stand her owner going off to work every day and leaving her alone.

Patricia and Wizard had spent the last four years apart while Patricia was away at college and Wizard stayed with a relative. A month earlier, Patricia had gotten her degree, landed a job, rented an apartment, and reclaimed her dog. The problem was that Wizard was having trouble adjusting to the lonely days in the tiny apartment. Whenever Patricia went off to work, Wizard would claw the front door and door frame—she had the splinters in her paws to prove it—or chew on the blinds. Wizard displayed all the typical symptoms of a dog who simply can't stand being alone.

While some clients sit back and wait for a list of orders, Patricia seemed willing from the beginning to move mountains in order to solve this problem. Short of moving—she had an iron-clad two-year lease—she would do whatever it took. All I had to do was come up with a plan.

"If only you could take Wizard to work with you," I mused, making some final notations on a form as we sat at her kitchen table. That would be a great way to start her first job after graduation.

"You're right," Patricia declared, jumping up and reaching for the phone.

"Uh, I didn't really mean to suggest . . ."

She dismissed my sputtering with a wave of her hand. "I'll call my boss at home right now," she said, punching in the numbers. She grinned at the horrified look on my face. She would probably end up spending all her time at home with the dog, once her boss got a load of my wishful thinking. That would solve the problem, all right.

I was beginning to realize that Patricia meant business. And to my amazement, her boss, after his initial incredulity wore off, said yes. But only once a week.

So every Wednesday, Wizard went happily out the door with her owner and had a grand old time being petted and pampered in the office. But that still left Monday, Tuesday, Thursday, and Friday as well as any time on the weekends when Patricia wasn't willing to sit at home looking at four walls.

Part of the problem, I suspected, was the configuration of the apartment. It was so small that no matter where Wizard was, she could watch Patricia get ready and go out the door. Wizard was already nervous about Patricia's absences. After all, one had lasted four years. Now as Wizard watched Patricia getting ready to leave, she got increasingly nervous. It was as though she were saying, *Oh, gosh, she's going to the light switch . . . she turned it off . . . now she's reaching for her purse . . . the keys are in her hand . . . oh, no, she's going. . . .* By the time Patricia finally left, Wizard was so filled with anxiety that the only way to get relief was to *do* something. So she would begin her destructive acts and keep doing them until her anxiety dropped to lower levels.

In many ground-floor apartments, there is a sliding glass door leading to a garden or patio as well as the front door. Sometimes the owner can slip out the glass door instead of going out the front. Varying the pattern of departures will often make dogs less focused on that one door and what happens when it opens and shuts. They understand that their owners are gone, of course, but they may be able to learn to cope as long as they haven't got that front-door stimulus knocking their anxiety into high gear.

Patricia did have a sliding glass door, but it was only a few yards from the front door. Wherever Wizard was—in front of the bedroom door, on the living room couch, or under the small breakfast table—she could see both exits. She reacted just as strongly when Patricia slipped out the patio door as when she used the front door. And Wizard had a long day to take out her frustrations on the nearest targets.

"Let me tell you what I've tried, and you can tell me if it was a mistake," Patricia began. I'm always glad to hear my clients' ideas for finding a solution to their pets' problems. After all, they know their dogs better than I do. Usually their ideas haven't helped much or they wouldn't need me. But it's not like I'm the boss and they're my assistant or employee. I'm a consultant, meaning my job is to help them change their dogs' behavior. Patricia understood that I welcomed her input and ideas, so she spoke right up.

"I thought it might help if I made Wizard's day a little shorter. So I started coming home every day at lunch. I'll just grab a yogurt and then play with Wizard for 15 minutes or so."

"It's great that you could do that," I said. "Did it seem to make Wizard happier?"

"Well, in a way, it made things worse."

"Twice as much separation anxiety, right?" She nodded glumly.

It wasn't too surprising. Wizard was obviously fixated on those things that led to the outside, where she could see her mistress disappearing down the street. That's why she clawed the door and chewed the blinds. With the lunchtime visits, Wizard now had two departures a day to set her off.

"Is there any location where Wizard seems to be comfortable by herself?" I asked. I was interested in coming up with a favorite spot where we might start out with Wizard in a very relaxed state, and then work to get her used to Patricia's departures. But the only time she would lie quietly by herself was when Patricia was home in the evenings, watching TV, listening to music, or talking on the phone.

"I usually keep the bedroom door closed for an hour or two, just to have some private time before bed," Patricia admitted.

"Okay, so you relax in your room, and Wizard lies outside. Where, exactly?"

"On the carpet outside the bedroom door."

"And she doesn't complain?"

"She doesn't complain."

"Hmm. If only there were a way to leave from the bedroom in the morning and come back the same way at lunch or after work, she might think you were still home and not freak out. Too bad you can't get somebody to chop a back door into your bedroom." I was thinking aloud again.

But I had said the magic words *if only*, and Patricia had another brainstorm. This one was way beyond the call of duty and could have gotten her hurt, shot, or arrested. But that didn't faze her one bit.

"That's it!" she exclaimed. "Come with me."

Uh-oh. She grabbed my hand and dragged me toward the bedroom as Wizard started to bark with excitement. I half expected to see her grab a hatchet and smash a hole in the bedroom wall to make a door.

She went directly to the window beside her bed and unlocked and opened it. Then she lifted up the screen and looked down at the ground below.

"What are you doing?"

"Well, I might mash a few tulips, and I'll have to put a step stool out there, but this is definitely doable," she said, a determined gleam in her eye. "I'll just shut the door and go out the window in the morning. Then I'll come in the window at lunch or at night and out the bedroom door as though I was here all the time. Think it will work?"

For a moment I was speechless, picturing this young woman, dressed in her business suit and high heels, crawling in and out the window. Someone would think she was a burglar and put a bullet in her butt. Or the police would haul her off to jail for breaking and entering. After all, her story would be pretty unbelievable.

"Well, it certainly might work, but what would the neighbors think?"

"The heck with them!" she replied happily. "Now you're sure that Wizard won't suspect that I've been in the bedroom an awfully long time?"

"Well, she might, but dogs are pretty hazy about the passage of time. Especially after they've had their exercise and aren't expecting another big event like food or a walk. And Wizard probably sleeps a lot at her age." Now that the shock had worn off, the possibilities were beginning to intrigue me. She might be able to pull it off.

"Do you ever have the radio or TV on while you are at home?"

"I'm doing that already," she said. Turning on a radio or TV helps mask outside noises that can make dogs nervous. Pets also associate the sound with the calmness they feel in their owner's presence, even when the owner isn't home. "It hasn't helped much," she added.

"The TV in the living room could keep Wizard company. Without you sitting in front of it, though, it might not help," I admitted. "The radio in the bedroom might fool her into thinking you were in the house, since you say you have it on all the time when you're in there."

"I get it," she nodded. "Well, let's give it a try. I'll start tomorrow morning."

"You're not afraid of burglars coming in the window?" I objected weakly.

"Nah," she brushed me off. "You worry too much." At least it was summer and she wouldn't be doing this in the dark. And whether it worked or not, she wouldn't be doing it for very long.

"Well, do you want me to help you . . . practice?" I asked.

"No, I'll be fine."

Whew. These measures were so extreme, I really didn't want to watch her going out the window. Or coming in, for that matter.

I did suggest, however, that she limit her absences to 20 to 30 minutes the first few times to see if Wizard would buy it. Then she could try it until lunch, or all day if she were too busy to get home at noon. I also suggested that she ask her vet for a mild anti-anxiety medication to help tide Wizard over during the experiment.

I asked her if she would be comfortable with this since many clients are dead set against using medication of any kind for behavioral problems. I explained that it would be a short-term tool to help Wizard cope. After a few weeks, we would begin reducing the dose as the problem lessened or was resolved.

"Whatever you recommend," she replied immediately. "I trust you." As I said, an animal behaviorist's dream.

"I know this is going to mean a lot of going in and out the window, at first," I said as I prepared to leave. "Are you sure you really want to go through with it?"

"Absolutely."

"Okay, then."

It was obvious that Patricia was determined. I always try to recommend what the owner can handle, and if Patricia could handle this, so be it. You have to be flexible. I walked to the dreaded (in Wizard's eyes) front door. This was the last time it would be used for a while.

"Call me tomorrow and let me know what happens," I said.

Patricia's over-the-top method worked like a charm. She didn't get burglarized, arrested, or shot, although she told me that one day she took some catcalls from some of the neighborhood kids when her skirt rode up as she jumped down. So she went out and shopped for pantsuits.

But, best of all, Wizard was happy. She actually bought the idea that her owner was spending a lot of private time in the bedroom. Eventually, the front door lost its significance, and she stopped chewing on it. She snoozed and puttered around until Patricia emerged from the bedroom, looking considerably more disheveled than the average businesswoman.

But like any best friend, Wizard didn't mind. And after several weeks, she was drug-free and relaxed enough that Patricia was able to start using the front door again.

That Wizard was one lucky dog.

I TRY NEVER TO BLAME AN OWNER for a dog's problems. Sometimes I have to bite my tongue to keep from doing that. But I'm the first to give the owner credit for the success of any treatment program he is willing to try. No matter how great an idea I have, or how many research studies there are backing me up, the fact is that it's the owner who has to carry out the program and work with the dog until the problem is resolved. And that's tough.

If the owner doesn't want to work with you, you're not going to have a good treatment program. But my philosophy is a little different from other people's.

Clients will tell me that they had such-and-such a trainer come in, or they took their dog to an obedience class, and they were told, "Here's the problem, and here's the solution." They were told they must do one, two, and three, and the expert would show them how to do it. And so they did one, two, and three, and often the problem did not get any better. Now they were told, "You must not be doing it right. Let me go over it again."

Then, human nature being what it is, the clients would likely get pretty frustrated and then angry because nothing was happening and they were being made to feel responsible for their dog's problem.

That's not my philosophy. My belief is that you can't take the dog problem away from the environment in which it occurs. The two are intricately related, and it does no good to cause the owner grief and blame him. He will only get defensive and be less likely to follow the treatment program you recommend.

If I'm correct to start with, then the success is theirs. It's theirs because they administer the program successfully from day to day.

They change when we need a change, and they persevere until we reach a point where the problem has been resolved or significantly reduced. The dog may go from something like totally damaging the household to just whimpering or whining for three or four minutes when they leave. Most owners would call that a success.

Sometimes it takes the compliance of a whole slew of people to have a successful treatment program—or at least the tolerance of a bunch of neighbors when the miscreant lives in close quarters with other apartment-dwellers. That was the case with Rags, a three-and-a-half-year-old mongrel who lived on the third floor of a retirement community building. His owner, Doug Ramsey, explained that Rags had a serious thunderstorm phobia. In this case, as with Wizard's, an apartment window played a key role.

It seems that Rags would get so scared during a storm that he would try to escape. When dogs are in the throes of anxiety during a severe thunderstorm, they don't sit down and analyze the situation. While they're running around in circles and freaking out *inside*, they don't seem to realize that they're going to be a heck of a lot worse off if they go *outside*. All they want is to escape their fear. And if the place they have to escape is three stories up, well, so be it. *I'm outta here!*

Rags was home alone one day during a booming thunderstorm. Doug was on his way in from the parking lot, hurrying to get back because he knew his scruffy little friend was always nervous during bad weather. He saw a bunch of residents from across the courtyard motioning to him from the shelter of a doorway in front of the building.

"Hurry!" the neighbors yelled, their arms pointing upward. "Your dog's about to jump!"

Doug looked up at his bedroom window and gasped. His little dog's head was poking out of the window. "Rags!" he yelled. "Get down!"

The screen was hanging loose at the top of the window. Rags didn't move, but he whined pitifully as the wind blew the rain across his dripping face. He was stuck.

Doug hurried into the building and up to his apartment. Bursting into the bedroom, he found the terrified dog with his hind legs on top of the bookcase below the window. His front paws were pressing against the screen and his head was out in the air, three stories up.

"That's when I decided that I'd better do something to help Rags cope with storms," Doug told me as we met for the first time. "I don't need a dog who thinks he's Superman."

"So then you bought the CD," I coaxed. Doug had seen an article in a magazine about a CD filled with sounds, which was used to desensitize dogs to doorbells, storms, and sirens.

"I got the CD and I started playing it," Doug explained. "I don't know if I didn't read the instructions or if there weren't any, but Rags started to get real nervous, just like with a real thunderstorm. But he didn't get used to it. In fact, he got even more frightened the next time it started to rain. That's why I called you."

These thunderstorm recordings have to be handled very carefully or things can go terribly wrong. Rags, unfortunately, was a case in point.

"Well, let's start over." I explained to Doug how the recordings are meant to work. The idea is to start the "storm" playing at a low volume that doesn't provoke anxiety, then gradually increase the volume while making sure the dog is still comfortable. The goal eventually is to be able to play the thunderstorm recording at a realistic volume and have the dog still be calm. Doug said he would start right away, at a much more gradual pace than before.

As he showed me out, he greeted several neighbors on the elevator and in the courtyard on the lower level. "Friendly building," I commented, as we shook hands at my car.

"Oh, yes, everyone's great here," he answered. "Ever since Rags almost took his famous leap, everyone's been asking me how he's doing."

The neighbors were soon to find out quite a bit more about how Rags was doing. For the first week or so, there was nothing notable coming from behind the door at apartment 3F. But then, every evening, tenants began hearing the most violent thunderstorms. Through cloudy weather and clear, with stars shining brightly or covered by fog, the sounds of a storm inside the building grew louder and louder. Finally, people started to complain. A group of eight neighbors arrived at Doug's door one night, wanting to know when the hell that racket was going to stop.

"I asked them to please bear with me," Doug told me on the phone. "But everyone's pretty sick of this thunderstorm booming out every night."

"But Rags is still fine with it?" I asked.

"Yes, he's doing fine. About one more week and we're done, right?"

"It sounds like it."

Well, the neighbors did hang in there. Nobody complained again, and everyone made sure to pet Rags whenever they saw him outside and to say some encouraging words to his owner. After six long weeks of listening to thunderstorms, the neighbors were finally rewarded with a great little dog who would no longer try to jump out the window when the rain started falling. Rags literally couldn't have done it without them. And that's the story of how it takes a village to pitch in and help a frightened pooch plant his four paws firmly back on the ground.

🐾 🐾

NOT EVERYONE IS AS COOPERATIVE as Doug and his neighbors, of course. I find it very hard to help people who want me to solve their dogs' problems but don't want to admit that their dogs are anything but perfect. And when they happen to have an entire pack of dogs, you know that has to be an unrealistic attitude.

Ben Strum had nine dogs and a severe case of denial. All the problems his dogs were having—and they were legion—were sure to be caused by some horrible neighbor or another. At least, that's the way he saw it.

Ben and his menagerie lived on the shore of a pretty lake in a community of summer cottages. It was the kind of place people go on the weekends to relax, maybe do some boating, swimming, or waterskiing, and to enjoy the quiet lakeside ambiance away from the frenetic city.

That was the idea, anyway. Those who happened to live near Ben's little hideaway told a different story. Every day, they were treated to a raucous gathering of howling, barking, aggressive dogs of all shapes and descriptions. And an owner who accused them of being dog-haters if they dared to complain.

Why would someone like Ben call an animal behaviorist for help? Well, he didn't. A trainer who had worked for Ben called me. Ben wouldn't listen to her, she said, but the dogs were totally out of control. Maybe he would listen to me. I agreed to meet with Ben to see if I could help straighten out the situation.

Ben and I both loved dogs, so I figured I would build on that common foundation to find ways to work with him. Still, memories of the trainer's frustrated complaints stayed with me all the way down to the lake. I was glad I had enough people psychology under my belt to cope with just about any type of owner a bunch of dysfunctional dogs could toss my way.

I planned on charging Ben a little more than usual due to the long travel time to get to his place. But if I had to do it all over again, I'm not sure I would take the job. Ben was a rather cantankerous lawyer who seemed to lose sight of the reason that there are laws and only looked for clever ways to get around them. This was a real challenge.

To my surprise, Ben was glad to see me. As I got out of my car, I was greeted by several of the dogs, none of which was leashed or restrained in any way. Ben didn't even have a fenced-in yard. A pit bull and a Chow-mix came to within a few yards of me and started barking. I stayed pressed against my car until I could figure out what they had in mind.

"Don't worry, they won't bite," Ben said. There it was again, one of the most famous speculative statements known to humankind. But I was uneasy. I was in a rural area, there were un-specified problems with several of the dogs, and there were no leashes in sight. But Ben was right: None of them bit me. He in-troduced me to Barney and Bailey and Laser and Miss Pepper and Rebel and Dijon. Tater, Turbo, and Elvis were around somewhere, maybe down the street.

He was glad to see me, Ben said, because he had this terrible problem. I got out my pen, wondering how he would pick out the worst problem from among the many an unrestrained pack of dogs like this could visit on the population at large.

It seems that one of the dogs was barking for an hour in the middle of the night and keeping Ben awake. All right, we could deal with that. I outlined some steps he could take to extinguish the barking. He was very fortunate that it was only one dog making speeches. What else?

"Oh, that's about it," he replied matter-of-factly. "Thanks for coming."

I set down my pen. "Really." He nodded. As we spoke, dogs were running into the street and barking at people walking by. Several of them were mixing it up in the backyard. He seemed oblivi-ous to all this.

"Your trainer, Liz, told me you were having a number of ag-gression problems with various dogs."

"Oh, that. That's not worth talking about," Ben smiled brightly. "You know, the people around here are so hyper. If a dog steps on a petunia, they want to call in the militia."

"I see." I could turn around and leave now, or I could try to pry the blinders off this fellow's eyes. I sighed. "Ben, I think there might be some other issues here that it would be a good idea for us to take a look at." Ben gave me a cold stare.

"Such as?"

"Well, I don't really know. I was hoping you could give me a little thumbnail sketch of how you deal with all of these great dogs every day. Tell me a little about them stepping on petunias and all that stuff."

With the greatest reluctance, he dredged up some of the high-lights of the past couple of weeks. Here are a few of the things I wrote down:

- Pepper bit neighbor at #43 as she walked to the mailbox.
- Ben rides bike while three to six dogs jog alongside. Barney broke from group and attacked man digging in his garden and singing at #28.
- Tater and Elvis haven't been seen for two days.
- Bailey hates Dalmatian at #104. Nearly broke glass in door lunging at dog.
- Bailey attacked Doberman at #52. Ben had to pay vet bills.
- Fined by animal control for having animals at large.

Finally, I made this notation about the Chow-mix that barked at me, the one Ben said wouldn't bite:

- Dijon spotted dog riding in pickup truck. Jumped up into truck and killed dog.

All righty, then.

In reality, the neighbor's petunias were the least of Ben's worries, and barking wasn't the only thing that should have kept him up at night. I wondered if he could spell l-a-w-s-u-i-t?

It turned out that Ben was already quite familiar with lawsuits, and I would hear from his lawyer when I got back home. The two of them were trying to evade responsibility for several past indiscretions committed by various dogs. Throughout it all, Ben maintained an air of aggrieved innocence, wondering why everyone at the lake was so uptight. But I was able to talk to him about getting the dogs into a routine so that everyone would be happier in the end.

I figured Ben wouldn't be able to handle anything too complicated with that many dogs, so I tried to work some changes into his normal routine. He went out in the rowboat every day, and many of the dogs loved to swim alongside. That gave them some good exercise, the cornerstone of harnessing all the energy that was wreaking havoc around the neighborhood.

The dogs would have to be brought inside when he went inside. The "safe" ones could run alongside as he rode his bike, but the worst offenders had to be walked on a leash. I gave him a bunch of commonsense instructions designed to bring order and discipline to the dogs. Some of the instructions, I imagined, were identical to the ones he got from the county animal-control officer, but he seemed more willing to accept them from me.

At any rate, things slowly started to change. To my surprise, Ben called frequently with progress reports. His attitude toward his neighbors seemed to improve, along with the reputation of his dogs.

After about a month, I got a call from the trainer who had sent me up to the lake in the first place. "Boy, I don't know what you did, but you caused a big change in that household," she told me. Actually, all I did was make some suggestions. Ben was the one who had the power to harness all that misdirected energy and improve those nine lives.

SOME CLIENTS ARE INCREDIBLY engaged in the whole process. They ask a lot of questions, try to understand why we're trying different things, and help me devise a treatment plan that's right for them. They're also the ones who will review a plan and scrap it for something else if things don't seem to be taking hold.

Betty Worley, on the other hand, seemed a bit mystified by the whole process of owning a dog. A retired third-grade teacher, Betty never questioned why she was doing certain things or what she hoped to achieve. Mistake was piled upon mistake. By the time she called me, I found a well-meaning woman and devoted dog owner who had become, quite literally, a prisoner in her own home.

From the tail-wagging, hand-licking greeting he gave me, it was obvious that Betty's dog, Gypsy, was an exceptionally friendly golden retriever. "I love him dearly, but he's making me insane," Betty said flatly. "I can't go on living like this." She sounded desperate, but the dog seemed so nice. Strange.

As I sat down in the nearest armchair, I noted that Betty, rather than sitting in a chair next to me, walked across the room and sat in the middle of a large sofa. Gypsy headed straight for my chair. "Oh, lord, there he goes," Betty said. I braced myself for a sneak attack of some sort. I didn't know how I had missed the telltale signals of an aggressive dog, but apparently something was about to happen.

Gypsy merely walked over and nudged my hand with his nose. He wanted to be petted. I obliged, feeling a sense of relief. I hadn't missed any signals after all. Gypsy wasn't aggressive at all. What was I doing here?

"Hi, there, Gypsy," I said, giving his head three or four smooth strokes. "What's up?"

"Now you're doomed," Betty said.

"What do you mean?" I asked, taking out my diagnostic forms and casually petting Gypsy again when he gave me another nudge. Sometimes owners are so dramatic. Gypsy seemed perfectly normal to me, but then, I rarely see my canine clients' worst sides. Those were usually reserved for their families or for strangers more threatening than I.

"This dog will not leave you alone," explained Betty. "Now that you've petted him, you might as well forget about doing anything else." The dog nudged my hand for a third time. I gave him a few strokes, then put my hand in my lap. Gypsy immediately shoved his nose under my hand. This routine *was* getting pretty annoying.

"No!" I said sharply, removing my hand. Gypsy looked up, startled.

"Lie down, Gypsy," I said firmly. Gypsy backed up a step, whined, and slowly lay down beside me.

"That's a good boy," I said. "I see he responds to commands."

"Sometimes," Betty said. Encouraged that Gypsy was able to lie down, breaking the undesirable behavior pattern, I picked up my pen again. Within seconds I felt a now-familiar wet nose under my hand. Gypsy had started to pant excitedly. I was beginning to understand the problem.

"Lie down, Gypsy," I said again. Gypsy whined and circled around as though to lie down, but instead stood looking at me. The brown eyes of a golden retriever, set in one of dogdom's most beautiful faces, are awfully difficult to resist. But I stood my ground. "Lie down."

This time Gypsy ignored the command, eyed my hands, and boldly pushed them with his nose again.

"He just never quits," Betty said.

"I get the picture." Gypsy had gotten into a habit of demanding that his owner do things to make him feel good. He depended on her to give comforting treatment. But I wasn't sure why he had come to me instead of her.

"I've already had a dog trainer come in here," Betty told me, "but Gypsy just got all hyper. Then the vet said that maybe you could help. I surely hope so because I don't like living in a cage like this."

"In a cage?"

"Come over here," she said. "Look at this. Don't trip, now."

I walked across the room to the sofa where she had stationed herself and looked down at the carpet. It took a minute, but then it all clicked in. No wonder Gypsy had turned to me instead of crossing the room to go to Betty. Surrounding the sofa was a wire, the kind that is usually buried underground and used in tandem with a shock collar to keep dogs from straying out of their yards. I had noticed the box on Gypsy's collar, but it hadn't occurred to me that anyone would use one inside their home.

"This is to keep Gypsy away from you?"

"You bet," she said. "Come on, I'll show you the only way I can get a good night's sleep." She stepped over the wire. "You know how goldens are. You can't shut a door on them or they'll cry all night." I had to agree. Isolating Gypsy wouldn't be the answer.

We walked through the house to a back hallway that led to the bedrooms. Tacked around the door frame leading to the hall was another wire. "I have some wire underground outside to keep him in the backyard, too."

"Really?" I said.

"Not that he would go anywhere," she added, confirming my suspicions. "He only wants to be where he can bug me."

"I understand."

"Before that dog trainer threw up his hands and left, he said the only way he could think of to keep Gypsy off me was to wire the house," Betty explained. "So I did. But I'm sick and tired of being a prisoner in my own home."

I agreed that this bizarre arrangement seemed unworkable as a long-term solution. I asked Betty to tell me a little bit about Gypsy's history.

Gypsy was about two years old, neutered, and obviously very attached to Betty. The problem had started innocently enough several months earlier. Betty would sit in the living room or at her desk. Gypsy, companionable fellow that he was, would plop down beside her, and Betty would occasionally pet his head. As time went by, Gypsy started craving more attention. The situation had evolved to the point where he would follow her around constantly.

"He'd follow me into the bathroom if I didn't shut the door," she confided.

As long as Gypsy was physically in contact with Betty, he was fine. But when she tried to create some physical space, Gypsy would get demanding. He would push his nose up under her hand or take her hand into his mouth.

Betty was a small woman, and she was getting bruises. She didn't care to have this continue any longer. Having spent more than $2,000 on the trainer and the wiring, she was left with a dog who stayed in the yard and a house that looked like a maximum-security prison. But Gypsy's problem remained—and sometimes got worse.

When Gypsy didn't get his way, he would become extremely excited. Rather than showing the typical laid-back behavior of this popular family breed, he would get nearly hyperactive. (Since then, I've encountered several other goldens who became hyper when their desires were thwarted.)

"The more I try to push him or shoo him away, the more he grabs my hands," Betty explained as we sat on the hot-wired sofa.

"He probably learned to do that to keep your hands from hurting him," I reasoned. Mouthing her hands allowed Gypsy to control her as well as the punishment. I noted that Betty really couldn't shove the dog away anyway. Any kind of physical restraint was just not possible with this anxious fellow, and it's usually not very effective anyway. The dog was big and the woman was little. I had to come up with something better than force or shocks.

I wondered how much additional damage the wiring had done to Gypsy's need for physical contact and attention. It was likely that the shock wires had made the problem worse. After receiving a shock, Gypsy probably needed even more to be in contact with his owner for comfort and reassurance.

"Has Gypsy gotten any better since you wired up the house?" I was pretty sure of the answer.

"No. He seems more determined than ever to get to me, and I don't think he likes getting those shocks, either."

That figured. The mild shocks were indeed making him anxious. The system Betty had purchased was an early one. It did not give a warning to the dog when he came close to the wire, so the shocks were almost unavoidable. Today's systems are somewhat better. They spare the dog a shock by warning him first with a certain tone. If the dog backs off, he hears a "good" tone and doesn't get shocked.

I really don't recommend the use of shock collars. But at the time, the technology wasn't as good as it is today, so I had to work with what we had. The challenge was to teach Gypsy first how to avoid the shocks and then how to find some good alternatives to constantly seeking comfort from his owner.

I began by making sure that Gypsy didn't get aggressive when he received a shock. Research has shown that animals given a shock will sometimes attack and bite whatever they associate with the discomfort. Betty confirmed that good-natured Gypsy wasn't one of these animals. He didn't reflexively bite; he just wanted to be petted.

Next we started teaching Gypsy how to stop the shocks. I gave Betty a word signal. About a second before Gypsy came to the wire around the sofa or door frame, she was to say, "Zing!" (Any word will do, as long as it's the same word each time.) If he stopped, she was to praise him and say, "Good boy!" These two utterances worked like the warning tone and the good tone used in current shock systems.

Gypsy soon learned that when he heard the word *zing*, a shock would follow in about half a second if he continued to approach. It didn't take the bright golden long to understand this new system. Gypsy began to lie beside the sofa away from the electrified zone. Betty could sit on the sofa or at her desk without fear of molestation.

There was an additional benefit to this training. When Betty was in a nonelectrified area and Gypsy approached to grab her hand, all she had to do was say "Zing" and Gypsy would immediately back off to avoid the shock that wasn't even there. But he didn't know that. Eventually, Betty removed the shock collar, and Gypsy would still stop in his tracks when she said "Zing."

As another part of the plan, it was important for Gypsy to get more exercise. This would help prevent him from becoming overly excited indoors. If he did get hyper, he was given a time-out outside. We were careful to avoid having Gypsy manipulate Betty into letting him go outside by getting hyper. In the best golden tradition, Gypsy wanted Betty's company, but that had to be indoors. So, when he was calm again, she brought him back in for another try.

I gave Betty some other strategies to use when Gypsy was trying to take her hand. Rather than leaving it soft and flaccid, which is something a dog can easily grab onto, she was to make a fist and slowly move her arm away from him. Dogs aren't crazy about trying to get their mouths around fists. (This is not a risk-free tactic, and I don't go around recommending it to every client.)

But Gypsy was fairly oral. He wanted to have something in his mouth a lot, like a baby with a pacifier. As a replacement for his owner's hands, we gave him a few substitutes, including rawhide bones and a large, hard rubber ball to hold in his mouth. He liked these a lot.

Within four to five weeks, Betty had a dog who backed off on command anywhere in the house. He worked off his excess energy appropriately and learned to calm himself to gain access to the house and his owner. And he played with toys instead of demanding petting. Now Gypsy sat contentedly near his delighted owner while she chatted affectionately, calling him a good dog and meaning it. Betty was no longer a prisoner in her own home. She called to tell me that she was taking great pleasure in the simple act of petting her devoted dog. And that, after all, is what it's all about.

THESE STORIES AREN'T ALL THAT UNUSUAL. All of the owners had their dogs' best interests at heart, or they wouldn't have called me in the first place. Most of them were more than willing to go the extra mile to make their pets happy.

There was Rhoda, who willingly ran mile after mile with her retriever-mix in order to help relieve an intractable case of hyperactivity. And the Warners, who stubbornly worked with a stray cocker spaniel for months to overcome a history of abuse. There was William Tegler, a retired cop who spent his days patiently getting in and out of a chair so that Zippo, his white spitz, would learn to be in the same room with someone walking around without freaking out.

Different problems, different dogs, different owners. But all of these folks had one thing in common: The determination to always look out for number one—their always-loved, always-worth-it dogs.

Chapter Six

The Dog Who Wouldn't Stop Singing

SOMETHING WAS VERY WRONG HERE. As I walked up a long, dusty driveway to see a new client who was in the business of breeding American basset hounds, I strained my ears for some hint of the melodious cry the breed is famous for. I heard nothing but a few faint, raspy bark-howls coming from the kennel area behind the ramshackle farmhouse.

Surely a pack of bassets wouldn't be making that sound. And what was that rasping noise all about anyway? I looked at Richard, a friend who was accompanying me for the day because he was interested in picking up a basset hound. His wife wasn't thrilled with the idea, but Richard was sold on the breed. So when I got the call from Brady Sinclair, the breeder, earlier in the week, I'd asked if I could bring Richard along.

"Sure," Brady said. "I might sell him a good coon dog, eh?"

Hunting was the furthest thing from Richard's mind. "I just love the way they wail," he said, opening up his mouth and sending forth a fair rendition of the basset's bell-like cry.

"Whoa, take it easy," I said, covering my ears. "No wonder Beth would rather get a kitten." Richard's melody faded, and only those croaking sounds floated back from the kennels.

"Why aren't we hearing any of that beautiful music?" Richard asked as we approached the front door. I shook my head and knocked.

A few minutes later, Brady was leading us to the breeding area and kennel behind the house. "You said you have a barking problem, but I don't hear it," I said as we neared the fenced-in area.

"The pups are inside, doing a lot of talking," Brady said, opening the door to the kennel. Inside there was a litter of seven or eight cute puppies and one sad-eyed dam lying in the corner.

"This is the problem," Brady said. As if on cue, the dam let out a series of howls to tell us what she thought of our visit. "That's more like it," Richard said, smiling appreciatively at the mother dog. Brady, on the other hand, scowled. "Tracker, shut up," he said.

He turned to me. "Doc, that bitch is one of my best breeders. But the neighbors on both sides say they're going to call the sheriff if this racket doesn't stop. One more complaint from those old biddies and I'm out of business."

I hadn't noticed before, but despite the long driveway, there were houses within 100 yards of where we stood.

"I read in the newspaper that you might have a better way to handle this kind of thing." Brady looked toward the back pen. When he turned back to me, he didn't quite meet my gaze.

While Richard played with the puppies, Brady and I walked outside, where there were several older bassets in a pen. "These are my retired dams," Brady said. "Still good for breeding, but not much else."

The bassets looked healthy enough, but they didn't sound like bassets. They were the ones making the rasping barks. I felt my heart sink. "What's wrong with these dogs?"

"I had to cut their vocal cords," Brady replied. "Didn't hurt them. Couldn't take a chance on losing my income."

"I see."

"So you say you have other ways of stopping barking? Come on back to the house. I'm all ears." Then he asked Richard, who had followed us outside, "Picked one out yet, bud?" Richard looked ill.

"No, sir, I sure haven't," Richard said. "John, I'll meet you in the car," he said and walked away.

"Guess your buddy doesn't like the looks of my pups," Brady said. "His loss."

I spent the next hour trying to explain some simple training techniques that would keep his dogs quiet without putting them under the knife. I knew that if Brady weren't diligent and willing to work with Tracker on a daily basis to quiet her barking—and somehow I didn't think he would be—she would suffer the same fate as the others. It's a terrible thing to do to a dog.

Brady eventually was shut down by the sheriff, and it was just as well. Dogs need their voices for more than making music. There hasn't been a lot of research done on what different kinds of barks or vocalizations mean, but most observant dog owners understand this kind of dog language, at least as far as their own pooches are concerned.

Sometimes, I'll walk into a client's house, and the dog will greet me enthusiastically. The owners will tell me that it's just his play bark or her someone's-at-the-door growl. I've gotten to know the language of the three dogs in my own house pretty well. RooRoo, the standard poodle, always "sings" when she starts playing with Charlie, the chocolate Lab. It's the only time she does that, and it's a very distinctive sound. If they start playing more aggressively, RooRoo will add a little growl to her song. But you can't generalize. One dog's barking doesn't appear to mean the same as another's. At least it's one code we haven't cracked yet.

On the other hand, there are some types of vocalizations that people can probably agree on if they've been around dogs for any length of time.

- "Yip, yip, yip" means *Gee, there's somebody out there. I'm a little scared. Why don't you come and help me look?*
- "Growl, bark" means *Somebody's out there and I'm really angry!*
- "Bark, bark, bark" means *There's nobody out there and nothing's going on. Boy, am I bored.*

Everyone is familiar with whining, which often indicates a dog's submissiveness. It's also used to get some attention from the mother or the owner, or to say, *Please let me out of here,* or *Get my ball out from under there.* Then there's the howl, which reminds us of the dog's heritage as a relative of the wolf.

Wolves howl as a kind of social greeting or an announcement. *I'm coming into the territory!* And the polite response from other wolves is to howl back the location. So when dogs howl (some breeds, like bassets and beagles, do it more than others), it might be prompted by their evolutionary history. It's almost a reflexive howling that they can't stop doing even if they want to.

Clearly, when we pull into the driveway, our territory, in our cars, we don't howl, and our pets don't howl back. But when dogs do howl, it can be very difficult to interrupt. You can't just say, "Stop howling!" and expect the dog to do it. But try explaining that to your next-door neighbor when he threatens to throw a shoe through your window if your dog doesn't shut up.

This is where I usually come in. Barking and howling can be serious problems for owners and their neighbors. It accounts for many dogs being kicked out the door, left on the doorstep of the local humane society or the side of the highway, or abused at the hands of their owners.

But there are ways to quiet barking, and doing so can have great benefits for the owner (or whoever lives nearby), whose frazzled nerves finally get a rest. It's good for the dog, too. Think of all the energy the dog uses in that relentless quest to tell the world all about himself. Owners sometimes call me to say that their pets seem much happier and more affectionate since their barking habit was extinguished. It's as though the dogs are saying, *Whew! Glad I don't have to do that anymore. I love you, man!*

When I get one of these cases, the first thing I need to figure out is why the dog is barking so much. For example, if the dog barks when the owner is gone, he could be suffering from separation anxiety. Or he could be barking and going crazy whenever the doorbell rings, which could mean he's being territorial or is simply excited by the novelty. Dogs also bark because in their minds, it's an effective way to establish who's in charge.

Dogs barking at the mailman have become a cliché. But there's a good reason for it. When the mailman comes up the steps, the dog starts barking. Then he runs to the window and watches the guy leave. The next day, he barks with even more enthusiasm. *Hey, it worked! My barking scared him away! That next guy better watch out!*

On the other hand, dogs will sometimes bark because they hear something outside that's scaring them. Or they could be uncomfortable or having a medical problem. Or it may be that they're just downright lonely or bored, especially if they spend their days tied in the yard. Boredom is a common cause of nuisance barking, which can go on for hours. That's usually when neighbors throw shoes or call the animal-control officer. And the desperate owners call people like me.

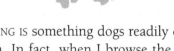

THE TRUTH IS, BARKING IS something dogs readily do and it's a fairly common problem. In fact, when I browse the pet-care message boards on the Internet, they are always filled with horror stories and owners asking for advice on stopping barking. It's always right up there among the most popular topics of conversation.

I can often get a pretty good clue as to what's going on by seeing what the dog looks like when he's barking his head off. If it sounds like he's going ballistic, but he's actually just standing there calmly and not showing signs of aggression, chances are he doesn't really have a target for his outburst.

On the other hand, when a dog barks when someone enters the yard, and maybe runs up to the visitor and then runs back, the bark is probably saying, *I know I've got a job to do, but I don't really want it.* Don't let this ferocious but frightened fellow get behind you, because he's probably going to be a butt-nipper, and your pride will be wounded, if nothing else.

But this type of dog is preferable to the quiet type who doesn't warn, boast, or complain but silently launches himself at intruders, running straight and true as an arrow, and simply nails them. I'll take a barker any day.

Luckily, a lot of barks don't signal aggression of any sort. And many clients are happy to learn that some barking problems can be addressed successfully with special collars that are made for the specific purpose of eliminating or reducing excessive barking.

I'm not much of a believer in gadgets. I prefer to help dogs learn while using as few commercial props as possible. But it's silly to dismiss all gadgets out of hand. There have been some very good aids invented in recent years that are both useful and relatively free of harmful side effects. For barking, three types of collars seem to work pretty well, especially when they're used in conjunction with some behavioral retraining. Dogs with separation anxiety or phobic reactions usually aren't good candidates for these collars because any type of anxious reaction is only made worse by punishment.

What do I mean by punishment? It doesn't mean physical torment. In behavioral language, a punishment is simply something that decreases the probability that the problem behavior—in this case, barking—will happen in the future.

Bark collars can be very effective punishers, especially for a small- or medium-size dog who is barking for no apparent reason other than that he is bored out of his skull. Bark collars have a built-in microphone. When the dog is getting geared up for an afternoon of barking and lets loose with his first woof, the collar emits a loud, short tone.

Here's what I think happens. The dog doesn't know where the tone is coming from. He looks around, perks up his ears, and listens for it to come again. Nothing happens, so after a while he barks again. There's that tone again! He listens a little longer this time, just to make sure. Then he barks again, not as loudly this time in case he might miss something. Once again, he hears the tone. Maybe he'd better take a look around. Eventually, he gets so occupied with looking and listening that he forgets why he was barking in the first place and simply stops.

Of course, it's not always this easy, but I've seen bark collars solve the problem in literally minutes. We don't think the tone is particularly unpleasant for dogs, but, of course, that depends on the dog and the sensitivity of his ears to the tone. In any event, this collar isn't designed to be used for an extended period of time. If it's going to work at all, it'll work pretty quickly.

And if it's not going to work, sometimes it's for no other reason than technological problems. I had a case some years back that always reminds me why I don't like gadgets too much. Back then, the tone collar was a new invention. The microphone picked up sounds pretty indiscriminately. That caused problems when I was treating Tippy, a black Labrador with a barking problem. And a snapping problem. And a lunging problem. And a disobedience problem.

In an attempt to control her behavioral problems, Tippy had been fitted with a Gentle Leader. This is a collar that goes over the top of the nose and around the back of the neck, then hooks beneath the chin. It's designed to help stop the dog from jumping around.

Because Tippy also had a barking problem, we were using a tone collar to see if it would help. Unfortunately, every time she moved a certain way, the Gentle Leader would rub against the microphone in the tone collar, setting it off. Poor Tippy must have thought she was surrounded by a mob of kitchen timers. She was downright frantic. After a day or two of this, her owner was beginning to think that the barking hadn't been such a bad deal.

Today's tone collars can be adjusted for their sensitivity to non-bark sounds. For the most part, technology has made it easier to help dogs with behavioral problems. That's not to say that the machine can outwit the crafty canine. A detective once told me that his police dogs were so bright that they could tell dummy shock collars with the batteries taken out from real ones. (Unlike tone collars, a shock collar gives an electrical jolt when the dog barks.)

Once a dog has been trained not to bark, owners will swap the live collar with a dummy replacement. The dog won't know the difference and so will continue to stay in line. But these highly sensitive police dogs weren't fooled, even when dead batteries were placed in the dummy collars. The officer couldn't tell what was tipping the dogs off—the smell of the live batteries, perhaps, or a slight vibration or sound just before the electrical current fired—but they quickly noted the change. When they were wearing the real collars, for example, they'd give a tentative bark to see if they were on. When the detective put on the dummy collars, they'd immediately bark their loudest. Those dogs were no dummies.

I have never used a shock collar for my own or anyone else's dogs. I prefer to stay away from electricity if at all possible. I'm much more likely to go with the tone collar or with a fairly new training device called a citronella collar.

Like a tone collar, the citronella collar is activated by barking Rather than a tone, however, it emits a spray of citronella-scented fluid. It makes a little *pssst* sound, which startles the dog for a moment and draws his attention away from his barking. In addition, some dogs find the smell of citronella somewhat interesting, and that also helps distract them. Recently, the collars have been equipped with a warning tone and the ability to be activated remotely by the owner.

Researchers at Cornell University in Ithaca, New York, have found citronella collars to be significantly more effective in reducing or eliminating barking than shock collars. It would be neat if the company that makes them added a variety of scents, such as lime or clove, just to keep the pooch on his toes.

While correction collars can work well when there's just one barking dog in the family, things get a little more confusing when you have two or three barking dogs. Unless the collars are adjusted precisely, they can "punish" the wrong dog if one of his companions is barking nearby. One colleague told me that the citronella collars he was using in a multidog household fired so frequently that they smelled up the entire house. The dogs couldn't get away from the smell and developed other problems on top of the barking. At least the family wasn't bothered by a lot of mosquitoes.

YOU DON'T HAVE TO RELY ON collars to treat barking problems, especially if you're willing to work with your dog before his normal barking develops into an annoying problem. You can play a little game in which you teach your dog to stop barking, then reward him with a "Good boy" and a treat when he shuts up.

In many families, however, people are too busy to take the time for training. And, of course, dogs often do their barking when no one's nearby to stop them. This was definitely the case with Snowy, a four-year-old female West Highland white terrier who was driving her owner and the next-door neighbors nuts with her barking.

Snowy would use the dog door to let herself out into the backyard every day. She would find some squirrels to bark at for an hour or so. Then she'd keep an eye out for the neighbors to show up on their back decks so she could bark at them, too.

"What have you tried so far?" I asked Mary Lou and Rob Russell, a pleasant, friendly couple in their late twenties.

"Well, we tried a couple of collars, but she seemed to pretty much ignore them after the first few times," Rob said.

"Yes, I've seen that happen," I said. "It's like sleeping in a strange place with a clock ticking. The first night, you lie awake wishing someone would shut the thing off. By the third night, you don't even notice it anymore." He nodded.

"What we do most of the time is just yell at her to stop barking," said Mary Lou. "She'll run up the hill to the back door as soon as we yell. Then she'll bark some more when she gets there."

"I've seen that before, too," I said. "What you're doing when you go outside and yell is giving her attention, which she probably likes, since it's boring out there and you're adding more stimulation."

"Even if it's negative attention?"

"Sure, it's better than nothing. You're yelling, 'Snowy, don't bark!' and she's thinking it's a nice family moment and you're encouraging her: *Oh, boy, you're going to bark along with me! Let's bark!*"

I suggested that rather than going outside and adding to the decibel level when Snowy was barking, they should just stay inside. It was possible that she would quit barking if she didn't have an audience. What happened then was one of those serendipitous simple fixes that lessened the problem behavior considerably.

Rob called the next day and told me that while they had tried not to respond when Snowy was outside barking, they were having a hard time restraining themselves. "Finally, Mary Lou couldn't stand it anymore and she rapped really hard on the windowpane with her ring," Rob said. "And guess what? Snowy stopped barking and looked up toward the house, trying to figure out what that was. She didn't see us because we were still inside, and she didn't bark again for 15 minutes. The same thing happened again just now. That was 15 to 20 minutes ago and so far, no barking."

"Great," I said. "Let's see if it continues, and then we can work on the other part of the problem. Did you have a chance to give those cheese treats to your neighbors? Are they willing to help?"

"Oh, yes," he said.

I could readily identify with the neighbors, who were greeted by the barking little dog every time they stepped outside to enjoy a little peace. I had been in the same position a couple of years earlier, only worse. My former home was just a few yards away from the house next door. When some new neighbors moved in, they brought with them their hyper, vigilant Chow Chow, named Pup-Pup. This was disturbing news for my two cats, who studiously avoided the neighbors' yard from then on and pretended not to notice when Pup-Pup threw himself against the fence, barking fiercely. But it was worse news for me, since I greatly valued the quiet of my property. So I set out to make friends with Pup-Pup. It wouldn't be easy, his owners warned me, but I was willing to try.

The next morning, I poured a large amount of dog treats into a bowl. My strategy was simple: I was going to throw him treats. People often believe that if you give a dog treats while he's doing something he shouldn't, like barking, you're going to reinforce the behavior. Very occasionally, that could happen, especially if you heap a lot of praise on the dog when he barks and then pop him a biscuit. And if you want to teach your dog to bark excessively, go ahead and try this. But dogs who are barking at people outside are usually barking pretty emotionally. That kind of barking can be controlled by what we call classical conditioning.

With a type of classical conditioning called countercondi-tioning, you use a word or some other stimulus, like a treat, to elicit a happy mood that's incompatible with the angry or fearful mood that's making the dog want to bark aggressively. In other words, the treat elicits the mood change that leads to the good be-havior. With a technique called operant conditioning, on the other hand, a dog will "emit" a desirable behavior (and then get a treat) at a time when he isn't being emotional.

Here's an example. A trainer says "Sit." The dog sits and re-ceives a reward. He gets the praise after the behavior. That's an ex-ample of operant conditioning. But if the dog is already misbe-having and that behavior is fueled by a lot of negative emotion, you use classical conditioning instead. You elicit a happy mood by let-ting him know that you stand for something that predicts he's going to get a treat. Treats make him feel good. He can't feel happy and angry at the same time, so you get a decrease in the emotional barking, replaced by a nice, submissive, happy tail wag as a result of the emotional change elicited by a food treat.

The first morning, I walked down the steps to my driveway. There was Pup-Pup, right on time, greeting me with his usual fe-rocious barks and growls. I didn't look at him or say anything. I just used an underhand toss to send a dog biscuit over the chain-link fence into his yard. Then I walked away, got in my car, and left. I didn't need to look in the rearview mirror to know there would be a rather confused look on Pup-Pup's face.

The next two mornings, I did the same thing. On the fourth day, I noticed that Pup-Pup only trotted partway to the fence, and the barking and growling were significantly reduced. I started to vary the routine a little bit. On the fifth day, I tossed the biscuit from my back steps. The next day, I walked over to the fence and tossed it. The day after that, I squatted down and poked the biscuit through the fence. Pup-Pup was so busy trying to take the treat from my fingers, he forgot to bark. I didn't let go of the biscuit right away. I held fast for a few seconds until he released his bite and tried again, then I let him have it.

I kept hand-feeding him after that. As soon as he'd latch on gently to the biscuit, I'd let him have it. This helped reinforce the gentleness. Soon I was giving him the biscuit and also adding a little eye contact, at which point he looked away. This meant that he was getting used to my being more and more assertive, while he became more submissive.

After 10 days, the angry, barking dog had been replaced by a nice, friendly dog who came out when I left the house and waited patiently for a treat, wagging his tail. So I wouldn't have to go through this routine for the rest of my life, I soon switched to an intermittent pattern of reinforcement, in which I only gave him a treat every once in a while. He continued to regard me in the same friendly manner, while hoping to get a treat now and then.

It had been a great success. The owners were happy, I was happy, and I believe Pup-Pup was, too. The only ones I'm not sure about were the cats, who continued to give Pup-Pup the cold shoulder for as long as we lived in that house.

I explained all this to the Russells, and they explained it to their neighbors. Snowy was soon getting a lot of treats, and, sure enough, she gradually began to lose interest in barking. To make her outside play more interesting, I told the Russells that they should take her out on a leash several times a day and give her some strenuous exercise. When Snowy had less pent-up energy, she was less likely to make mischief.

MANY DOGS WILL BARK AT WHATEVER they perceive as an intruder, which is anything from the sound of the doorbell to the school bus coming up the street. This type of barking usually isn't difficult to control. What I usually do is make a tape recording of the school bus, the doorbell, or whatever, and put it on a loop so it keeps playing.

The first time you play the tape, your dog will launch into his noisy routine as he always does. Your job at this point is simply to be calm and ignore it. After your dog settles down—I've seen dogs carry on for 5 to 10 minutes—play the tape again briefly, or until he starts barking. (I have to warn clients using this method to brace themselves to put up with a lot of barking and doorbell or school bus sounds for a week or two.) Let him calm down and then do it again.

After 15 to 20 times, your dog will get the idea that the sounds on the tape don't mean anything, so he'll start to ignore them.

After a few weeks, during which you may have played the tape 30 to 40 times a day, there will gradually be less barking and fewer episodes of leaping around and getting overexcited. Eventually, your dog will be able to sit quietly when the doorbell rings or the bus chugs into the neighborhood.

This isn't always foolproof, of course. Some of my colleagues have reported that this kind of routine can backfire and actually make the dog more sensitive. That's why it's important to work with a professional instead of trying to change your dog's behavior on your own. This is especially true when there's more than one behavioral problem, as there often is.

I remember a dog who had a doorbell *and* a UPS problem. Dusty, a handsome Airedale, lived at the end of a cul-de-sac, so trucks were constantly pulling up and turning around, and this excited him considerably. He'd really go nuts when people rang "his" bell. Dusty had been known to lunge at the windows and chew the door frame when the doorbell rang. In fact, it was well-known on the street that Dusty simply wouldn't let some people into the house.

"And with good reason," his owner, Bill Wendell, said as I wrote down some notes.

"Why is that?" I asked. This type of problem often develops out of the blue. It wasn't all that often that I could find a precipitating event that started things going downhill.

"A couple of months ago, our house was broken into," Bill told me. "The guy must have rung the doorbell first and found out that we weren't home. He pretty much trashed the house. Dusty had never reacted to visitors before that."

Bill leaned down to pet Dusty, who was standing uneasily by his side, looking at me suspiciously. To give me a little more legitimacy in Dusty's eyes, Bill had suggested that I meet him in the driveway so we could walk in together. Sure enough, Dusty didn't bark or jump, but he still wasn't too thrilled that I was there.

"Poor old Dusty had blood on him when we came home," Bill said. "He's been watching for that guy to come back ever since so he can finish him off." Dusty was only six months old, but he was taking his responsibilities very seriously. He was going to protect his family, whether they appreciated it or not.

We were able to help Dusty in a couple of ways. The first thing I did was ask Bill to always keep the ceiling fan or a radio on to mask sounds coming from outside. I figured that Dusty wouldn't always feel on duty if he couldn't hear the potential perpetrators coming. Then I had Bill hook up the doorbell to a little button, which he could press from a chair. This made it easy to ring the bell often as part of a training program.

After a few weeks, Dusty had stopped going crazy when the doorbell rang. Bill and I then worked on getting him to sit and stay when Bill went to the door and opened it. When Dusty succeeded, he was praised and rewarded. Eventually, he got to the point where he wasn't going crazy when the delivery man or other visitors came to the door. When people came inside, Bill asked them to sit down while Dusty came up and sniffed them, if they didn't mind. This was his reward for being compliant and not barking. Dogs think sniffing is a big deal, so this was a pretty good reward.

Finally, Bill put up signs outside asking visitors to come to the side or back door and knock quietly instead of ringing the doorbell. This helped to confuse the issue a little bit in Dusty's mind and took his mind off the target area at the front door. I suspected that Dusty would always be at least a little bit suspicious of strangers. But since his behavior was now under control, it really wasn't a problem. And as long as the visitors didn't smell like a burglar, they had nothing to worry about.

BARKING CAN BE A TERRIBLE problem for those who live in condos or apartments. It's difficult enough for owners to live with dogs with behavioral problems. They do it because they love the dog, no matter what. Neighbors, on the other hand, have no such bond to keep them from turning downright ugly and forming committees designed to throw owners and their noisy mutts out on the street.

Such was the case with Lilly Lubell and her little Maltese, Angel. Angel consisted of about five pounds of hair done up with matching red bows above each ear, two little beady eyes, and about the most annoying bark imaginable. She was Lilly's pride and joy.

"Why are all those mean people complaining about my little Angel?" she asked, holding the yipping little dog a few inches from her face. Angel stopped barking long enough to snap at the tip of her nose. "You entertain Dr. Wright while I get him a cup of café au lait."

She set Angel on the couch next to me and swept into the kitchen, her long chiffon scarf billowing behind her. Lilly was quite a piece of work. I believe she spent her days in some kind of theatrical workshop, whether as an instructor or an aspiring performer, I hadn't a clue. All I knew was that Angel was causing a lot of trouble, and I was supposed to keep the two of them from being evicted.

While waiting for my coffee, I leafed through a coffee table book about the "Chien de Malte." I learned that, for all its diminutive size, the Maltese seems to be without fear and that its trust and affectionate nature are very appealing. I looked over at Angel. She was huddling and shivering at the end of the sofa.

"Is that so, Angel?" I whispered.

"Yap, yap, yap!" At the sound of my voice, she trembled even more. She jumped down from the couch and scampered after Lilly. I saw that her nails were painted bright red to match the bows in her hair. I closed the book and waited for Lilly to return.

After we had talked a bit, I began to appreciate the scope of the challenge before us. The list of things that made Angel bark, which I jotted down on my notepad, was nearly endless.

Barks at strangers. Barks at cars backfiring. Barks at door shutting in hallway. Barks at shopping bags. Barks at boxes. Barks at any noise outside.

After a few minutes, I said, "It might be easier if I wrote down the things Angel doesn't bark at. Is there anyone or anything she seems comfortable with?"

"Well, not really," Lilly said. I put down my pen.

"We have our work cut out for us," I admitted. "There are a number of things we can try to make Angel more comfortable with new things." The dog was clearly neophobic, afraid of anything she hadn't seen before. Since she was also pretty curious, she was constantly scaring herself half to death. And she definitely didn't trust people, except maybe her owner.

We were able to help Angel in many ways. I gave my usual advice to keep the radio on when Lilly was away. Some people assume that "music hath charms to soothe the savage breast," but my money goes on the fact that it helps block out other sounds that a dog would ordinarily react to.

I also recommended that Lilly ask a friend to come over and help Angel get used to the idea of having other people around. After much deliberation and negotiations by phone, Lilly invited a friend of whom Angel wasn't afraid. The idea was to play a sort of musical chairs, with people getting up, walking around, and sitting down again until Angel became less nervous about people moving around. At the same time, the constant shuffling helped her relax a little bit when Lilly was out of sight. Within a week or two, we found that Angel was less likely to stare at Lilly constantly and track her with her eyes.

Once Angel was comfortable with two people in the house, we repeated the procedure with someone she wasn't as familiar with. Then we did it again later with a stranger. Angel got better and better at coping with various people and was less likely to raise a ruckus every time someone came around.

While we had some victories, I felt our program was only marginally successful. Angel never really calmed down entirely, even when she wasn't upset. She seemed to have a generally fearful personality, and that drove just about everything she did. When a dog has this type of temperament problem, desensitizing her to any one particular event or stimulus just isn't as likely to work. So I asked the vet to prescribe an anti-anxiety medication to help her cope a little bit better.

By combining the medication with the behavioral program, we were able to make Angel less anxious, tense, and annoying to the neighbors. Although I would have preferred to use the medication as a very short-term solution, Angel's fears came back as soon as we quit using it. So we all agreed that the best thing was to keep Angel on very low maintenance doses of the medication indefinitely, or until her vet found a way to wean her from the drug entirely.

I first met Angel quite a few years ago, and I thought then that she was a surprisingly nervous Nellie. But then, I hadn't yet met the phobic bunch of dogs that I found hiding in bathtubs or chewing on their paws, which I was to encounter later on.

Chapter Seven

The Dog Who Was Scared to Death

PIXIE WAS A LITTLE THING WITH a big, overwhelming fear. The three-year-old Yorkshire terrier weighed in at four pounds soaking wet, which, if dogs had sweat glands, she would have been every time she saw Joe. Joe was Maria Stone's boyfriend, and Pixie was terrified of him.

"I can't understand it," Maria told me when we met. "Pixie just can't handle men. Nobody ever did anything to her, especially Joe." Maria was recently divorced, she told me, and she expected to be seeing a lot of Joe. Everything was going great, except for the Pixie problem.

Pixie scampered away as soon as I came into the house, and I didn't expect to see her again. But I had a pretty good idea of what to expect, even without seeing her cower.

"I told him not to take it personally," Maria said. "But how would you feel if your girlfriend's dog peed all over you when you picked her up?"

I agreed that I might be a bit offended.

"The last time he tried to pick her up," Maria added, "she tried to bite him."

I shook my head and continued taking notes.

"I don't know how much more he's going to put up with," she said. "There are lots of girls out there with nice dogs and cats. He doesn't need this."

I was disappointed that Maria's concern seemed to lie with her boyfriend. I figured he wasn't much of a catch if he held the dog's problems against Maria. I would have preferred that she have a bit more empathy for Pixie, who, after all, was the one who was suffering the most.

I suspected that the little dog was trying to assert herself when she saw this giant (to her) man on her turf every day. Maria told me that Joe visited frequently and was planning to move in soon. But it wasn't easy for Pixie. She yelped whenever Joe walked by and then retreated to a corner to quiver. The few times Joe tried to pick her up or pet her, she would quiver, urinate, or bite.

"She even barks at Joe's shirt on the bed after he leaves," Maria added. "What am I going to do?"

I had to admire Pixie. Though she was clearly terrified, the dog was coping as best she could. "I wish that Joe had joined us, but he had to work," Maria said.

"How does Joe approach Pixie?" I asked since I couldn't observe his manner for myself. "Is he very loud or rough?"

"Not at all," Maria answered. "Like I said, he's a cream puff."

"Okay," I said. "Can you ask him to walk very quietly and not try to pick up Pixie anymore? And not to bend over her or even try to pet her?"

"Well sure, if that's what you want, but I don't know how that's supposed to get them to be friends."

"I'm not really worried about them being friends right now," I explained. "We have to reduce the fear that Pixie is feeling, and to start with, that means she's going to have to avoid the guy who's scaring her. I don't suppose you'd consider not seeing Joe at your house for a while, until we can get Pixie a little healthier?"

"Isn't that a little drastic?"

"Well, I think Pixie would do much better if she only had to cope with, say, his shirt for a week or so. If we can get her to be comfortable with one article of clothing—and I can tell you how to do that—we'll be able to slowly get her to accept Joe's presence and eventually Joe himself."

Maria stood up. "Let me get this straight," she said, running her hand through her hair. "You want me to make do with Joe's shirt for a week, instead of Joe? And what'll I get next week, maybe a sock?"

She was beginning to get a little steamed. I had a feeling that this was going to be one of those cases where the dog ends up with the short end of the stick, despite the owner's insistence that she wants to solve the problem.

I explained the rationale for the treatment program as best I could. Taking it slow and easy was essential. Helping Pixie get desensitized to Joe's shirt was just the first step; getting used to Joe himself would come later on. I gave Maria some other specifics to start off with. For example, it would be a good idea for her to wear one of Joe's used shirts periodically, which would mix his "frightening" scent with her "acceptable" one. She wasn't thrilled with this idea, either, but she agreed to do it and to call me once a week to chart Pixie's progress. I wondered if she'd really ban her boyfriend from the house long enough for Pixie to begin to calm down. As I went out the door, I caught one last glimpse of Pixie, a little shivery head poking warily around the corner of the hallway.

Maria didn't call back. I waited two weeks and then called her. A soft, friendly male voice answered. Maria wasn't there, but he'd be happy to take a message. I told him who I was. Oh, yes, Maria had said something about not picking up the dog anymore. But he had really wanted to make friends with the little critter.

"I guess Maria didn't tell you what happened?" He gave me the bad news and said he'd tell Maria I called.

I hung up the phone and looked down at Pixie's diagnostic form on the desk in front of me. I noted sadly that she was only three years old. No one could have predicted that she would simply collapse one day after eating. I picked up my pen and made a notation on the sheet:

Pixie died of a heart attack.

I put the form in my file. After a while, I took a long walk in the park.

PIXIE'S STORY IS VERY UNUSUAL, and there's no way of knowing if anything could have been done to save her life. But her almost disabling fear certainly must have contributed to her untimely death. Since then, I have seen and treated dogs with profound fears and phobias that were making their—and their owners'—lives miserable.

Although a fearful temperament is one of the most heritable traits we see, dogs are not born with specific fears. If they are exposed to a wide variety of enjoyable experiences and new objects and people in the early weeks of their lives, they are less likely to be afraid as they mature. Dogs who don't have any interaction with people until they are three months or older are very likely to have fearful reactions to all the people they meet from then on.

My colleagues and I once studied two groups of puppies. Those in one group were raised in the usual litter, and the others had a lot of interaction with people. We wanted to see how outgoing and exploratory the two groups would be. We put them in an eight-foot-square box. The box was divided in half with a small doorway in the middle, which allowed them to pass back and forth freely. One half of the box was empty. The other half was filled with a variety of objects—a balloon on a string, for example, and a ticking metronome. One by one, we put the puppies in the empty half and watched to see how long it took them to explore the other side.

The litter-reared pups, who hadn't been exposed to people or very many objects, huddled in the corner. They didn't want to explore the stimulating side of the box at all. The people-reared pups, on the other hand, spent most of their time on the exciting side. They were more curious and outgoing and less afraid.

What this means is that dogs who weren't exposed to a variety of things early on were naturally fearful, not just of one or two things but of all new things. Fear becomes a natural part of their personality. And it rarely goes away, but generally gets worse as a dog gets older.

It's natural for dogs, and people, to be nervous about things they think will do them harm. For example, many puppies are afraid of stairs. This kind of fear is normal since the puppy, quite reasonably, doesn't want to take a tumble. In most cases, he'll quickly learn to feel comfortable scampering up and down. On the other hand, when a mature dog refuses to go near a flight of stairs or starts to pant or shy away even at the sight of stairs, that isn't normal. It's an out-of-control phobic reaction.

How does a puppy cautiously working his way up and down the stairs turn into that poor, panting dog? It happens either because it's a personality trait or because there was a traumatic event. Maybe he was pushed down a flight of stairs or simply took a bad fall. Many times, we have no idea why the fears developed.

Dogs, like people, can be afraid of just about anything. My files are full of notes about dogs who were terrified of male voices, staple guns, people walking around a room, and even pieces of paper. One of my big-city colleagues tells me that he often encounters dogs who live 20 stories up and won't step onto an elevator. In the country, dogs who have been zapped a few times by underground fencing may have to be dragged outside in the future. Not that this makes their fears any better.

Dogs will do anything possible to avoid whatever it is they're afraid of. This is known as avoidance learning. Lots of dogs, when they encounter the wrong thing, will pant, squint, shake, pace, try to hide in or under things, go outside and come right back in again, bark, or bite out of sheer panic.

None of this is a pretty thing to have your dog suffer through, and it's not something that he'll grow out of or be able to cope with successfully by himself. One of the most widespread fears in dogs involves thunderstorms. We're not sure exactly what it is that scares them so badly. Is it the crash of thunder? The flash of lightning? The sound of the rain on the roof? The wind whipping branches against the window? All of the above? Or maybe it's none of the above. Some dogs start panting and pacing half an hour before the first raindrop. Can they sense the negative ions in the air? We really don't know.

What we do know is that many dogs suffer big-time during stormy weather, and they all have different ways of coping. I remember a four-year-old beagle-mix named Aspen who would hide in the bathtub when it started storming. She loved baths, and this represented a safe haven to her. Curiously, despite her love of baths, she was terrified by water that produced any kind of rain sound. The sky could be bright and sunny, but when the lawn needed watering, Aspen was in trouble. The sound of water from the sprinklers hitting the windows would be followed by the sound of dog hitting porcelain as Aspen dove into the tub.

Another dog with an intense fear of thunderstorms was Koko. His problem began when a cleaning lady, annoyed at his getting underfoot, banished him to the cellar, a dank, dark place he had never been before. Coincidentally, there was a thunderstorm going on at the same time. The noise of the storm, combined with the lack of an escape route back to his safe, familiar surroundings, frightened him badly. Thereafter, he was so terrified when it stormed that he would lick his paw for comfort. He licked so much that he developed a bad sore. He also bloodied himself when he clawed at the bedroom door, trying to get in so he could hide under the bed. Poor Koko.

Then there was Aslan, a golden retriever who, if caught outside in a storm, would cower and shake, looking nervously up at the sky as though waiting for something to fall and strike her dead. The only thing that would calm her even a little was to wedge herself between the toilet and the wall in the bathroom.

Many dogs will try this type of squeeze play in order to calm themselves. It's almost as though keeping themselves from moving somehow lessens the fear. Or perhaps they're telling themselves, *If I hide, maybe it will go away.*

I also remember Rocky, a three-year-old keeshond, who would break through the kitchen screen to get inside and away from the storm and then would break right out again. He was one of those dogs who could predict a storm before the first clap of thunder, and he'd start panting and squinting and going inside and out.

The only thing that gave Rocky comfort was snuggling in his owner's arms, or actually, under her arms: He would bury his nose in Clara's armpit until the storm subsided. "Any port in a storm," Clara said brightly when I commented on Rocky's unusual behavior. She ended up building Rocky a little den—a small kennel covered with a blanket inside a darkened bedroom. It seemed to work at least as well as her armpit.

The worst thunderstorm phobia I ever encountered was harbored by Taffy, a four-year-old yellow Labrador retriever. Taffy lived pretty much in the lap of luxury across the street from a ritzy country club in the suburbs of Atlanta. But money can't buy happiness. Taffy was an easygoing dog most of the time, but when it started to storm, he would shiver, shake, pant, and go looking for a place to hide.

His owner, Angela Tulander, called me one sultry evening in considerable distress. Taffy, it turned out, always knew when a storm was coming, and he didn't like it one bit. But one night things took a turn for the worse.

"My husband and I went out to dinner, and it poured and thundered all evening," she said. "We stayed and had dessert until the worst was over. When we got home and walked into the kitchen, all of our pots and pans were strewn all over the kitchen floor."

"Uh-oh," I said.

"And there was Taffy," she continued, "hiding inside the new pecan cabinets we had just finished installing. He had chewed through the frame."

This sounded familiar. It's not at all uncommon for dogs with thunderstorm phobias to do considerable damage when they're in the throes of panic. So we made an appointment to talk things over.

The next day I grabbed a cassette tape ("The Ultimate Thunderstorm"), a strobe light, and a stick of room deodorant and went to see the Tulanders. I always consider the recording and, in some cases, the light to be essential for coping with thunderstorm phobias. Using the deodorant is my own invention, and not all of my colleagues bother with it.

I sat down with Thornton and Angela Tulander, a handsome, refined couple in their fifties, and said hello to Taffy, who, since it wasn't storming at the time, acted pretty much like any other Labrador. I was glad to see he didn't have a generally fearful personality, which meant that we had just one problem to deal with. I couldn't have guessed by looking at him that Taffy would prove to be the most difficult thunderstorm-phobia case I ever encountered.

While the Tulanders and I discussed his problem, Taffy sat politely nearby and watched the proceedings with interest. Little did he know that we were going to seed the clouds for him any minute.

The Tulanders had tried a number of things to solve Taffy's problem, including erecting a chain-link fence around the backyard. They did this because Taffy would try to escape his fear by running away whenever he heard thunder. They also bought a beautiful doghouse for him to hide in. It was the size of a child's playhouse and had wood clapboard siding painted to match their own southern colonial. I'm sure they meant well.

"I had our architect draw up the plans for that," Thornton told me.

"It's beautiful," I said. "It looks brand new." Actually, it looked completely unused.

"Taffy doesn't seem to like it all that much," he admitted. "Can't fathom why not."

I explained that dogs don't often like doghouses. They are too isolating. Most dogs would much rather be sitting with their people.

"He really hates the doghouse when it's storming out," Angela added. "He only tried it once, and he shot out of there like a bullet as soon as it started to pour." The sun glinted off the roof of the doghouse.

"That a copper roof?" I asked.

"Oh, yes," Thornton answered.

The roof was beautiful, but I knew that it would greatly magnify the sounds of the raindrops during a storm. Any dog inside who was already phobic to rain would probably hightail it out of there at the first drop. The Tulanders were being sabotaged by their own good intentions, not to mention their impeccable taste.

After we talked a bit, I got out the thunderstorm recording. I explained to the Tulanders that the program I had in mind would most likely take between two and six weeks to achieve a noticeable result. I'll explain how this behavioral program works, but it's not something you can do at home unless you've been trained by a professional. If it's not done right, it can backfire and make the dog worse.

"That's all right. We have all the time in the world," Angela said. "Although I would like him out of my kitchen cabinets as soon as possible." And so we began.

THE IDEA BEHIND THUNDERSTORM recordings is pretty simple. By playing the recording—first at low volumes and then gradually louder—and giving the dog plenty of time to adjust and stay calm, he'll gradually become desensitized to the noise. This isn't the same as forcing him to face what he fears and hope he'll get over it. That's called flooding, and it rarely works.

What I usually do is have the owner sit with the dog in a darkened room with a stash of whatever treats the pooch normally likes. The room has to be equipped with a CD or tape player. In addition, during the first session, I uncap the room deodorant, something like Glade Solid, and put it near the sound system.

This is not my uncouth way of suggesting to the owners that the room needs deodorizing. What it does is give the dog both a visual and an olfactory cue that he can associate with the other elements of the training session. It may be that the air freshener is the only stimulus that allows the dog to tell the difference between a real storm and the recorded storm in a training session. If he acts relaxed while the aromatic item is in the room, he may relax in the future as well. Other behaviorists suggest using a small rug that's been saturated with something like oil of cloves. It doesn't matter what odor is introduced, as long as it is novel and distinctive, and the people can stand it.

The air freshener is left out only during the training session. After the behavioral program is finished, it can be opened and set out whenever a storm is expected. This allows the dog to associate the smell with the feeling of calmness he experienced during the program. If the fragrant item is left out all the time, it won't be associated with any particular feeling and will lose its effectiveness.

When starting the program, we need to find out whether or not we can fool the dog into believing he is listening to a real thunderstorm. As a test, we turn on the first "storm," using a moderate volume. If the dog starts panting and pacing, we know we can use the recording. If he looks at us blankly, as though to say, *What? Are you kidding?* we have to adjust the conditions until we have more credibility. The dogs I see are generally phobic enough to swallow the simulation hook, line, and sinker.

I generally start the first training session with the sound pretty low. If the dog remains relaxed, he is praised and given a treat. So the very soft thunder, instead of predicting something scary that will trigger the pacing, panting, and shaking, predicts something the dog enjoys. The idea isn't to force the dog to face his fears. It's to help him associate the soft claps of thunder and falling rain with the idea that he is going to get something good to eat.

The entire recording lasts about 40 to 50 minutes. I've found it works best to mass practice, or play the entire storm, rather than space practice, in which you play it for 5 minutes, stop, do another 5 minutes, stop, and so on. I tell the clients that if the dog is still relaxed when half of the storm is completed, they can turn up the volume ever so slightly for the remainder of the recording.

At some point, if the dog isn't getting worked up at all, I'll turn on the strobe light. The combination of the recording, a dim room, and the light bouncing off the wall means we have a pretty realistic thunderstorm. After the initial session, in which I teach the owners what to do and what to look for, the program has to be practiced every day. It's a bit of a commitment for owners and dogs alike.

After a few weeks of practice, the dog should be getting pretty comfortable with the storms. At that point, I instruct the clients to have a session in which they open the air freshener but don't play the recording. This allows the calming effects of the training environment to carry over even when nothing is going on. When a storm does come up, this will help remind the dog that everything is okay.

Animal behaviorists have had many successes with this procedure, which has evolved through trial and error over the past decade or so. The fancy name for it is counterconditioning with systematic desensitization. The same type of procedure works for other types of fears as well. Again, the idea isn't to force the dog to confront his worst nightmare. With repetition, by exposing him gradually and gently to that which he fears, you can help make the threat benign.

Of course, even the most successful program can have setbacks when real life intrudes on the charade we so carefully set up to lull the dog into a false sense of security. Remember Rocky, the armpit nuzzler? He was doing fine with the program until lightning hit a transformer near his home. There was a big explosion and the power went out, along with several weeks of newfound confidence. So we had to start over. It's a good idea to begin training during a stretch of clear weather because a real thunderstorm could have unfortunate consequences.

I EXPLAINED ALL THIS TO THE Tulanders and asked them to lead me to the media room. I was sure we could rev up a thoroughly realistic thunderstorm with the sound equipment this obviously wealthy couple probably had.

Thornton led me to the lower-level family room. "Will this do?" he asked.

I looked around for the gigantic sound system I was sure was there. I was amazed to see a cheap little tape player about a foot square, with four-inch speakers. "Our son has a much nicer system, but he took it off to college," Thornton explained.

"That's okay," I said, trying not to sound discouraged. It would be a miracle if Taffy were fooled by the anemic thunder that was going to come from those puny speakers. He probably wouldn't even notice the sound at all. I hated to let down a client and, worse yet, not be able to ease an animal's suffering, but I wasn't too confident about this one anymore.

"Let's give it the old college try," I said, trying to dredge up some enthusiasm. After having Taffy sit, I put on the tape and adjusted the volume to the test level. I waited for him to give me a blank stare and start looking around for his rubber hot dog.

But to my utter amazement, he didn't laugh in my face. He actually bought it. Within seconds, even with the laughably unscary thunder coming from the speakers, Taffy started panting, pacing back and forth, trembling, and drooling. I had never seen a more instantaneous, severely anxious reaction to the recording. Or to the real thing, for that matter.

"There he goes," Thornton said. "Poor old Taffy!" He didn't sound all that sorrowful. In fact, he was beaming with approval. "Guess you'd better turn the volume down a tad, no?"

"Yes." I quickly turned it off. It took about 15 minutes for Taffy to calm down enough to try the recording again. I set the volume as low as it would go. The thunder sounded mainly like static coming from the tinny speakers. I looked at Taffy. He was listening, all right. And starting to shake.

I quickly turned it off again. I had nothing to work with here. Other tricks, like the strobe light or cake pans in the shower, a neat way to amplify "rain" sounds, were totally out of the question. I couldn't believe it. Thornton was talking about getting together for golf when the sessions were over, and I couldn't even start the first procedure. All I knew for sure was that it was going to be a long road to recovery for Taffy.

Eventually, I advised the Tulanders to get an anti-anxiety medication from their vet, which would help reduce the severity of Taffy's fears during storms. As another storm precaution, I told them to put Taffy in their comfortable basement, turn on the washing machine and dryer, and add some soft music. Masking the noise was our only hope.

Oh, we still tried using the recording. We tried it for several days at the lowest volume, putting Taffy as far away from the speakers as possible. Each time, Taffy got frantic, and it took him up to 20 minutes to simmer down after a session. He was just beside himself. This was not the way it was supposed to go. So we went the drug route, and this gave Taffy some relief. I'm just thankful that the son didn't come back from college and put the thunderstorm recording on his top-of-the-line system. That probably would have driven the poor dog over the edge.

FEARS AND PHOBIAS HAVE NO favorite breeds. But I had reason to be alarmed when I got a call from the owner of a Shetland sheepdog, who explained that his dog was having severe phobic reactions to noises outside—so much so that he would only leave the house by the back door, the one farthest from the noise. Shelties are wonderful little dogs, intensely loyal, affectionate, and responsive to their owners. But the American Kennel Club has described them as sometimes being prone to shyness, timidity, and nervousness as well as snappiness or being ill-tempered. Not the kind of dog you'd want living half a mile from a colossal air force base, where there was the constant, ground-shaking rumble of transport jets taking off and landing and the crash of weapons firing during range practice.

I wasn't surprised when the dog's owners, Bob and Jane Morgan, told me that Sarge frequently trembled, chewed the door frame in attempts to escape, and—no surprise—snapped at them. It was useless to speculate whether a laid-back mutt or a gun dog of some sort might have been better prepared to cope with that type of environment. Or maybe an older dog with severe hearing loss would have been the best bet. But they had a sheltie, and there was nothing I could do now but try to help him.

When I drove to visit the Morgans, I saw, or rather heard, that they hadn't been exaggerating. As I got out of the car, I could feel the vibrations as a plane lifted off. The noise was deafening.

The Morgans were both retired from the military, and this was the first new house they'd ever owned. They had a built-in swimming pool, and they weren't moving again. They greeted me with obvious relief, and I looked around for their little companion. He was nowhere in sight.

"Where's Sarge?"

"Well, a big one just took off, so he's probably in a closet somewhere," Bob said. "Sarge, come!"

I wasn't surprised that there was no response.

"Will he usually come when you call him?" I asked.

"No, but I keep trying," Bob said. He led me to the front bedroom. "Take a look at this," he said. A mangled wire kennel was beneath the window. "Last time, there was firing range practice." He pointed out the window. "Sarge worked himself right out of here. I've never seen anything like it."

I had. Very motivated, very panicked dogs will do that. It wasn't all that surprising. The placement of the kennel, right under the window where the shots were very audible, had been a bad choice.

"We found Sarge hiding in here," Jane said, showing me a walk-in closet stuffed with clothes and boxes. "Why, here you are!"

She bent down and peered into the clutter. "Come on out, Sarge," she coaxed, reaching into the closet. I heard a low, warning growl.

"I wouldn't stick my hand . . ."

"Ouch!" She jerked her hand back and stood up quickly, rubbing a finger.

"I guess he's not ready to meet company just yet." She patted her graying hair. "Coffee?"

It was a bad situation, but despite the constant noise, I was able to help Sarge overcome his fears and learn to enjoy retirement living. Bob willingly did everything I asked, including getting the base schedule for daily events. We worked out a program of desensitizing Sarge to the front and side of the house and yard. Aided by the flight and firing range schedule, we were able to use a system of treats, soothing talk, and strokes to help Sarge adjust to his explosive environment. It would never be the French Riviera, but after six weeks of militarily precise drills, as Bob called the sessions, Sarge was feeling much better and the whole family was able to relax by the pool and enjoy life a little more.

I NEVER RECOMMEND THAT DOGS with phobias who aren't used to kennels be forced to stay in a cage, especially when their owners are gone. A cage will prevent damage to the house, but some dogs will panic and wind up cutting their gums or their paw pads when they try to escape. Some dogs will go further and internalize the stress, sometimes triggering ulcers or other digestive problems.

When I think of what not to do with a fearful dog, I remember Ginger, a two-and-a-half-year-old Airedale. Her family meant well, but they did all the wrong things to cope with Ginger's problem.

They called me on the 28th of July. I get a lot of calls in July from frantic owners who need help with their fireworks-phobic dogs and cats. You've probably heard public service announcements reminding people to keep their pets inside on the Fourth. Everyone keeps them inside, all right. They put them in a room or a cage or, as in Ginger's case, leash them to the leg of a piano and go off to enjoy hours of picnicking and fireworks, thinking their dogs are safe from harm.

The next day, I get calls from bewildered, desperate people wanting to know why their pets hurt themselves, wrecked the home, or have been cowering under the bed all day and won't come out. If they don't call me on July 5th, they call by the end of the month when their dogs are still acting funny or have generalized their fear of firecrackers to fear of other noises like thunderstorms.

I had to feel sorry for Ginger, because she had been through the mill. Her owners tried a series of stopgap solutions that nearly were disasters in themselves. They started with an electrified fence to prevent her from escaping from the yard. That kept her in the yard, all right, but then she was desperate to get into the house, and she chewed through a door in order to get in. To prevent the chewing, they tried chaining her. She quickly wrapped the chain around a tree, got trapped, and was actually elevated off her front legs. As her owner put it bluntly, "She almost hanged herself." The next thing they tried was leashing her to the leg of the piano. When they got home, the leg was a mass of splinters, damaged beyond repair, and Ginger's gums were torn up as well.

Soon after this, they called me. I don't think Ginger could have taken many more "solutions."

I couldn't really blame the owners, because they just didn't understand what they were doing. They obviously weren't aware that a pet must not be forced into a situation in which she will only become more upset and frightened. Tying her up, shutting her in a cage, or trying to drag her from under a bed cannot help the situation and may be dangerous for the pet or the owner. Dogs should be rewarded for showing calm behavior and never be punished for being afraid.

THE ENGLISH SPRINGER SPANIEL IS one of the world's foremost bird dogs. Even springers who have never seen a rifle or spent their days retrieving grouse, woodcock, pheasant, and duck have those hunting genes built in. Which is why I can't help but be amused by a springer I once met who was terrified of his own backyard.

The problems began when the dog, named Hunter, got dive-bombed by a blue jay. The peck on the head rattled him so much that for three weeks, he wouldn't set a paw into the backyard. His owner, Sam Weldon, had to walk him to a vacant lot down the block to do his business. This was obviously inconvenient as well as a little embarrassing. Sam wanted help.

I asked Sam what steps he had taken to solve the problem. He told me that he had spent a lot of time on the patio, tugging on the leash to try to get Hunter out of the house and down the step. This is what most people would have done, especially when they knew their dog's phobia was ridiculous. After all, the blue jay had moved on. There was nothing to be afraid of.

But, Hunter didn't see it that way. He must have thought, *No way I'm going back into that combat zone!* Sam's tugging on the leash only frightened him and made him more stubborn about going outside.

My solution to this problem was to make it a little more pleasant outside. By this I mean that we started throwing treats just outside the back door. I had Ricky, Sam's 10-year-old son, do the honors since I was afraid Sam's image had been slightly tarnished in the eyes of his best friend.

At first, Hunter would grab the treats, then run back into the house. After a while, he realized that no one was forcing him outside anymore. Then we started throwing the treats farther and farther away from the door, always allowing him to come back into the house and praising him all the time. We eventually got him to go as far as the edge of the grass.

Next, I asked the members of the family, including Sam, who was by now back in Hunter's good graces, to scatter treats in a circular pattern, starting with a tiny circle and then expanding it until Hunter was going to all the corners of the yard and every portion in between. After about a week, he discovered that nothing in the yard was hurting him anymore, and since he wasn't forced to be out there, he had nothing to rebel against.

Hunter isn't the only dog who was afraid of his own backyard. Duchess was a six-year-old retriever who stayed in the backyard during the day when her owner was at work. Everything was fine until her owner installed an electronic bug zapper near the porch. In case you haven't seen them, bug zappers are tubular affairs with a neon light. They emit a very loud "zap" whenever a bug is electrocuted. People get used to the noise, but some dogs get unnerved.

No one explained the bug zapper to Duchess. In short, it scared her silly. She refused to go in the yard voluntarily. One day, after her owner had dragged her out, she chewed the vinyl siding off the house in an attempt to get inside and away from that weird, scary thing. I was able to help her, but her owner still had to shell out several hundred dollars to repair the siding.

Then there was Foxy, a three-year-old Australian shepherd who had one of the strangest fears I've ever encountered. Foxy was willing to go outside, but only in the dark. During the day, even if it was overcast, he would reluctantly leave the house to relieve himself, then scamper quickly back in. When it was bright and sunny, however, he was much worse. He had to be dragged or carried outside, and his owner had the bites and scratches to prove it. This unhappy fellow needed a technique in which we "fade-in" the light.

I simply had his owner, Brad Straber, begin by taking him outside when it was dark, then shortly before dawn, then right at dawn, and so on. The idea was to get him used to being outside in the daylight without hitting him all at once with it. I think perhaps this dog was actually afraid of what he would see once it was bright out, rather than fearing the light itself.

Whatever was the cause of Foxy's light phobia, it wasn't the only thing he was afraid of. There was a lamppost at the end of the front walk that totally freaked him out.

There is some research to show that wolves are afraid of unfamiliar, stationary, vertical objects and will naturally shy away from them. It's one thing to be afraid of a farmer running toward you wielding a shovel and quite another to be afraid of a lamppost. But who am I to say? We tried to desensitize Foxy to vertical objects, but it was an excruciatingly slow process. Brad, to his credit, understood that Foxy couldn't be rushed into accepting activities that other dogs did pretty much on autopilot.

While dogs like Ginger and Duchess are trying to scratch and chew their ways back into the house, others are desperate to get outside. I'm thinking of two dogs that I treated when they were six months old—different breeds and different households—but both were terrified of motorized objects around the house.

Between them they were afraid of the vacuum cleaner, food processor, buzzer on the clothes dryer, dishwasher, blender, can opener, garage door opener, hair dryer, electric razor, and air conditioner, to name a few. In fact, one of these dogs, named Rascal, was so afraid of the kitchen that she wouldn't even go in to eat. Now *that's* a fearful dog!

The method I used to help them conquer their fears is essentially the same as the one I use for thunderstorms or doorbells. It requires lots of slow, gradual habituating to the sounds or objects that frighten them and owners who are patient, nonpunitive, and willing to put in the time to make their pets happy and well-adjusted.

In Rascal's case, which was featured on *PM Magazine* several years ago, I asked her owner to show me how the dog reacted to the can opener. This is normally a welcome sound that beckons dogs to dinner. Rascal knew what the whirring sound meant, and she wanted to eat, she really did. But it was hard for her. She would run toward the kitchen and then run away, again and again. Finally, she'd run away or hide under a table.

The solution we decided on was to run the can opener 30 to 40 times a day. Rascal, incidentally, only got her food at mealtimes, and the can opener was empty the rest of the time. Rascal's owner was to feed her just outside the kitchen initially and then gradually move the bowl into the kitchen. If there's one thing that makes dogs feel more comfortable, it's food, and Rascal's fears gradually began to fade away.

Solving phobias is rarely easy, but most owners will do anything to help their troubled pets. They certainly don't want to give them up. They'd sooner throw the pasta machine and coffee grinder out the window and go to live with their dogs in a cabin in the woods.

Chapter Eight

The Dog Who
Practiced Voodoo

WHAT DO YOU MAKE OF IT, DR. WRIGHT?"

I was standing with Bill and Betsy Turner, a pin-striped marketer and a fashion designer, respectively, in the living room of their opulent house in the suburbs of Atlanta. We were looking at a bizarre stain on the cream-colored wall-to-wall carpet. The carpet wasn't cheap, and I could see why they were concerned. What I didn't have, at least right away, was an answer.

"Well, it sure is unusual," I said, stalling for time. "I've actually never seen anything like this."

"We call it voodoo," Betsy explained, smiling weakly.

The stain in question had a rather intricate design. About a foot in diameter, it consisted of a circle of urine with reddish lines going out from the center like spokes on a wheel. The strange markings had started appearing about six months before, the Turners explained. "I remember the first time we saw this was the day after Silky had some minor facial surgery," Betsy recalled. "We wanted to stay home with her while she recuperated because she seemed sort of unhappy, but, of course, we had to go to work." Since then, the markings would appear as often as four times a week or as seldom as once a month. The one constant was that they always appeared during the day, when the Turners were away from home. It was a strange thing to come home to, and they wanted to know what in the world was going on and how to stop it.

It hadn't taken them long to figure out that one of their pets was responsible, Bill told me. A sniff test proved the spot was urine, but they hadn't been sure who was the culprit—Silky, their 12-year-old spayed cockapoo, or Mitts, their black-and-white cat. And they were absolutely baffled by the strange design as well as the reddish, nonurine streaks.

Several weeks before, they hit on the idea of setting up a video camera to tape what happened while they were at their offices, earning a buck to pay for the fancy carpeting that was now on its way to ruin. I had to admit that it was a good strategy, but the circumstances that made it necessary were less than ideal. I've seen dozens of clients in the last 15 years who spend so much time working that their pets spend most of their time alone. Unfortunately, one of the by-products of long hours and lonely pets is more business for animal behaviorists like me. Clearly, this couple's number had finally come up.

"Would you like to see the video?" Betsy asked.

"By all means," I said. Actually, I could hardly wait, because this one had me stumped.

We settled down on the sofa to watch the tape, which showed a long shot of the living room. Silky was asleep on the carpet, and Mitts was curled up on the floor by the fireplace. So far, so good. Then we watched Silky wake up. She stretched, yawned, and started sniffing the carpet. Eventually, she went to the spot in question, squatted down, and urinated.

That eliminated Mitts as a suspect.

Silky walked off a little way when she was done and sat down. A minute or two later, she went back to the spot and began her "voodoo" ceremony. Beginning outside the urine spot, she put her nose down and pushed it along the carpet toward the spot. Then she stopped, went to another spot, and pushed her nose along the carpet again, making another "spoke" in the wheel. Even on the tape, I could see that all this activity was too much for her sensitive little nose. It was bleeding a little bit, which accounted for the reddish markings.

After completing the circle, Silky looked over her handiwork. She seemed satisfied and walked off-camera toward the kitchen and her bowl, presumably because she was thirsty after her morning's creative efforts.

Bill turned off the tape, and he and Betsy looked at me expectantly. I needed to kill some time in order to think about the strange behavior I'd just seen. "Let's see that pooch's nose," I suggested. Bill brought Silky into the living room. "Is your nose raw from scraping on the carpeting, puppy?" I stroked her head and took a look. Indeed it was.

"Well, what do you think?" asked Betsy. It was time to come up with some rational explanation for this clearly irrational behavior. I thought for a moment. "You say she never does this when you're around?"

"Never," Bill confirmed.

"And she can normally hold her urine?"

"Yep, for 12 hours sometimes if she has to," Betsy said. "That's why we figure it must be because she's lonely when we're gone. She must be trying to tell us to stay home."

The "accidents" always happened during the week, when the Turners were gone. Most dogs don't have any trouble coping with being alone, but Silky may have been an exception. I suspected that she started getting nervous as soon as Sunday night rolled around.

I had another theory as well. "I wonder if a clue to this behavior might be connected to the cat."

"Mitts? I don't see how he can have a role in this," Bill said.

"Show me where he makes his 'pit stops.' Can Silky see Mitts scratching the dirt and covering everything when he's done?"

"I suppose so," Bill said. "But I've never caught her watching with an interested look on her face."

I laughed. "Well, it's just one theory."

It seemed pretty unlikely, actually, that the dog would be imitating the cat. While cats are well-known for their fastidious bathroom habits, dogs generally don't bury their droppings. But they get a big kick out of burying other things, like bones, which they dig up and eat or play with later. I thought of my own dog, Charlie, who buries bones in the soft ground in the woods around our house. After burying a bone, she often pushes leaves and dirt over the place with her nose—much like Silky was when she put her nose to work on the expensive carpet. It was possible that Silky was responding to an ancient behavioral imperative of some kind and was trying to bury the urine.

I decided to share this line of speculation with the Turners, who were probably wondering by this time if I knew what I was doing.

"It could be that when the urine soaks in, Silky thinks it is buried and she needs to cover it up," I suggested.

"That makes sense," Betsy said, much to my relief. I don't like speculating, but it's often the only way to get an inkling of what's going on in the dog's mind.

I also had to consider the possibility that Silky's behavior was caused, at least in part, by a physical problem. "Has Silky had a medical exam lately?" I asked the couple.

"No," Betsy said. "Do you think there is something wrong with her?"

"Not really," I said. "But before I try to attack this on a strictly behavioral level, we need to know if there could be a medical or physical reason why Silky is using the living room as the ladies' room. I just need to rule out a urinary or kidney infection."

I recommended that they ask their vet to do a complete workup to see if anything physical could explain Silky's lapse in training. But the fact that Silky could go all day most of the time without a problem made me suspect that there was a behavioral issue at work and that some simple retraining would be more valuable than medical intervention at this point.

Betsy called me back a week later. As I suspected, Silky got a clean bill of health, so we had to consider some other possibilities. Since the problem only occurred when the Turners were at work, it seemed likely that Silky was having a problem being left alone. Millions of people go to work every day, and most dogs don't have a problem with it. But some dogs, like some people, have a real need for frequent companionship. When they're left alone for a long time—and for some dogs, five minutes can seem like a long time—they start getting bored, anxious, or frightened.

Veterinarians and behaviorists see a lot of pets with separation anxiety, which in severe cases can cause dogs to chew at doors, destroy the furniture, or even jump out of windows. "It probably is a separation problem since you and Bill are gone all day," I said. "But I'm not seeing the anxiety part. Silky is waking up from a nap and urinating, not tearing up the house and then losing control."

"Is that what most dogs with separation anxiety do?" Betsy asked. At this point, I figured she might know a bit about anxiety herself.

"Usually," I said. "It could be a lot worse, believe me. Dogs who are really suffering from missing their owners act out in all sorts of ways. This voodoo stuff probably wouldn't be happening if you were home during the day, but you're not, so let's work from here."

My files are full of sad tales of "latchkey dogs" filled with anxiety, an unfortunate consequence of today's two-paycheck families. While we take pains to find the best day care for our children, much less attention is paid to the plight of our dogs. They're often left home alone all day, five days a week. And dogs are letting us know in no uncertain terms that this is unacceptable.

Dogs used to live in packs, and they are genetically prepared to be with others, either other dogs as in the past or with their owners. When we go off to work all day, some of them just can't handle it. They'll start to whine and cry as soon as their owners close the door. Or they'll urinate or defecate in the house. Or they'll engage in all kinds of destructive behaviors.

These are the same dogs who can be perfect ladies and gentlemen when you are home or they're out for their evening walks. Unfortunately, obedience training flies out the window when anxiety strikes. Many people try to cope with their dogs' separation problems by rushing out and taking obedience classes, thinking the problems will stop. In my experience, they simply won't.

Destructive behavior and house-soiling aren't always caused by separation anxiety. Sometimes boredom is the culprit. A dog who is ignored or left in one room for many hours will eventually try to entertain himself. His idea of a good time is not likely to be the same as yours. Or he may spend hours trying to escape from a place that he doesn't like. Or he could be frightened by something, a noise outside, for example, that causes him to act out. Occasionally, several of these factors come together at the same time, causing a horrible, or at least weird, sequence of misbehaviors.

I figured the best solution, in this case, was to attack the problem from two angles: by giving Silky more company during the day and by reducing the amount of urine she had available for her impromptu artwork. I recommended that the Turners take her outside more often than they had been and leave less water out during the day. (You should always talk to your vet before restricting your pet's water, however.) When Bill explained that he worked just a few miles from the house, I suggested that he come home at lunch and give Silky some extra attention, along with a walk. I was pretty sure that these simple steps alone would go a long way toward solving the problem.

Since dogs don't like to play and eliminate in the same place, I asked the Turners to make Silky's "spot" a play area for tossing balls and so forth. For extra insurance, I advised them to put a plastic carpet runner over the area and leave a few toys on top of that. This would reinforce the idea that this area was distinctly not for urinating.

This was one case I never solved completely, although the simple changes we made did make a difference. Betsy called several weeks after our visit and told me that the voodoo had all but become a thing of the past.

UNFORTUNATELY, IT'S NOT ALWAYS that easy. Dogs don't need to be entertained all the time, but many of them can become very upset when they're separated from their owners. I wouldn't dismiss Silky's problem as insignificant—it certainly wasn't—but compared to dogs who have full-blown separation anxiety, it wasn't anywhere near as severe as it could have been.

I remember, for example, a 10-year-old toy poodle named Sunny. Her owner, Barbara Franklin, had spent four years working at home, which meant that she and Sunny were constant companions. Then she took a job outside the home and quickly discovered that hell hath no fury like a poodle scorned. A walk through the debris-strewn apartment showed that Sunny was clearly busy during the hours she spent alone. I actually wondered where she found the time to feel lonesome.

Although Sunny was unusually destructive, the basic pattern was fairly typical of dogs suffering from separation anxiety. As soon as Barbara left the house in the morning, Sunny went to work. She would go to the front closet, tear open Barbara's shoe bag, and pile all the shoes in a heap. At some point, she would scoot into the bathroom, knock over the brass magazine rack, shred all the magazines, and drag the bathroom carpet into the hallway. Sometimes, for variety, she would just pull the magazine rack into the hallway instead of tearing up the magazines.

The next stop was usually the bedroom. Sunny would go to the storage bag under the bed, unzip it, pull out a blanket, and then put the bag on top. That accomplished, the little handful of fluff would tear up the linoleum in the kitchen, put some of the pieces in her food bowl, and then shove the bowl around the kitchen.

We didn't have to work too hard to find a solution because Barbara eventually decided to stop working and spend her days at home again, at which point Sunny's destructive enterprises immediately stopped. But most people don't have the opportunity to spend their days at home. They leave for work first thing in the morning and often don't come back until late at night. Their dogs and their possessions sometimes pay a terrible price.

Dogs who tear up the house in their owners' absence are often coping with more than just the fear of being alone. There may be other precipitating factors that occurred around the time of the original misbehavior. Not surprisingly, owners usually don't understand what's happening or how to deal with it. Even when done with the best of intentions, their home "treatments" aren't always appropriate and can make things worse.

Such was the case with a pleasant, seven-year-old German shepherd named Atticus. Atticus's owners, Leo and Bonnie Mansfield, had recently returned from a military assignment in Korea. Upon coming back to the States, they retrieved Atticus from Leo's parents, where he had been staying for several years. They had a pleasant reunion, and everything was fine for a few months, until New Year's Eve.

Although it's not as bad as the Fourth of July—which is every animal behaviorist's nightmare—New Year's Eve can be pretty hairy for the mental health of animals because people are setting off firecrackers, banging on pots and pans, and the like. In addition, people usually go out, leaving their pets alone. When the noise starts, no one's home to comfort the terrified canines, and destruction often results.

That's exactly what happened with Atticus. While the family had been out celebrating, some neighbors set off firecrackers, and Atticus's reaction was fairly predictable. When the Mansfields came home after midnight, they were shocked to find deep scratches on every door that led to the outside. So they let Atticus "have it," and things rapidly went downhill.

When I met with the Mansfields at their home in Atlanta's western suburbs, I was stunned by what I saw. Atticus's face was scuffed and scraped, and he was lying listlessly on the floor. I wondered if his owners had beaten him up. "What happened to this poor dog?" I asked.

"It's a long story," Leo told me. But rather than telling me the details, he handed me a sheet of paper. "I have it all documented," he explained.

"Let's see what you have," I said thoughtfully. The sad chronology went like this.

- New Year's Eve: Firecracker scares dog. Scratched every door. Punished with rolled-up newspaper.
- February 5: Atticus accidentally shut in bathroom. Opened window with nose—first successful escape.
- March 3: Doors scratched again—salesman in the neighborhood. Locked dog in crate for an hour and a half. Problem solved?
- March 4: Atticus kept in crate all day. Ripped up towel in pen and ate it. Threw up later.
- March 5–12: Keeps eating towels. Salivating heavily and licking himself. Coat soaking wet.
- March 13: Kids find Atticus on kitchen floor and crate open!
- March 15: Atticus out again. Bloody nails, bloody gums. Carpet in living room ripped. Punished with newspaper.

I read through the rest of the list, each item more upsetting than the next. Poor Atticus, I thought. "That brings us to today," I said. "Want to give me the rest of it?"

In an attempt to keep Atticus from escaping and to stop the almost-daily destruction, Leo had installed a heavy lock on Atticus's crate. The next day, when the children came home from school, Atticus was still in the crate. But he'd tried mightily to get out. His head and neck were swollen and raw from trying to push through the wires. He was whining with pain.

It was a sorry state of affairs. It was very clear to me from his behavior—scratching at the doors, salivating heavily, trying to escape from his crate—that Atticus was terrified of being alone and was highly stressed. German shepherds are among my favorite breeds, and seeing this dog suffer because of his owners' insensitivity made my blood boil. I had to keep in mind that I was here to help, not judge.

"A couple of observations," I offered. "When you punish a dog who is suffering from anxiety, it generally will add to his stress. It will not cause him to stop the bad behavior. It may seem as though it has had some effect when there are no incidents for a while, but the stress is still there and building. There was no relief from that for Atticus. Putting him back in the cage each day, not to mention hitting him with the paper, was definitely punitive."

"I understand what you mean," Leo said, "but I felt we had to teach him a lesson. And our vet told us to put him back in his crate."

"Your veterinarian probably didn't realize that Atticus was suffering from a severe nervous disorder," I said. "And what you really want to teach him is rules, not a 'lesson.' Atticus needs to learn that he'll be okay when you're gone and that he should remain calm until you come back. But he can't do that in the brig, as it were."

Now, I have nothing against crates in general, provided the owner introduces the dog to the crate gradually and without force. Atticus had probably been willing enough to check out the new environment at first. But once he got scared, and after his first breakout attempt, the crate must have felt like a prison.

The fact that Atticus had begun salivating heavily about a month after his involuntary crating told me that he was internalizing his stress. When dogs get really nervous, they start to pant. If they pant enough and salivate enough, their fur gets wet, which they respond to by licking their coats, making them wetter.

This was a terribly upsetting case. It was clear to me that while the family, especially the kids, was concerned about the dog, the primary source of their unhappiness was the scratches on the doors. So here was this beautiful dog, his head swollen and cut, and his owner was mainly concerned about getting him to stay in his crate. In fact, Leo told me that he was planning to build a stronger cage until Atticus gave up trying to escape, unless I had a better idea.

Actually, I had several. The trick was going to be finding a way to stop Atticus from destroying the house when the family was gone, while at the same time keeping him out of jail. I looked at Atticus, who was still lying on the floor. He had a dazed look on his face. I figured it would take a while before he got that indomitable shepherd spirit back. We were obviously going to have to take things slowly and carefully.

The firecracker incident had probably sparked Atticus's fear of being alone, I told the Mansfields. After that, it didn't take much— a stranger ringing the doorbell, perhaps—to put him over the edge. One of the easiest ways to help him calm down again would be for the kids to take him for a good walk before they left for school in the morning.

"If you guys help Atticus get rid of a lot of energy in the morning, he won't have that energy available to fuel his anxiety or his frustration with being alone," I explained. At the same time, it was important not to keep him in the crate, because that clearly fueled his anxiety more than anything else.

It was also important to assuage Atticus's fears about being left alone each day. The best way to do that, I explained, was not to make a big fuss over him before they went out the door. Quite the contrary. They should leave the house as though nothing were happening. "Try tossing a little treat of some sort over his head and away from him," I added. "That way Atticus can start munching while you make a quiet exit."

It would be helpful to leave doors open inside the house during the day because this would make the whole environment feel less confining. When Atticus was acting calm, I said, they should praise him. And if they could occasionally take him along when they went somewhere, that would be ideal. Leo said he could take Atticus with him to work a few days a week, which sounded great.

And, of course, I had to tell them to stop all punishment. I really couldn't believe that after looking at this dog, with his swollen face and cut paws, they actually would punish him for breaking out of his crate.

In the end, however, I had to respect the family's willingness to step back and try new things. They realized that what they'd been doing hadn't worked, and they were eager to learn ways to treat Atticus more like a member of the family and less like a problem pet. This case, as I learned after several follow-up meetings and phone calls, turned out to be a very successful one. Within two months, Atticus had the old spark back in his eye, and the family had gained a happier, more confident pet.

EVEN THOUGH ATTICUS AND SILKY both had problems being separated from their owners, neither one suffered from true separation anxiety. How can you tell the difference? Well, most dogs will greet their people enthusiastically when they come back home—and after 30 seconds to a minute, it's all over. Dogs with full-blown separation anxiety, however, can go a little berserk with pleasure. They'll pant, leap around, and keep jumping up for 5 to 10 minutes before they run out of steam. After the initial, overly exuberant greeting, they'll still try to stay close—so much so that owners start to feel as though they have a perpetual shadow.

I remember a four-year-old mixed breed named Shorty who was a textbook case for separation anxiety. Shorty's owners, Travis Kent and his girlfriend, Billie Speidel, had recently adopted Shorty from the local humane society. "She's just a doll, but very sensitive," Travis said when we met at their apartment. "If you even look at her and say the word 'no,' she just cowers."

It's not unusual for shelter dogs to have some initial difficulty adjusting to a new home or to form an overly dependent relationship with their new owners. It's probably not the shelter itself that causes these problems as much as the dog's uncertainty about where this new change, or the one after that, is going to lead.

Dogs get anxious when they feel that they can't predict what's going to happen next in their lives. And this anxiety may lead to destructive behavior when they're left alone. In Shorty's case, this meant tearing up blinds, digging holes in the carpets, chewing on doors or window frames, or even unlatching doors.

Shorty was so terrified of being alone that she was even reluctant to go outside to relieve herself. She would only go as far as the little gardener's flat on the back deck, and even then she had quivers of anxiety until she got back inside.

"Watch this," Travis said, urging Shorty to go outside to do her business. She reluctantly went to the small plot of dirt, looking backward while Travis stood in the doorway. When she was done, or so I thought, she quickly scampered back into the house.

But this was only the beginning. Shorty was so eager to get back inside, I discovered, that she often dashed in before she finished what she went out to do. "Now I have to say, 'Outside again?'" Travis explained. With some more coaxing, Shorty went back out and used the garden flat again. Then she scampered back into the house.

"Go back? Go back?" Travis persisted. Shorty went out again. Done at last, she ran past Travis into the house.

This odd ritual meant that Shorty was never gone from Travis for very long. Although he didn't go outside with her, he always stood in the doorway, encouraging her, sending her back, and encouraging her some more. This scenario was repeated every time the dog went to the bathroom. I could only imagine what Shorty went through when Travis went to work, leaving her alone to cope with her terrible anxieties.

Actually, I didn't have to do much imagining. The damage inside the house told the story pretty clearly. Many dogs with separation anxiety will do damage when they're home alone. What made Shorty's story so unusual was that she often tore things up when Travis and Billie were home but were out in the yard put-tering around or gardening.

Shorty's behavior was a little extreme, but the solution was pretty simple. I recommended that the couple put Shorty's bed in front of the dining room window and make sure the blinds were up when they went outside. Once Shorty was able to watch her family in a relaxed setting, she quit going crazy all the time. This wasn't the only element of the program, but it went a long way to-ward stopping the frustration and acting out.

PEOPLE ARE PREDICTABLE. MOST OF US follow a pretty set routine. In the morning, for example, we put on the coffeepot, run the shower, and lower the thermostat. We feed and water our pets and take them out. We put on our jackets and take our keys from our pockets or purses. Then we go out the door, turning the lock be-hind us.

Most of the time, we do the same things in the same order. Nothing remarkable about it. But our dogs are watching and lis-tening and sniffing, and they're not stupid. When they're prone to separation anxiety, they start getting emotional at the first cue that a departure is about to happen. They get progressively more emo-tional as each additional cue occurs. By the time their owners fi-nally get to the door, they may be so upset and desperate that they'll grab onto a wrist or leg and not let go, or even deliver a painful bite.

Take Snoopy. This timid basset hound would follow his owner around the house all morning, getting more and more panicky as the time for her to leave approached. Then he'd bite her when she tried to go out the door. This isn't the goodbye most people have in mind when they decide to get a dog.

Other dogs, incidentally, have the opposite reaction. Rather than trying to physically restrain their owners, they become de-pressed and don't move. They lie down, put their chins on their legs, and refuse to eat until their owners get back. I've seen both extremes, and there's no way to tell how different dogs will react. But the key to stopping both reactions is to confuse the dog about the leaving ritual.

The idea is this: By changing your routine on a regular basis, it becomes much harder for a dog with separation anxiety to predict when you're actually leaving. This is important because once these dogs have identified your patterns, they'll start getting more and more anxious as each item in the pattern is ticked off. By the time you leave, the anxiety may be so high that they're unable to control it. And so, they'll act out.

Most of the destructive behavior, the panic, barking, or whatever, occurs within 5 to 30 minutes after the owner leaves. Some dogs will continue to bark or act up for hours, but even then the misbehavior will occur without the emotional frenzy of those first few minutes.

On the other hand, some dogs have the worst behavioral problems right before their owners get home. This is not necessarily caused by a renewed burst of anxiety about being alone. On the contrary, it may occur precisely because the owner *is* coming home. This is especially true when house-soiling is involved.

Dogs who make messes in the house tend to be punished. And they can anticipate this. I suspect their thinking goes something like this: *I see that stuff on the floor, I smell it, and pretty soon he's going to be coming home, and he's going to see and smell it, too. I don't feel so good. Maybe tearing up the couch will make me feel better. Oh, no, here he comes. I don't like the look on his face. I'm going to get my nose shoved in it, but I don't know why. What did I do?*

Dogs catch on pretty quickly. After a few repeats of the crime and punishment, a dog's anxiety levels will start to escalate whenever his owner is about to come home. By the time the owner actually walks in the door, the dog may be scared to death. He'll automatically tuck his tail between his legs and slink away. The owner will think, "Aha! He knows he did something wrong and feels guilty. I'd better punish him so he won't do it again." But of course, the dog does do it again. All the punishment does is make him dread the arrival more the next time.

I have a hard time convincing people that what they perceive as guilt on their dogs' faces is in fact no such thing. The dog may have deposited the "gift" hours before and no longer really feels responsible for it. When people balk at accepting this explanation, I often show them a little experiment, one I call the "impending doom" demonstration.

Some years ago, I tried this approach with a woman named Sharon Mulliner, who was at the end of her rope with her eight-year-old miniature poodle. The poodle, named Dandy, had been urinating and defecating in every room in the house except the living and dining rooms, which were kept closed off. Dandy had also destroyed the carpeting and two doors.

Sharon and her husband reacted the way many people do: They'd either scold Dandy or rub his nose in the mess. Dandy always looked guilty, she said, so she knew he understood what he'd done. "But that hasn't stopped him from doing it again, sometimes right in front of us," she said.

So I recommended that she try my experiment. "What if I could show you that Dandy really isn't feeling guilty and that the punishment might be backfiring?" I said. "Would you be interested in taking another approach?"

When she agreed, I opened my briefcase. "Exhibit A," I said, taking out a realistic-looking plastic dog dropping I had found at a novelty shop. "You never know what tools you are going to need in this business," I said when Sharon started to laugh.

I told her to leave the house for a few minutes. "Go out the door you usually use," I said. "Then come back in about five minutes. Dandy and I will have a surprise for you."

"I'll bet," she said, shutting the door behind her.

"Well, Dandy, it's just you and me now." Dandy had been lying in the kitchen, but he rose to his feet in consternation when Sharon left. "Don't worry, Dandy," I said, feeling rather helpless. Like two-year-olds who cry when Mommy goes out, dogs aren't comforted by strangers. That's why pet-sitters aren't always a solution. To dogs, human beings just aren't interchangeable.

I petted Dandy a little, then coaxed him into the living room with a few small dog treats, which he reluctantly sampled. When he was done chewing, he looked up and noticed the fake dropping, which I'd put on a spot where he often made his messes. Dandy went over to the dropping, eyeing it suspiciously. He stood over it for a few seconds, then cautiously sniffed. *It certainly doesn't smell like what it looks like. Hmm.*

At this point, Sharon came back into the house. "Check this out," I said. Dandy looked up, saw his owner, and immediately hung his head, tucked his tail, and tried to sneak out of the room. It was a perfect imitation of a poodle who has made a mess on the rug.

"Wow," Sharon said. "You don't think Dandy believes he made that, do you?"

"He isn't stupid," I said. "I think Dandy knows he didn't produce that stuff, whatever it is. But he reacted the same as if he had because he associates the presence of the 'mistake' with you coming in the kitchen door. So he slinked off in a fearful, submissive way to try to avoid getting his nose rubbed in it." I looked at the plastic mound. "Or on it, in this case."

"So I'm probably making him more anxious by punishing him." Sharon scooped up Dandy and gave him a hug.

"That's okay," I said. "Let's just go from here. I think you'll see better results without the punishment."

And she did.

Separation anxiety is one of the toughest problems for owners to deal with because nothing is more heartrending than the idea that your pet is falling apart the minute you walk out the door. Replacing chewed-up rugs or damaged door frames isn't a lot of fun, either. So it's not surprising that some people go to considerable lengths to try to figure out what's really going on when their dog is home alone.

One of my clients, Betty Smythe, was so worried about her little terrier-mix, Snowdy, that she turned on a tape recorder when she left the house. The crying, she discovered, started a few minutes after she left and didn't stop for at least an hour, until Snowdy, apparently exhausted, quieted down.

Once she witnessed firsthand the dog's pathetic crying and barking, Betty knew she had to do something. So she started calling home during the day and leaving messages on the answering machine. Hoping Snowdy was listening, she would tell him that she loved him, hoped everything was going okay, and she'd be home soon. It was all pretty heartbreaking, she said.

When I arrived for our initial consultation, Betty told me Snowdy's sad story. The dog was 14 years old, nearly blind, and had recently lost his longtime companion, a dachshund named Becky. Snowdy spent most of the day on an orthopedic bed, and he wasn't used to strangers. I looked over at the bed. Sure enough, Snowdy was looking suspiciously in my direction, shivering and shaking all the while.

"I'm feeling so sorry for him," Betty told me sadly. "His best friend just died, he can barely see, and he hates it when I'm gone."

I knew this was going to be a tough one. At 14, a dog isn't going to be too flexible. And Snowdy's health was clearly fading. He had a lot to be upset about. But I did have an idea.

"He can't see very well, so let's take advantage of his other senses to involve him in a more interesting activity than crying," I said. "The next time you are at the grocery store, I'd like to you buy an assortment of doggy treats—all different kinds. Try them out and see which ones Snowdy gets excited about."

The idea, I explained, was for her to stash the treats around the house before she left in the morning. By laying out a trail of treats, like Hansel and Gretel winding through the forest dropping bread crumbs, Betty would be starting Snowdy's day with an exciting treasure hunt.

I really wasn't sure if this was going to keep Snowdy calm or not, so I was pleased when Betty called a few days later. She said that Snowdy had spent a fair bit of time sniffing out the various treats and had postponed his crying for 10 to 15 minutes after Betty left the house.

This was encouraging. To make the treasure hunt more exciting, I said, she should buy a few chew toys and use them in addition to the treats. Not only would finding the treats keep Snowdy busy, but chewing the toys would help relieve some of his anxiety.

Although it was unfortunate that Snowdy had lost some of his sight, I thought we might be able to use this disability to our advantage. I suggested to Betty that she vary her departure routine, leaving from different doors on different days. It was possible, I said, that Snowdy would think she was still in the house and would be less likely to be anxious.

To further confuse Snowdy, I recommended that Betty periodically act as though she were about to leave—by turning off the television, for example, which is what she always did when she left the house—and then stick around instead. Or she could open a door, go out for a moment, then quickly come back in and sit down.

In most cases, you want to calm dogs by creating reassuring rituals so they're less anxious and afraid. For dogs with separation anxiety, however, it's often better to do the opposite. If you take away their anxiety triggers, all those little predictable cues that tell them you're about to go away, they're less likely to have their stress rise to uncomfortable levels.

After a few weeks of treasure hunts, chew toys, and fake departures, Snowdy was much calmer than he had been, but the crying and barking continued to some extent. Betty's veterinarian began treating Snowdy with antidepressant and anti-anxiety medications. These helped a little bit, but still the problem continued.

Finally, Betty came up with a solution on her own. I hesitate to mention it because it's not one I would usually recommend. But it's hard to argue with success.

Betty thought it would be helpful to get another dog—a puppy who would help fill the empty spot in Snowdy's heart left by the death of his longtime companion. This is usually a bad idea for dogs with separation anxiety. Animal behaviorists have studied the levels of stress hormones in dogs and found that dogs get much more stressed when they're separated from a person than from a canine companion. Humans set out long ago to make dogs man's best friends, and the evidence is pretty clear that we succeeded. The solution for separation anxiety is unlikely to be getting another pet. In fact, getting another pet may cause additional problems, such as competition for attention, that will only make things worse.

·I was pretty skeptical when Betty said she was going to get another dog. I explained every reason why she shouldn't, but I couldn't stop her. After all, our efforts hadn't been entirely successful. And Snowdy obviously missed his old companion and often walked around the house looking for her or sat or lay in spots that they used to share.

So Betty went out and adopted a very ugly, very tiny, one-year-old mixed breed. She said that her looks didn't matter because Snowdy was nearly blind anyway. That little dog, which Betty named Beauty, wasn't put off by Snowdy, either. Beauty would walk right up and lick Snowdy, and Snowdy really enjoyed that. He stopped crying and barking and spent his last years in contentment with his new companion.

You just never know.

Chapter Nine

The Dog Who Killed Her Toys

THE NOTE I HELD IN MY HAND SAID, "soiling the carpet and barking out the window." I had had a very brief phone conversation with my new client, Sharon Rodman, a few days before and had come to see her at her garden apartment in the heart of Atlanta.

The moment I stepped into the foyer, Lass, a pretty two-year-old miniature sheltie, began telling me all about herself. I realized that "barking" didn't adequately describe the problem. Lass was going berserk. "Yap, yap, yap!"

She ran from window to window and door to door, even though I was standing right in front of her and was clearly the one who had caused all the commotion by ringing the doorbell. She started twirling in place, barking, and pawing at the air with her front paws. She wasn't focused on me at all. Sharon looked at me helplessly and shrugged her shoulders. The racket gradually died down and Lass, exhausted, sank to the floor.

"At least she didn't pee on the carpet," said Sharon, by way of introduction.

"That's good," I said lamely. I had no idea what was bugging this dog, but I wanted to find out. Both Lass and Sharon looked like they were sick of the whole business. I got right down to it.

"Please tell me what's been going on with Lass," I said. The dog's overreaction to a visitor gave me some clues, but I wanted to hear the whole story.

It seemed that Lass responded in this exaggerated fashion to everything there was to respond to. As Sharon went through the litany of noises and events that would set Lass off like a Roman candle, I realized that my first impression was correct. Anything from the slam of a car door to the flutter of a curtain was enough to trigger her routine.

And what a routine it was! She would leap up, run to her chew toys, and shake them as if she wanted to destroy them. Sharon called this behavior "killing." Then Lass would spit out the toys and race around the apartment. This was followed by something even more bizarre. Lass would slam into the front door, pick herself up, shake, then run to the back sliding door and slam into it. She would pick herself up again and run around the apartment again, barking and yelping all the while.

A passing jogger could get her started. So could the sound of a garage door opening. When the phone rang, she attacked the wire. When Sharon took away her toys, Lass attacked the furniture. When Lass got sufficiently worked up, she often urinated as well.

I immediately thought that this might be a seizure-related problem and suggested that Sharon and Lass see a veterinarian. But there was no evidence of seizures, Sharon told me, citing a recent exam. Another possibility, though a remote one, was that Lass was hyperactive. This is actually a rare condition. Most dogs that people think are hyper are merely in need of more exercise and are trying to discharge their excess energy. But Lass got plenty of exercise, Sharon told me. Even when they came home after a long walk, Lass would launch into her routine at the slightest provocation. The poor dog must have been exhausted. In any event, her vet didn't think that hyperactivity was the problem.

"I guess you can't take her many places," I said, making some notes about Lass's histrionics.

"Well actually, it's funny," Sharon said. "When I take her to a friend's house or even to the kennel, she acts perfectly normal."

Curiouser and curiouser. I thought about Sharon for a moment. I noticed that she was a bit more nervous than my usual client. She wrung her hands often and fidgeted on the couch. I had to wonder if her temperament somehow might be rubbing off on the dog. But I could only speculate.

I wondered if Lass's troubles stemmed from something in the apartment itself. I looked around. What could be setting off this firestorm every time there was a noise or movement?

Lass was pretty small. She couldn't see out the windows, and there wasn't furniture she could jump on that would give her a view outside. The sliding back door led to a tiny patio surrounded by a brick wall. The arrangement gave Sharon plenty of privacy but essentially shut out the world for the little sheltie.

"Sharon, let's proceed on the premise that Lass isn't nuts and isn't hyper," I said. "Maybe she's frustrated as all get-out by hearing things and not being able to see what's causing them, where they're coming from, and, above all, by not being able to do anything about them."

"Okay," said Sharon. "I guess I'll buy that."

"Your dog's temperament is such that maybe she's attacking toys and running through the house as a way of releasing her frustration."

"How do you know she's not just scared?" Sharon asked.

"Well, her body language tells me she's not having a fearful response," I said. I had watched Lass closely when I came in. Her social signals—a smile face, tail up, ears forward—showed me that she wasn't really afraid of the doorbell or a stranger entering her home.

"When she hears noises, she's probably thinking, *Let me get at this thing. If I can't get it, I'll attack something else and shake it around and kill it, which gets rid of this bad, helpless feeling.* Have you ever tried to stop Lass from zooming around?" I asked.

"Oh, yes," Sharon said. "I've even stood in front of her. She just zips by or jumps up and ricochets off my legs. Then she starts her twirling."

I made a few notes. The environment clearly wasn't ideal for Lass, but there wasn't anything we could do about that. In any event, it didn't really matter what was causing the behavior if we could devise some strategies to stop it. The urinating in the house, for example, could be solved with some basic retraining, more frequent walks, controlling her fluid intake under the vet's supervision, and so on. But Sharon wasn't paying me for some simple advice on how to housebreak a dog. I had to look at the big picture.

As I probed a bit further into their daily routine, I found another possible cause for the dog's nutty behavior. One thing I'd noticed was a baby gate at the bottom of the stairs. Sharon explained that she put it up to keep Lass out of the bedroom, where she might tear up the pillows or eat Sharon's clothes. The gate also served to keep Lass in the bedroom at night. I wondered if that might be causing some of the problems.

At bedtime, Sharon explained, she closed the gate and put Lass on a short leash and hooked it over the bedpost. "I don't want her bouncing off the walls all night and waking me up," Sharon explained. This arrangement meant that Lass couldn't jump on the bed or even move around very much. It would help explain why she was hyper during the day.

The nighttime confinement seemed a little extreme, I told Sharon. After all, Lass couldn't even go get a drink of water. Being tied up might be very frustrating for her and could partly explain why she was so overactive during the day.

I explained to Sharon that allowing Lass a little more freedom at night would probably help decrease her overall sense of frustration, which would help her to control herself during the day. But this was only a small part of the solution, I knew. I really wanted to find a way to interrupt the pattern of going nuts at the slightest noise or movement.

I recommended that Sharon try a Silencer collar. These are ingenious gadgets that emit a tone when dogs bark. The tone startles them temporarily, which stops the barking. And because dogs dislike the tone, they often decide that constant barking isn't worth the consequence. We also discussed the possibility of creating a masking noise—by leaving the TV on, for example—in order to cover up outside sounds. But Sharon had already tried that, with little success.

"Lass just seems to hear right through the television," she said. "And of course, sometimes it isn't a noise at all that sets her off— it's just the curtain moving." So we decided to go with the Silencer.

I also suggested that Sharon take away Lass's favorite toys, which included rubber hamburgers, knit balls, a squeaky mouse, and two old tennis balls. This may sound cruel, but I wanted to remove Lass's temptation to "kill." Besides, I was going to replace them with something better.

I asked Sharon to leave a bunch of rawhide chews around the apartment. I hoped that Lass would attack these with the same enthusiasm that she showed for her former toys—with this difference: Instead of "killing" the rawhide, I figured that her tastebuds would take over and she would chew it rather than merely assault it. Not only would this put the brakes on her running around, but the chewing would help her work off some of her excess energy and frustration.

I was hoping that this hypothesis was correct and that making these few simple changes would take care of most of the problems. Sure enough, Sharon called two weeks later and reported that the program was working pretty well. Whenever Lass got startled, which still happened all the time, she would work off her anxiety by working over a rawhide chew instead of running around and bouncing off the windows. And the collar was helping to control the compulsive barking. So far, so good. Sharon and I talked often on the phone, making slight changes and adjustments as necessary.

For example, after a few weeks, I suggested that Sharon take advantage of a time-out area where Lass could settle down for a few minutes after an episode. Putting Lass in the small, quiet, dark lavatory off the entranceway helped her get her nerves back together. I also asked Sharon's vet to give a short-term prescription for an anti-anxiety drug. This would make it easier for Lass to adjust while she was learning her new ways.

Finally, I decided to have Sharon block the path to the front door with another baby gate. This way, even if the "killing" behavior got started, the second part of the frenzy, throwing herself against the front door, would be short-circuited by the gate.

The combination of removing the favorite toys, giving Lass something to really sink her teeth into, blocking the path to the door, providing a time-out area, and giving her medication helped us get off to a very good start. Eventually, Lass was able to sleep in Sharon's bedroom without being tethered to the bedpost.

Some months later, Sharon called to tell me that she and Lass were moving to a new place. "There are plenty of windows and no walls blocking the view," Sharon said.

"Good!" I replied. Although moving can cause problems for some dogs, I told Sharon I would be there if she needed help. I never heard from her again—knock wood.

LASS'S SITUATION WASN'T ALL THAT unusual. Dogs have an intense need to control their surroundings, which they achieve in part by identifying or predicting various stimuli, such as sounds. When they don't have this sense of control, because they can't see outside an apartment, for example, they may experience a lot of stress. And dogs often cope with stress by acting in destructive or self-destructive ways.

Dogs don't adjust to change as quickly as people do, so even minor disruptions or novelties in their lives can cause a lot of stress. Getting a new roommate or even a new piece of furniture can be very upsetting for some dogs. So can adding another pet to the family or changing your usual routine.

One dog who had enormous difficulty adjusting to new things in her life was Jenny, a two-year-old bichon frise. Jenny's owner, Gillian Rudolph, had lost her husband to a heart attack six months before. Gillian recovered fairly quickly. She had met a new man and was now engaged to be married. Jenny, on the other hand, went into a tailspin after her owner's death. And Gillian's new romance didn't help. Jenny had a problem. A big one.

"Love me, love my dog." That's usually a reasonable expectation when two people come together, and Drew, Gillian's fiancé, was ready to do his best. But Jenny wasn't doing her part. "They started off on the wrong foot right away," Gillian told me when we got together to discuss her problem. In fact, Drew told her that Jenny wasn't going to move into his house until she showed an attitude adjustment.

"What exactly happened?" I asked, pen in hand.

"Well, whenever Drew would get close to me, Jenny would try to break it up."

"It's not the first time I've heard that," I said, "if it makes you feel any better."

"Jenny was a great chaperone," Gillian continued. "She would just get in between us or sit on my lap."

"It could be that Drew made her really uncomfortable just by being new to her," I suggested. "Did Jenny do anything else to show that she might have found the situation stressful?"

"Does peeing on the rug when he reaches down to pet her count?"

"I'd say so," I smiled. "How long has that been going on?"

"About a month," Gillian said. "And this is a really big problem because Drew refuses to have Jenny in his house while she is doing things like that."

"I see."

"I can't really blame him," she said, giving Jenny a pat. "Still, I think he should be a little flexible."

"Well, let's see if we can clear that up so it won't be an issue anymore," I said. There was a bit of resentment in Gillian's voice, and I wondered how much the dog had become an issue in their relationship.

Unfortunately, there was more than just the occasional accident and possessive behavior going on. For example, Jenny would occasionally launch into a wild frenzy of barking at the television. "What drives her up the wall," Gillian explained, "is a jingle that accompanies a carpet cleaner commercial. Most of the time, Jenny enjoys television," she added. Her favorite show, fittingly enough, was *Lassie*. Jenny would lie on the glass coffee table for a solid half-hour without moving, fascinated by the collie and his master, Timmy.

I wondered if Jenny might be using the television to zone out, like 10-year-olds who stare blankly at the TV after school. Watching TV and going into zombieland might be a self-medicating type of behavior that Jenny used to cope with all the problems in her life.

I was pretty interested in this possibility. There is no definitive research on dogs and television. Some dogs ignore it completely, and others seem to watch it and react, especially to dogs and the sounds of barking. In recent years, technology has virtually eliminated the flicker of the television signals. One of my colleagues has predicted that as television achieves more realistic images and sounds, dogs are going to believe that the image on the screen is real. So Jenny's type of behavior—barking at the screen—is probably going to become more of a problem with dogs in the future.

At any rate, Drew didn't mind the fact that Jenny enjoyed watching TV. He didn't even mind that she used the coffee table as a viewing stand. But the uncontrollable barking at the TV drove him up the wall. Before Jenny moved into his house, he told Gillian, this too would have to stop.

"He's trying not to take all this stuff personally," Gillian said.

"But maybe it is personal. Maybe Jenny's trying to tell me something."

I wondered how much she had thought about the message Jenny was sending, but I decided not to go there. The couple's personal relationship was beyond my purview. I only handle dogs and cats.

Jenny had one additional problem that was a source of profound embarrassment to Gillian. At least once a day, Jenny would start whining and wrap her legs around Gillian's arm and start humping. Gillian found this extremely distasteful, and, needless to say, so did Drew. I recognized this as a classic sign of overstimulation. Along with the other strange behaviors—barking compulsively at the TV or, conversely, going into a near-catatonic state while watching *Lassie*. This was one way for Jenny, who was clearly stressed out, to get rid of nervous energy.

There obviously wasn't much we could do about the underlying cause of the stress; namely, Drew's involvement in the family. Rather, I decided to look for ways to distract Jenny from her problem behavior.

The first thing I asked Gillian to do was think of a list of words that made Jenny happy. For most dogs, these revolve around the same sorts of things, like food or a walk. The next time Jenny was staring at the TV or barking up a storm, I told Gillian that she should interject with one of the happy words and offer Jenny a treat or a walk. It's difficult for dogs to misbehave when they're feeling happy. Behaviorists refer to this phenomenon as the theory of competing motivations. Killer isn't going to bite you when he's being petted, and Jenny wasn't going to bark like crazy when she was eating or being offered a walk.

I also wanted to get Jenny out of the habit of lying on the glass coffee table. I suggested moving the table from in front of the television and providing Jenny with an equally comfortable place. Jenny seemed to like cool, hard surfaces, so Gillian brought out a leather chair that she could use. If Jenny didn't feel like using the chair, I said that Gillian could encourage her to lie on a tile floor nearby by putting some of her toys there and petting her when she lay down.

Sure enough, Jenny started to settle down. After a few weeks, she was doing much less barking at the TV. To reduce the barking even more, I suggested a new way to cut it short. Previously, Gillian and Drew chimed in with a chorus of no's when Jenny started making a racket—a chorus she pretty much ignored. I told Gillian to respond instead with a sharp, "Ah, ah, ah!"

Animal behaviorists have tried all sorts of sounds to see which are most effective at getting dogs to look up and pay attention. *No* is used so often by owners that it is practically meaningless. Making the alternate sound, I explained, would get Jenny's attention and stop the barking for a second, at which point they could praise her and help her relax.

I also suggested that they make an audiotape of the commercial jingle that got Jenny so excited. Once or twice a day, I said, they should play the tape, preferably in an area away from the television. The idea was to play the jingle at a low volume while giving Jenny something else to occupy her, something that wasn't compatible with wild barking, like a couple of dog treats. Jenny couldn't eat and bark at the same time and would gradually learn that the music was a sign that something good was about to happen.

Much more unpleasant was Jenny's habit of urinating when Drew greeted her. I sized this up as submissive urination, which contains an element of fear. Jenny didn't know Drew very well, and he clearly made her nervous. The best solution seemed to be to change the way Drew approached Jenny so she'd be less nervous and have a better chance of maintaining her dignity.

As I mulled over this problem, I was reminded of a dog I met several years ago. Max, a two-year-old Airedale, was also afraid of the man in his life. Barry was a large, imposing man with a very deep voice. When he came home after work, he'd boom out, "Hey, Max," and bend over to give Max's head a rough pat. The poor dog would often lose it right there. Sometimes, in fact, Max was so tense that he would urinate just from having Barry look at him. I had to teach Barry to speak in a higher, lighter tone and to toss Max a dog treat rather than just lunging in with his hand extended. I also recommended that he set a clock radio that would turn on just before he came home every day. That way, Max would have a little time to prepare for his entrance.

Drew was neither imposing nor did he have a deep voice, but that didn't stop Jenny from reacting just as Max had. I asked Drew not to look directly at Jenny when he came into her presence, at least until this problem was straightened out. He needed to look away and squat down and wait for the dog to approach him.

"I guess I could do that," Drew said. "Anything to stop her from peeing all over my shoes. She probably knows I don't like her much," he added.

"Well, let's see if we can make her more likable." I smiled, but at the same time, I was thinking that from Jenny's point of view, he wasn't such a prize, either.

I wasn't sure how I was going to handle the arm-humping, but fortunately, I didn't have to. When Jenny's stress levels declined and her other misbehaviors came under control, she didn't have the need anymore to release her excess energy in this socially unacceptable way.

I would like to say that this case was resolved to everyone's satisfaction. Certainly, Jenny learned to behave in more appropriate ways, and Gillian was grateful that she was able to lower the amount of stress Jenny was experiencing. But I wasn't too surprised when Gillian left a message on my answering machine several weeks into the program.

"I just wanted you to know that Jenny's much better," she said. "But Drew still doesn't seem to like her much. . . ." There was a nervous laugh, followed by, "Well, we'll send you a wedding invitation. Talk to you soon."

I'm glad I didn't hold my breath, because the invitation never came and, I learned later, the wedding did not take place. I'm sure there were lots of complicated reasons for this, but at the very bottom of it all, I believe that Gillian loved her dog more than she loved Drew. And that was the end of that.

HEALTHY DOGS WHO SEEM TO BE HAPPY with life almost always get a lot of affection from their owners. They count on that affection and look forward to it. And since they get affection on a regular basis, they can predict when it's going to happen, and they learn to behave in certain ways that help them get more of it. *If he throws the ball and I go get it and bring it back, I will be petted. Hey, this is great!* This gives dogs a sense of control. It's very comforting.

Dogs are always ritualistic; they like to know exactly what's coming. It's fine to change the kind of affection or exercise you give your dog as long as he knows what's coming at the end. Dogs who feel secure in this way are better able to put up with minor changes in their daily routines since they know they can count on the important certainties.

While Jenny's case ended happily, even though her owner was left circling the personals, others aren't so easy. There are times when I can see right away from the environment a dog is in that the owner will have a hard time changing things to help the dog feel more confident and secure.

Cooper was a great little four-year-old beagle with a people problem that caused him a tremendous amount of stress. The problem began when he was a puppy and he ended up, in my opinion, in the wrong household with the wrong people. I was asked to try to fit this square peg into a round hole before someone got hurt.

Roxanne Bell was a good mother and a very nervous person. Her two children, she explained when we met, had a variety of emotional problems. I soon learned that everyone in the family, except for her husband, Brian, was taking some sort of mood-altering medicine for a variety of symptoms, including impulsive behavior. This was not the ideal atmosphere for a dog like Cooper.

Cooper had a strange history. I heard all about it and more because Roxanne was a nonstop talker who rarely paused for breath. I recently looked back at the diagnostic form and could barely decipher the pages of notes I took trying to follow her rapid trains of thought.

The Bells had purchased Cooper from a breeder. He was supposed to be a purebred beagle, but the breeder didn't offer them the papers. This should have set off an alarm right there, but it didn't right away.

"The fellow told us that this dog wasn't like the other puppies in the litter. He was sickly and everything," Roxanne said. "So he kept the poor little thing in the basement all the time. I don't think he really walked him very much or let him go anywhere, except to his spot in the basement. Poor little Cooper."

When she paused for breath, I asked, "Do you know what was wrong with Cooper?"

"He didn't really say he was sick. You know, he just said he was sickly," Roxanne said. "We thought he was so cute, and he was the only one left, so we decided to take a chance and bring him home. He was only six weeks old, but of course, we didn't realize how long he'd been cooped up in the basement—that's why we named him Cooper."

"I get it," I interrupted, trying to gain some control of the meeting. "Let's go over what this kind of early experience meant to Cooper so we can understand a little bit about his nature." I looked at Cooper, who was hiding under the coffee table, looking nervously at Roxanne's children, who were roughhousing on the carpet nearby.

Dogs who are kept in isolation during the first weeks or months of their lives perceive stimulation differently than puppies—or people, for that matter—who are raised with normal amounts of social contact. When they go out in the world and are exposed to a wide variety of people, places, and sounds, they perceive it all as being too much to handle, and they try to avoid it.

"Is that why he's always hiding under things and snapping at the boys?" Roxanne asked.

"Very likely," I said. I didn't blame the dog. This environment was starting to make me nervous, too. Dogs like Cooper, I explained, are often anxious and neophobic, meaning they're afraid of new things—anything from people on the street to a new toy in the house. And because they're afraid all the time, they're often reacting, growling, or snapping at the slightest excuse.

"I don't like him biting and snapping at the kids, and I'm afraid he's going to bite someone else, especially another child," Roxanne told me.

I realized this was more serious than I originally thought. "Roxanne," I asked, "has Cooper always been like this?"

"Well, pretty much," she said. "He'll snap when you take away his food and he'll growl or bite the kids when they pull on his tail a little."

So the children pulled the dog's tail and picked up his food while he was eating, I thought. Great. "What else do all you kids do with the dog?" I asked.

Instead of answering me directly, Brad, the younger one, said, "Come on, Cooper. Let's play dead."

"Don't play that horrible game," Roxanne said. "He's going to bite you."

"Can you guys explain the game to me?" I asked. After a few false starts and a lot of giggling, the boys explained their favorite game.

When they had friends over and everyone was tired of video games or watching TV, they'd call in Cooper and play the game "drop dead." The game was simple. If Cooper was feeling friendly enough to come over and invite a petting, all the kids would fall over and pretend they were dead. Cooper would get very worried and would begin to nose their limp, still bodies. They got a kick out of that and would start to giggle and jump around. Cooper, who probably thought his family was gone for good, would be terribly startled. He reacted, quite naturally, by growling or snapping at the sudden motion. That would end the game, of course, and Cooper would be banished to another room.

This is one case I don't like remembering because I wasn't able to do much for poor Cooper. I told the family that it was essential to leave Cooper alone and give him his space, especially when he was eating. Because of his early confinement, I explained, Cooper was never going to be the sort of dog who would relish a lot of attention, especially the teasing kind of attention he was getting.

To keep everyone safe, I recommended that they introduce Cooper to a Gentle Leader, a special collar-harness combination that fits over the nose and neck. When the dog starts to lunge forward, the loop pulls his head sharply down, which can cause him to tumble head over heels if he's really moving quickly. This and similar collars, like the Snoot Loop and Halti Headcollar don't hurt the dog and are great for dogs who tend to pull their owners along. After a few false starts, they learn to stop that kind of behavior very quickly. I figured the collar would help the Bells gain a measure of control without endangering themselves. Plus, it would help Cooper learn to stay calm around the children. Unfortunately, Roxanne's youngest thought the loop looked cruel (which it isn't), so they didn't try it.

This was a very unfortunate and unusual situation. Most of my clients are very concerned about their pets and will do just about anything to keep them happy and well-adjusted. The Bells were concerned, too; otherwise, they wouldn't have called me. But they didn't have the resources or commitment to really follow through.

Although Cooper's case was somewhat extreme, it shows what can happen when a dog feels he has no control over people or events. Cooper was treated almost like a play toy, and no one really thought how he must feel when they were grabbing his tail, taking away his food, or suddenly jumping up and scaring him.

We think of stressful events as being dramatic, or at least obvious, events in our lives. And they are when they affect us. But dogs operate on an entirely different plane. Things that we would never notice or would dismiss as insignificant can be very stressful for them. A ringing doorbell or clap of thunder can be just as stressful for a dog as the thought of heart surgery might be for us.

Of course, some of the same things that kick our stress levels into overdrive can have the same effect on our dogs. I'm thinking of moving. Moving to a new house can be incredibly stressful. For the human members of the family, moving means that everything's out of whack for a few months. You can't find anything, money is probably tight, and whatever you happen to need right now, like your toothbrush, is always packed away in the bottom box.

But at least you can understand what the move is all about. Try explaining to your dog that the move is a good thing because you're getting a new job or moving to a better house in the sub-urbs. All your dog knows is that all of sudden, his entire life is disrupted and he hasn't the foggiest notion why. And the fact that the human members of the family are also stressed doesn't make his feelings of anxiety any better.

Some years back, I saw a little Maltese who holds the record among my clients for having moved the most times in a brief period. The dog, Mi-Mi, had flown over from Japan with her American owner, Jane Bigelow. Upon returning to the States, Mi-Mi and Jane moved to Philadelphia, Florida, New York City, and Atlanta, all within three months.

Mi-Mi had coped well at first, but by the time she got to Atlanta, she was beginning to come unraveled. I met with Jane in her apartment—temporary, as it turned out, because she was waiting for a permanent assignment from the large corporation she worked for. The moves, she explained, had made her life totally unpredictable, and Mi-Mi was barely able to settle into one routine before she was uprooted again.

"Mi-Mi is so stressed out," Jane said. "I don't know what to do with her. She has started barking all the time, and when I come home at night, she follows me around constantly."

"I can't blame her," I said. "This little girl probably doesn't know from day to day whether you're going to show up or where she's going to wake up tomorrow."

"You're right," she said. "And she's never heard so much English before."

"Wow, I never even thought of that," I said.

Even though dogs don't understand a heck of a lot of our conversations, the very different sounds of the English and Japanese languages could have been just one more new thing for little Mi-Mi to adjust to—sort of a dog's culture shock. Any number of cultural differences between Japan and here could be confusing to her. I thought for a minute. "Why don't you try speaking Japanese to Mi-Mi?" I suggested. After all, that was her "native language."

I knew that Jane was going to have to do a lot more than say "Sit" in Japanese before Mi-Mi would start relaxing. Dogs crave predictability in their lives. Moving even once is stressful. Moving four times in three months is enough to trigger emotional chaos.

Whenever possible, it's a good idea to take your dog to visit the new place before you make the move. Not only will this give him the opportunity to get the lay of the land—*Hmm, smells like a cat was here. I like these rugs. They're a lot easier to walk on than the hardwood floor*—but he'll also be able to recognize his own scent when you make the actual move later on. Anything you can do to make the place seem familiar and friendly will help keep his stress levels down.

Of course, it's not always possible to arrange previsits. All you can do then is try to make the new home feel just as comfortable and familiar as the place your dog just left. It's a good idea, for example, to bring along some of your dog's favorite possessions, such as chew toys or his special dog bed. When you get to the new place, see where he relaxes, then put his toys and the bed in *his* spot. Not only will he associate these objects with good feelings, but letting him choose the place will restore some measure of control in his life.

None of this was going to help Mi-Mi at this point, at least until the next move, but I suggested a few other things that Jane might want to try. It was clear that Mi-Mi was suffering some degree of separation anxiety, which is why she stuck to Jane like a shadow in the evenings. It wouldn't hurt, I said, for Jane to plan a system of graduated departures, in which she would periodically leave the house, then return almost immediately. If Jane did this fairly often, Mi-Mi would soon discover that nothing bad happened when Jane left. More important, it would help her understand that Jane always came back.

It would also help, I told Jane, if she would try to re-establish the same routines that she had in her previous residences, like getting up at the same time and taking the same walk after breakfast. Dogs love familiar, predictable routines because they make them feel as though they have control in their lives, and that's by far the best way to keep stress levels down.

Jane agreed to give all this a try. She called about two weeks later to explain that while Mi-Mi was still having trouble adjusting, she was clearly getting better. In the background, I could hear some soothing Japanese music.

"That's for Mi-Mi," Jane said. "I can't stand it, but she never barks when it's on." It was clear that Mi-Mi needed a somewhat Asian environment, at least for a while, to reassure her that she was home. The music wasn't going to solve all her problems, but it was one more way to make life predictable. And for dogs, that makes all the difference.

Chapter Ten

The Dog Who Lived
in a Birdcage

I COULD HEAR BIRDS CHIRPING AS soon as I opened the car door. As I approached the front door of the modest bungalow on the outskirts of Atlanta, the sounds grew louder. I looked in the large front window and saw parakeets everywhere, hanging from perches, hopping around on the floor, and flying from one room to the next. I had never seen anything like it.

"Dr. Wright! Thanks for coming!" A small, gray-haired woman flung open the door and greeted me enthusiastically. "Welcome to the birdcage. I'm the bird lady." She stuck out her hand. "Say hello, Hi-Fi and Tweety." She was evidently speaking to the two parakeets perched on her shoulder. One complied with a loud

"Hi-hi-hi-hi-hi," and the other just cocked its head and looked at me curiously.

"Hi, guys," I said, scanning the hallway for a dog. Usually, they're the first ones on the scene when I make a house call. "Is Zero around, Mrs. Moseley?"

"Oh sure, he's in the living room—and just call me Birdie," she said.

As we entered the living room, I saw that she had converted the bay window into a huge birdcage. The door was open and birds were flying in and out, lighting on curtains, the fireplace mantel, the armchairs, and Birdie herself. I could tell that conversation was going to be difficult because of the cacophony of chirping. The floor of the enclosure was pretty clean, but the whole place still smelled like a pet shop.

I finally saw Zero, a nice border collie–beagle-mix, looking up at me eagerly with his tongue hanging out and a smile on his face. He shared the room with the birds but apparently didn't enjoy the same freedom they did. One end of a six-foot leash was attached to his collar, with the other end anchored to a wire crate. His loud panting told me he was under a great deal of stress. The reason for that was no mystery, I mused, as a pair of green, beating wings zoomed past my nose. "Whoa!"

"Don't worry, they always miss," Birdie said.

"Does Zero chase the birds?" I asked, noticing that she made no move to let him off the leash.

"Oh, he's tried it, but I can't allow that," she said. "That's why he's tied up." She frowned. "Actually, I think he's a bit afraid of them. Sometimes they pretend to dive-bomb him."

"Poor little guy," I said, kneeling down and scratching him under the chin. His eyes gleamed with appreciation, and his bushy tail swung his whole rear end back and forth.

"Watch it," Birdie said. "He might bite."

I saw no evidence that Zero was getting ready to bite. He just seemed grateful for the attention. But Birdie had called me because she was concerned that Zero was overly excitable and aggressive and had been nipping her with maddening frequency.

"Can we sit down somewhere and talk about Zero?" I asked. The birds were getting on my nerves. The two on her shoulder had been replaced by three others, including a pretty pale yellow parakeet.

"Bad dog, bad dog," the parakeet chanted.

"Sure, let's go into the kitchen," Birdie said. She brushed the birds from her shoulders and turned to walk out of the room, making no move to release Zero from the leash. He looked after us longingly and barked once or twice.

"There he goes," she said as we stepped into the relative quiet of the kitchen and adjoining family room. "Always a comment." The barking continued for a minute or two, but it was barely audible over the noise of the birds.

I sat down and began taking notes. Zero, Birdie told me, was one-and-a-half years old and neutered. She had adopted him about six months before and didn't think he'd been obedience trained. He was overly hyper, Birdie told me. He jumped up, nibbled fingers, nipped, and barked. Occasionally, he clasped her leg and did "disgusting things."

What Birdie wanted was for Zero to be calm and passive. She had enough activity with all the birds flying around, she explained.

I asked Birdie about Zero's daily routine. She walked him every morning at about 7:00 A.M. Then she put him in his crate in the living room and went to work. At 11:00 A.M., a handyman dropped by and took Zero for about a 15-minute walk. Birdie took him for another walk after work and again at midnight. The walks usually took about 30 minutes, and she took the same route every night.

"Four walks a day is good," I commented, as I wrote down the information. "Now when you are home after work, what do you and Zero do?"

"I keep him tied up mostly. Otherwise, he'd be jumping at the birds."

I put down my pen. "Let me make sure I understand you. Zero is basically confined all the time when he isn't being walked or is eating?"

"That's right," she said. "It's the only way I can keep control of him."

"Does he spend the night in his kennel?"

"Oh, no," Birdie said. "He comes up to the bedroom with me."

Well that was something, at least.

"I hook his leash over the bedpost so he can't get into trouble."

"Oh," I said, jotting it down.

I tried to get a picture of how she dealt with Zero when he misbehaved, although it seemed that his opportunities for any kind of misbehavior were few and far between, considering his circumstances.

Birdie said she'd yell when he did something wrong or take a rolled-up newspaper and hit it against the couch to frighten him into stopping whatever he had been doing.

"Does that make him stop?" I asked.

"You bet," she said. "He stops for a minute, anyway."

"When Zero does behave calmly, do you reward him?"

She thought for a moment. "Not really. Although I am glad when I don't have to yell at him. Do you mean I should give him treats?"

I explained that a reward could be anything from a pat on the rear end or saying, "Good dog" to taking him for an extra walk or playing with him for a few minutes. It didn't have to be food. It only had to be something that would make him feel good and help him learn that if he behaved a certain way, he would be rewarded instead of punished.

"Oh, I see. Well, I suppose I could do that."

I thought about the situation for a minute. The pattern of yelling and frightening Zero with the newspaper bordered on psychological abuse, in my opinion. The dog was essentially held hostage. As a mixture of sporting and working breeds, Zero came equipped with a tremendous amount of energy and enthusiasm, which had absolutely no way to be expressed.

I occasionally see mismatches like this in my line of work. Birdie would have been better off without a dog, or at least with an older, docile pet who would just lie at her feet snoozing. Zero would have been better off with an active family that loved to be outdoors throwing Frisbees or going hunting or playing ball in the backyard. But as usual, I had to deal with the situation at hand. It's not my practice to suggest to people that they find a better home for their pet without first trying to make the dog's life better where he was.

I explained to Birdie that Zero was not acting terribly unreasonably. She was a bit offended at first, but after I explained that he needed a lot more exercise and some freedom, she said she'd never really thought about it. That was obvious to me the moment I walked in.

If she were to give him a lot more praise for good behavior, I said, it would start to shape and mold his behavior into a more healthy pattern. Birdie agreed to do it. "If I can find anything to praise him about," she added.

"Well, when he is calm and not jumping on you or nipping, you can say in a soothing voice, 'Go-o-od bo-o-oy,'" I said. "Since he's been showing signs of aggression, don't look at him when giving the praise." Direct eye contact can be stimulating to many dogs, especially dogs who are already prone to aggression.

"What else?" she asked, taking out a pencil and piece of paper. It always amazes me that some people have to write down instructions on interacting with their dogs when other people know how to do it instinctively, but I spelled it out for her.

Zero only wanted to be close to her, I explained. When he was good, she should reward him with a 5- to 10-minute play period or an extra walk. "Don't let him demand things by barking or whining," I added. The idea was to give him a framework of activities during the day so he would have things to look forward to.

In addition, I recommended that she let Zero off the leash more often, as long as he was complying with her wishes and remained calm, which he likely would if she gave him more chances to work off his energy by running around and playing outside.

Finally, I suggested that she stop keeping Zero and his crate in the living room. That would get him away from the chirping and dive-bombing that was probably driving him nuts. I helped her move the crate into her bedroom, and she agreed to let him stay there at night with the door open as long as he behaved.

When I talked to Birdie a few weeks later on the telephone, she told me that Zero was definitely calmer. The worried look had disappeared from his face, and the incidents of misbehavior had dropped off considerably. Zero now had the run of the house, she told me, but he avoided the living room entirely. "Isn't that something?" she said. Somehow, I wasn't too surprised.

Birdie saved the best news for last. "Listen to this, Dr. Wright," she said. I could hear spirited chirping in the background. "Come on, Daffy," she coaxed. Then a raspy new voice came over the phone.

"Go-o-od do-o-og, go-o-od do-o-og."

I laughed with delight. Now that the birds were on board, I knew that Zero was going to be just fine.

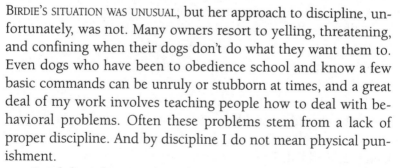

BIRDIE'S SITUATION WAS UNUSUAL, but her approach to discipline, unfortunately, was not. Many owners resort to yelling, threatening, and confining when their dogs don't do what they want them to. Even dogs who have been to obedience school and know a few basic commands can be unruly or stubborn at times, and a great deal of my work involves teaching people how to deal with behavioral problems. Often these problems stem from a lack of proper discipline. And by discipline I do not mean physical punishment.

Good discipline involves showing the dog which behavior is right and which is wrong. You don't show him by smacking him or hurting him. You do it by being consistent—by showing the dog what he's supposed to do and then praising him when he does it.

Suppose a dog urinates on the rug. Rather than beating him, which will probably cause him to sneak off and pee in the next room in order to avoid you, you need to catch him in the act and say, "Ah, ah, ah!" This is a gentle correction that gets his attention.

Then you gently but firmly take him to the door, lead him outside, allow him to go there, and praise him after he does.

If you do this consistently, the dog will soon learn the rules: *When I feel like I have to pee, I go to the front door, I go outside, it feels good to let it go, and I get praised for doing it there. Hey, that feels good!*

People make the most progress with behavioral problems when they use gentle discipline and corrections. They make the least progress when they use the threat of physical punishment or actually strike the dog. The rolled-up newspaper Birdie used to threaten Zero was bad enough. It's even worse when it's in the hands of someone who is actually prepared to hit the dog. In fact, hitting can cause a minor behavioral problem to escalate into a serious case of aggression.

That's what happened to the Whitlock family when they decided to bring out the heavy artillery to deal with their Welsh terrier, Skippy, after she made the mistake of urinating on the living room carpet.

"I used to just yell at her," said Kristin Whitlock when we met for a consultation in her small Atlanta apartment. "She's been to obedience school, so I didn't think she'd be going on the carpet."

"Well that's not a skill they usually teach at school, unfortunately," I said.

"That's true," Kristin admitted, "but it's really maddening to have to clean it up and smell it afterward."

"How do you deal with it?" I asked.

"Well, Joe and I used to yell at her, but she would growl," Kristin said.

I looked at Skippy, who was eyeballing me suspiciously from under the dining room table. The growling should have been their cue to stop yelling. Since they didn't understand discipline issues, however, they took precisely the wrong approach and escalated the battle.

Another problem, it turned out, was that they yelled at Skippy whenever they discovered the accident, even if it was hours later. "She knows what she did," Kristin said.

"Well, she probably doesn't," I said. We've all seen a guilty look on a dog's face, which we interpret to mean they know they did something wrong. But in fact, that look is actually anticipation of the punishment they know is coming when their owners show up. Dogs can have a hard time linking their behavior to the angry reaction they get later. They just learn from experience that when their owners come home, they're often mad. They don't have a clue why.

In any case, Kristin and Joe's yelling had caused Skippy to growl. So the next time there was an accident, Kristin rolled up a newspaper and swatted the little dog. Now, Skippy wasn't as good-natured as Zero when confronted with a rolled-up newspaper. In fact, the spunky little dog saw no reason to be attacked for something she had nothing to do with (the fact that she had urinated on the carpet was long forgotten by then). So she lunged at the newspaper. All of a sudden, Kristin and Joe had their hands full avoiding nips and bites from a dog who had never been aggressive before. It was their mistake—which, in my opinion, was a lot worse than Skippy's reaction—that brought me into the picture.

Skippy's aggression didn't stop with that one incident. In the months after the initial display, she began lunging and snapping at Kristin and Joe whenever they yelled at her. "Don't forget when we just look at her," Joe said. "And if we walk too close to her when she's lying in the hall. She's gotten pretty touchy."

She had also gotten very intolerant of newspapers. She had begun attacking any newspaper she saw, even when Kristin or Joe was merely sitting on the sofa reading the sports section. Skippy had obviously been terrified by the initial discipline and was mounting preemptive attacks.

"I'm afraid you both contributed to that by not knowing how to discipline her effectively in the first place," I said, feeling like I had to defend the dog. I didn't like to hear her being blamed for something her owners, admittedly with the best intentions, had brought upon themselves.

This case was unfortunate because it was so unnecessary. Since Skippy sometimes went on the carpet even when the Whitlocks were home, they had ample opportunity to deal with the problem in a way that would help Skippy understand that she was supposed to take her business outside. By using an inappropriate correction, however, a simple house-soiling problem had become an aggression problem.

In the future, I said, they should watch Skippy closely. When they saw her preparing to urinate inside, they should calmly say, "Come on, pup, let's do it out here," and gently propel the dog toward the door and go outside with her. Then they were to praise Skippy for going. It was as simple as that—and, I learned a few weeks later, it worked like a charm.

I was gratified that the Whitlocks were willing to go back to the drawing board and start over. Some people aren't so flexible, especially when it comes to traditional corrections like a rolled-up newspaper, which too many people continue to use even today.

Another type of inappropriate punishment is the old standby of "rubbing his nose in it." As distasteful as it sounds, and is, dogs around the country are having their noses shoved in messes on a regular basis, and most of them are probably pretty bewildered by this turn of events. Even when they actually know that they made the mistake, they don't deserve this kind of treatment. And it doesn't work anyway. The kinder, gentler techniques that I taught the Whitlocks do.

A good approach to misbehavior is often the time-out, and 30 seconds to two minutes is most effective. With a time-out, instead of running after the dog and shouting or hitting, which gives the dog the attention he is looking for, even if it is negative attention, you take away the social reinforcers that keep the bad behavior going. Instead, he's in a room by himself. When you let him out, he'll usually behave better and receive praise as a consequence. Over time, he'll learn to discriminate between acting out and getting yelled at and lying peacefully on his pillow and getting praise or treats.

Some people use a crate as a time-out spot. That's okay if the dog is really comfortable in the crate. But if he has separation anxiety or regards the crate as a punishment zone, then it won't work, and you'll have to find some other quiet room.

Unfortunately, many people don't understand the fine points of training. In addition to the swat-him-with-a-newspaper or rub-his-nose-in-it schools of training, I've seen some pretty bizarre scenarios that people develop for teaching obedience.

I REMEMBER A THREE-YEAR-OLD springer spaniel named Mingo. Mingo was acting aggressively toward her owners, who unfortunately took her to the wrong expert. Instead of recommending a time-out, the doctor recommended a technique that was in vogue several years ago but which has since been rejected by most responsible veterinarians and trainers.

Their veterinarian told them to take a choke chain and leash and, when the dog was misbehaving, pull her into the air until she was hanging off the ground. The idea was that the owners needed to establish themselves as the alpha dog in the family pack. Hanging the dog in the air was meant to show her who was boss.

What the vet didn't mention was that doing this could damage the dog's spine or trachea or cut off circulation to the brain. How a medical person could recommend it, I don't know. It is simply inhumane.

Unfortunately, many owners have used this technique for punishment purposes. In Mingo's case, her owners, Tom and Sally Baker, thought it would help stop her from barking or challenging them in the bedroom at night. Not surprisingly, it didn't work.

That's when they called me. It turned out that Mingo had developed the habit of defending the bedroom. She wouldn't let Tom or Sally back in the bedroom if they happened to leave at any time during the night or in the morning. She would bark and growl, and they were afraid of her.

It's not uncommon for owners to get more and more aggravated when confronted with this type of recalcitrant behavior. They tend to want to challenge the dog rather than back off until she's calmer. Tom had tried grabbing Mingo by the collar, but that resulted in a bite. So he changed his tactics. He would say, for example, "Get off the bed!" When she didn't, he would stare at her. Staring is very confrontational to some dogs, and Mingo responded by growling and showing her teeth. That's when Tom would get the blanket, throw it over her, and try to drag her from the room without getting bitten. These were not happy campers.

As it turned out, Mingo was smart and easy to work with. I taught the couple not to challenge her or force compliance but to let her experience something that was more pleasant than being on the bed. I suggested that they keep some of Mingo's favorite chew toys, along with a huge rawhide bone, in the bedroom and only allow her to chew them there. This helped distract her from guarding the bed.

In addition, I helped Tom develop some nonconfrontational and nonpunitive signals. Despite Mingo's history of being hanged by a choke chain and dragged in a blanket, she actually responded very well to other signals. By the third week of the program, she would reliably jump down from the bed when Tom snapped his fingers and then happily receive his praise. It just shows the amazing resilience of our companion animals. In the end, they just want to please us.

SOME YEARS AGO, I RECEIVED A CALL about a couple of escape artists. The two dogs, one a year-old Labrador-mix, the other a three-year-old German shepherd, were famous in the neighborhood for always getting out of their backyard pen during their owner's absence. The owner, Marvin Bigelow, was upset about the veterinary bill he had recently received from the next-door neighbor after the shepherd, Hero, escaped from the pen and attacked the neighbor's dog.

I'm always amazed at the lengths some people will go to when confronted with things like vet bills or bills for damaged property, without regard for the dog's mental health or motivation. It is only when they are at their wit's end with bills mounting up that they consider consulting a professional.

Marvin was determined to keep those dogs in the backyard pen no matter what. He started out, he told me, by fencing the pen with barbed wire, but that hadn't worked. They jumped right over the top. After he raised the fence a few times, the dogs couldn't clear the top anymore. So they started digging.

"Was that successful?" I asked.

"Oh, yeah, that was successful," he said. "So I put the barbed wire on the bottom of the fence."

Uh-oh, I thought. Really bad idea.

"Hero tore himself up pretty good trying to get out," he said. "I'm still paying the vet for that."

"He's okay now?"

"Oh, yeah. A few scars. Anyway, then we decided to leave Honey outside because she only tries to get out when he does. We put Hero in the basement."

"Okay, how did that work out?"

The big man shook his head again. "He went crazy down there. The neighbors were complaining about all the racket. Barking, whining, yelping, and whatnot."

That's when Marvin came up with the idea of matching harnesses. By now I had put my pencil down and was just listening with horrified fascination.

"What did you do with the harnesses?"

"Well, we put the harnesses on the two of them out in the pen, and then we attached them together with some rope."

"You attached them together?" I asked weakly.

"Yeah, and then I got some weights and tied them to the harnesses, so if the dogs did dig out, they couldn't get away very fast and attack somebody's dog."

I realized that Marvin was trying to keep things under control without really considering that there were two living, feeling animals here that were being damaged. In addition to making nearly constant pen renovations, Marvin often resorted to punishment. When the dogs escaped and came back home, he would take them back to the pen, show them the holes they made, and then hit them. Pretty soon they learned not to come back after they escaped. He had to hunt them down. And now he was using weights to slow them down.

In some ways, the dogs were responding very logically to the situation. Why go back when you're called if you are going to be hit? So now they were stuck with weighted harnesses and bound together like a bizarre pair of Siamese twins. At least the dogs liked each other and the harnesses hadn't driven them to fighting. It was the only silver lining I could think of in this tale of horror.

To help the dogs, I had to help Marvin and his wife, Debbie, understand why the dogs were escaping in the first place. After all, not every dog hates being penned up, especially when he has a buddy to keep him company.

"I'm surprised every time I come home and those dogs have gotten out," she said. "They always seem so content when I look out the window."

"They don't try to get out at all when you're here?"

"Never," she said. "They know I've got an eye on them."

This was my first good clue. I had a growing feeling that separation anxiety, not being penned up, was the real problem.

"When you leave the house," I asked them, "which door do you leave from? The back one?"

"That's right," Debbie said.

"So the dogs watch you go?"

"Absolutely. And we give them plenty of warnings about what they're not going to do while we're gone," Marvin said.

"Which they ignore," Debbie added.

This was further evidence, I believed, for separation anxiety. Marvin and Debbie were giving the dogs a pretty big goodbye when they left the house. Then, after getting all this attention, the dogs saw their owners leave. That's probably when their feelings of

anxiety and arousal caused them to start digging. They were probably saying to themselves, *Hey! Where's everyone going? It's scary
being alone, so let's get out of here!*

I tried to help the Bigelows see things from the dogs' point of
view. Yes, the dogs were causing problems for the couple, but it
was not because they were bad or malicious. They simply missed
their owners and were coping with their anxiety by digging and escaping.

I put together a program for them that included lots more attention and regular walks. I also recommended that they plan
random periods of separation in which they'd leave the house for
anywhere from a minute to an hour. This would make it harder for
the dogs to predict when they were going to be gone all day. As
long as they thought their owners would be coming back any
minute, they would be less likely to be lonely and anxious.

Further, I told them that it was less important to give the dogs
attention for their escape behavior, even negative attention, than it
was to give them lots of good attention for their positive behavior.
In other words, they were to reward the dogs for staying in the pen
and not for trying to escape.

"What's that supposed to do?" Marvin asked.

Sometimes people actually reinforce or encourage more bad
behavior when they pay a lot of attention to it, I explained. It's like
the teacher in school who constantly yells at the class troublemaker: "Billy, sit down. Billy, go to your seat. Billy, sit down right
now." She's not punishing the roaming, despite her intention to do
so. By giving Billy attention, she's actually reinforcing his behavior.

"I'm with you so far," Marvin said.

"Okay," I said. "Now if she ignores Billy's wandering, and no
one else reinforces the wandering either, then what we call extinc-
tion of the behavior will take place. In other words, he will sit
down. Like Billy, the dogs will respond a lot better if you don't
dwell on their mistakes by giving them attention for misbehaving."

As a final step, I recommended that they have Hero neutered.
This would decrease his urge to roam and pick fights when he en-

countered other dogs. When I left, I figured I had given the Bigelows a new way to view and understand their pets' misbehavior and also the tools to correct it in a humane and caring manner. The rest was up to them.

MOST OWNERS, OF COURSE, do their best to manage misbehavior without resorting to cruel or strange punishment methods. The problem is that people often don't have the slightest idea how to control their dogs or shape their behavior. They're unclear about how to use rewards and punishments. The result may be a dysfunctional adult dog who has no concept of limits. Sometimes you can't really blame the owners. You can only feel sorry for them and try to help them, and their pets, get out of the jam they've gotten into.

Take Munchkin. A six-year-old white toy poodle, Munchkin was essentially in charge of her exquisite Atlanta home, which came complete with Munchkin's owners and a housekeeper, who did their best to make sure the dog's needs were taken care of. After interviewing Eleanor and Alan Morton, it was clear that they had precious little time left over for themselves.

From the time she got up in the morning until the time she went to bed, Munchkin didn't hesitate to let the Mortons know when she wanted something, which was most of the time. When she wanted petting, for example, she would jump on Alan's lap. If he stopped petting for a moment, she would bite him. When Eleanor talked on the phone, Munchkin would bark angrily until she hung up. She would also snap at the housekeeper when she tried to remove Munchkin's blanket from the couch. In short, the dog was doing whatever she darn well pleased.

Munchkin was house-trained, but she didn't like the feel of wet grass on her dainty paws, so she often used the lavish living room, dining room, or master bedroom as a bathroom. To contain the "accidents," the Mortons put barriers all over the house to keep her in sight as much as possible. Baby gates make effective barriers, but when they're scattered through a home loaded with crystal chandeliers, silk lampshades, and oriental carpets, they make an incongruous sight, to say the least.

Munchkin would demand to be taken out so frequently that the Mortons were often exhausted by the end of the day. Yet they felt they couldn't refuse to take her because there might be more messes in the house.

Munchkin was an obvious candidate for obedience school, but when I broached the subject, Eleanor told me that she'd already been, briefly. She had barked, howled, and disrupted every class. It was obvious that the dog was a nervous wreck. The Mortons had tried giving her tranquilizers prescribed by their veterinarian, but without behavior therapy to go along with them, the drugs didn't work very well. Their vet finally recommended that they call me.

I knew what Munchkin needed was a little order and discipline in her life. I recommended that Eleanor buy a short leash, which she could use in the house to keep Munchkin under control. I told Eleanor and Alan to practice making Munchkin sit and stay—the two things she had learned in obedience school—in front of the front door before letting her out. Munchkin didn't like it, but she also knew she wasn't going to be allowed outside unless she did what she was told. So she learned to behave a little better when she was on the leash.

I also recommended that they get rid of Munchkin's bed on top of the couch. Instead, they should let her sleep only in the bedroom, but with a catch. They weren't to allow her in unless they led her on a leash. This further increased the balance of power in their favor.

When I first talked to the Mortons, I wasn't too confident that they were going to be able or willing to make the necessary adjustments. I was pleasantly surprised to get a note from Eleanor several weeks later. The note said:

Thursday evening, my daughter came for a visit. Munchkin was such a pest that I finally put on her leash and fastened it down low on my chair, and she instantly calmed down. Finally, she just curled up on the floor. In a little while, I removed the leash and she behaved much better.

Clearly, Munchkin was learning that there were limits and consequences. And I know the owners felt better having established some control over their little tyrant.

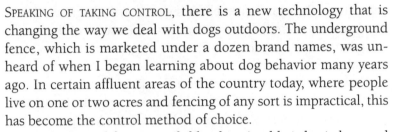

SPEAKING OF TAKING CONTROL, there is a new technology that is changing the way we deal with dogs outdoors. The underground fence, which is marketed under a dozen brand names, was unheard of when I began learning about dog behavior many years ago. In certain affluent areas of the country today, where people live on one or two acres and fencing of any sort is impractical, this has become the control method of choice.

Underground fences work like this: A cable is buried around the perimeter of the property—or at least that portion of the property where owners want their dogs to stay—and a metal box is hung around the dog's neck. When the dog gets too close to the buried wires, he hears a warning sound from the metal box. If he ignores the sound and keeps going, he receives a mild shock. Most dogs get the message fairly quickly and learn to stay away from the borders of the yard. As with any technology or technique for controlling animals, however, it isn't foolproof.

For example, some dogs will see something exciting on the other side of the border and bolt right through, shock or no shock. Then they're reluctant to come back in because they know another shock is waiting for them.

Another problem with these devices is the electricity itself. Although the shocks are described as mild, there is no way of judging the pain threshold of any individual dog. More worrisome is the fact that some dogs will begin to associate the shock with an entire section of yard or in some cases, with their owners, and thereafter avoid them like the plague.

There's a more subtle problem as well. I sometimes worry that people who use them have a tendency to think of them as electric baby-sitters. They put their dogs outside and basically forget about them. But dogs need a lot of personal interaction with their owners, fence or no fence. People who forget this simple fact may find themselves with a dog who never gets out of the yard but has other behavioral problems that they'll have to deal with eventually.

A couple of years ago, I visited a family in the suburbs of Atlanta. As I drove up, I could see small flags fluttering along the perimeter of their yard—the telltale signs of an underground fence. As I soon discovered, the fence was just one aspect of the hands-off relationship they had with their dog, an attractive black Labrador named Boomer.

It was clear almost from the start that Boomer was utterly mismatched with his human family. He was an energetic, loving dog. His owners, however, were apparently focused a lot more on their respective career tracks than on Boomer's needs. John and Susan Parker left the house before 7:00 A.M. and didn't get home until after dark. Their children—two boys and two girls—were either in school or playing in the neighborhood and often didn't traipse in the front door until after their parents got home.

Surrounded as he was by busy humans, Boomer didn't get a lot of attention. Even on weekends when everyone was home, he was often locked up in the sunroom, where his indoor doghouse had been turned to face a blank wall. Boomer couldn't see what the family was up to most of the time, and he certainly didn't feel like he was part of the family. He was only let out in the yard a few times a day to do his thing. As for walks on a leash, forget it. "We have the underground fence," Susan said.

Not surprisingly, Boomer was almost desperately eager for attention. Whenever anyone came by or when someone in the family would pause for a moment to pat his head, he would run around, bark, or jump up, often scratching them in the process. Naturally, this hyper behavior wasn't appreciated, so he'd usually be yelled at or banished to the yard or sunroom. Or he'd be threatened with a rolled-up newspaper.

The real problem, I discovered, was that none of the Parkers had ever spent time around dogs. Boomer was their first pet, and they didn't have the slightest idea what he needed or how they should care for him. It was obvious that I was going to have to teach this family the most basic principle of all: Dogs are members of the family and they need a lot of attention. They also need some basic training to learn that jumping up, barking, or other forms of overly exuberant behavior aren't appropriate. The Parkers had the idea that Boomer would automatically behave, sort of like the automatic electric fence.

Boomer only wanted to be integrated into the family's life, I explained. "He isn't trying to be a nuisance," I told them. "His behavior has to be molded and shaped, and he has to have consistent praise when he does the right thing. He just wants to be included and treated as an equal."

To their credit, the Parkers were dismayed to learn that they hadn't been the perfect parents. They peppered me with questions about what Boomer really needed in terms of exercise, attention, and so forth.

Exercise was clearly the first thing. Labradors are energetic dogs, and unless they burn off some of that energy, they're going to be a lot harder to control. Putting a dog alone in a big yard, with or without an underground fence, isn't enough because he'll just lie around and wait for someone to play with him. So I had to explain the importance of regular walks and play sessions.

Not surprisingly, none of the children was eager to be enlisted for this chore. But after a few rounds of objections—and one demand for money—we were able to work out a system in which different children would take Boomer for walks several times a day. The exercise would do more than keep him calmer, I explained. It was also a great way to integrate him into the family.

"Boomer doesn't feel much like part of the family right now, and he doesn't know what to do when everyone yells at him or pushes him away," I explained to the children. "So try to give him something else to do—throw a ball or something when he comes

over to play with you." They all nodded. "And I hope you'll remember Boomer when you're planning stuff to do," I added. "Dogs
don't like to be left out, either."

There was another chorus of okays, a little more enthusiastic
this time, I thought. One step at a time.

The next step—and the easiest one—was to get that designer
doghouse turned around. The sunroom wasn't the worst place for
Boomer to spend some of his time, but it was absolutely critical
that he be able to watch the family. Dogs crave companionship,
and they need to know what's going on around them. The way the
doghouse had been set up, Boomer was automatically cut off from
things, and it must have felt like punishment to him.

Finally, I asked Susan if they'd thought about taking Boomer
to obedience classes. "Absolutely," she said. "We just haven't had
time to do anything about it."

"It's worth doing," I said. "You'll all enjoy him a lot more when
you're able to play with him and walk him without getting
mauled."

"So there's hope for this dog?" John asked.

"Sure," I said. "Especially with all your kids. He's going to be
in great shape after a few games of soccer or Frisbee."

I've learned over the years that it's not always easy for people
to change, and if the people don't change, the problems with the
dogs rarely change, either. But when I left the Parkers' house that
day, I knew they had the interest and energy to follow through.

A few months later I was in their neighborhood, and I thought
I'd just quickly drive by. Sure enough, there was Boomer in the
yard, chasing after a basketball, surrounded by the exuberant
Parker boys and three of their friends. They all looked like they
were having a great time. And mischievous as they all were, I'm
pretty sure that none of them, including the dog, was getting
swatted with a rolled-up newspaper. And that, I have to figure,
spells progress!

Chapter Eleven

The Dog Who Laughed at Her Buddy

WHEN A PROFESSIONAL DOG TRAINER calls an animal behaviorist for help, you know the problem is serious. When two trainers call, they must be in real trouble.

John and Cindy Frankel devoted themselves to dogs seven days a week. Where pets were concerned, they held to the view that more is merrier. As they discovered, however, when one dog becomes two, or more, and a cat or two is thrown into the mix, things can become a bit complicated. Like anyone else, a dog trainer, or a behaviorist, can have a superbly trained dog with impeccable manners—a virtual showcase for his work—and still have to deal with behavioral problems, especially when there's more than one pet involved.

All too often, multiple-pet households become hotbeds of conflicts, role wrangling, or simple personality differences. My job is
to help people understand some of the basic concepts of managing
multiple pets so everyone will function as one big, happy family
instead of a dysfunctional one.

I haven't been asked very often to give advice to trainers.
Trainers and behaviorists have different backgrounds, training, and
approaches. I was a little bit apprehensive about stepping on the
Frankels' toes. I knew I would have to deal with their belief systems—gained from years of experience training dogs a certain
way—while still being true to my psychologically based point of
view. I only hoped I'd be able to help without crashing into a brick
wall of conflicting theories.

The Frankels welcomed me warmly, saying that a former client
of mine had given them my name. The problem, they explained,
was that two of their dogs weren't getting along, and they hadn't
been able to figure out how to patch things up.

"Come on and meet the dogs," John said, leading me through
their sprawling split-level home.

"Excuse the mess," Cindy added.

The house had clearly been set up for the comfort of the dogs
as well as their owners. The Frankels had converted their garage
into a combination office and den. A desk strewn with papers was
surrounded by dog crates and pillows. And lounging there were
their pets.

Dixie, a five-year-old husky–Australian shepherd-mix, trotted
up to greet me, while India, a three-year-old husky–collie-mix,
looked up warily from her pillow by the desk. India looked a little
beat up, and I wondered if Dixie had something to do with that. A
third dog, Candy, was a Pekingese-mix. She ran around for a while
checking out all the humans and canines, then settled down on a
chair to oversee her turf. In addition to these three pets, the
Frankels were foster parents to a parade of dogs that came in times
of need and left when they were ready to join a new family.

"Buster, our last foster dog, just found a home, but we still
have Ghost over there," Cindy said. Ghost, a spitz-mix, gave us a

bored look and didn't bother getting up. "She spends a lot of time sleeping in her crate," Cindy said. "Waiting for a home, I guess."

"So there are various numbers of dogs in your house from time to time?" I asked. "That can make things pretty interesting."

Just then, yet another pet, a large orange cat, jetted into the room. "Here's Smedley," John said. At the sight of the cat, Dixie stopped licking my hand and took off in pursuit. The room quickly became a helter-skelter affair of barking and flying fur. The Frankels waited patiently until their various pets settled down. Apparently this was par for the course. "Smedley keeps things interesting," John said.

"So what can I do for you?" I asked.

The problem, John explained, was that after three years of perfect compatibility, there had been a number of incidents between Dixie and India.

Incident number one. The various dogs had been lying on the living room floor one evening. Each dog was gnawing away on a rawhide chew. Candy left her chew for a moment in order to sniff something in a corner of the room. India, having tired of her own chew, figured she would sneak over and finish Candy's. That's when Smedley raced through the room, teasing Candy to chase her. Candy rose to the occasion just as Smedley ran past India, who was suddenly caught with Candy's bone in her mouth. Busted!

Candy changed course and made for India and the stolen bone. Now Candy wasn't much bigger than a cat and posed no threat to India. But India became flustered and pinned Candy to the ground. The little Pekingese howled in pain and fear.

"We grabbed India and put her out on the porch for a time-out," John said. What they didn't realize was that Dixie had watched the whole business. Dixie liked Candy and didn't appreciate her being picked on. So the stage was set for future problems.

Cindy and John didn't waste any time reacting to this first sign of trouble in paradise. They decided to take away all the rawhides. When there's an object that causes a fight, it makes sense to remove the object—which is fine as long as you replace it with something the dogs can enjoy in its place. But they didn't, and that's when the dogs began getting a bit testy and irritable. "They were probably beginning to compete for your attention, hoping you would give them a rawhide," I said.

Things started going downhill after that. "We had to stop using the split leash and walking them together because Dixie had started getting in India's face," John said. "Whenever India would bark or whine, Dixie would growl at her."

"Has Dixie always been the top dog on the ladder?" I asked.

"Yes," said Cindy. "But after India pinned Candy, India started getting more assertive." During walks, she said, India's tail started going up when Dixie got too close. The Frankels recognized the warning signs.

"Yeah, that sounds like trouble," I said. I was grateful that they were in the business and well-versed on dog communicative behavior. They would have no trouble recognizing the signs a dominant dog displays.

I thought back to a couple I met several years ago in rural Georgia. They didn't have a clue what their two dogs were up to. One dog, a gentle golden retriever, was regularly attacking their other dog, a German shepherd. We watched the dogs for a few minutes. I saw the shepherd trying to play with the golden, and the golden would respond by giving her a huge hip slam. This is when a dog leans into another dog and bumps him with his hips or rear end. They'll do it with people, too, when they're trying to get the upper hand. This type of behavior can lead to aggression— it's what wolves do. But of course, most people don't recognize this. They just think their dogs are leaning on each other for fun.

But back to Dixie and India. When the status between two or three dogs becomes too similar and competition for resources heats up, you have a higher likelihood of aggression. That's what happened after rawhide-time was canceled.

Incident number two. Dixie was in the kitchen, and Cindy tossed her a treat. It went over her head, and Dixie put her nose in the air to catch it. She fell over, hit her head on a bowl, and yelped in pain. India innocently wandered into the kitchen, and suddenly Dixie was all over her.

"India was laughing at Dixie for falling over and hitting her head, and that's why Dixie attacked her," Cindy said.

Well, I thought to myself, here it is. We had finally gotten to a point where I was going to have to suggest a different interpretation of what happened. It's quite natural for people to attribute human emotions to their pets, but the reality is usually different.

"I'm not sure dogs actually laugh at the misfortune or downfall of other dogs," I said, picking my words carefully. "But India could have had a bigger smile face than usual because she felt kind of fearful and submissive. That tends to make more teeth visible, and it would surely look as though the dog were laughing."

Cindy considered this theory silently.

"I doubt if Dixie actually was humiliated by being laughed at," I said, "but it's possible that she did associate the sudden pain from the fall with the appearance of India in the kitchen and maybe decided India was responsible."

"That makes sense," John said, to my relief.

"Was there another incident?" I asked.

"There were three fights before we decided this was more than we could handle," John said.

Incident number three. Everyone was gathered in the master bedroom—and I do mean everyone. The couple had no children, but they had plenty of companions to put to bed. Unlike trainers who keep their dogs and their personal lives entirely separate, this couple invited all of their pets into the bedroom at night. It was not unusual to find one or two of the dogs or a cat hanging out at the foot of the bed. This particular night, Candy was at the foot of the bed, Dixie was on the bed to John's left, and Ghost had made a rare appearance in the room and had jumped up on the bed to lick John's face.

Happy with his affectionate pets, John made the fatal mistake of inviting India up on the bed, too. That's when Dixie started to go ballistic.

"She started whining and barking and becoming very agitated," John said.

"The whining and barking isn't unusual," I said. "It's what some dogs do when they've been in a fight with another dog and then they find themselves in the situation again."

It's as if the dogs know something rotten is going to happen, but they can't stop it from happening. The barking is their way of saying, *Get out of here; you're not supposed to be doing this,* and the whining means, *We're going to get in a fight.*

But things happened too quickly for the Frankels to interpret all this dog talk. As soon as India put her paws on the bed, Dixie let her have it. John found himself in the middle of a dogfight. While Ghost and Candy quickly leapt out of harm's way, Smedley knew a good time when she saw it. She catapulted onto the bed and latched onto John's arm.

At this point, Cindy jumped out of bed and dragged India into the bathroom.

That awful night ended with an emergency trip to the vet, where India had to be sedated and stitched up. She suffered a torn lip and some loose teeth and was still recovering on the day I arrived.

After the Frankels finished their story, I noticed Dixie watching us from the sunroom, where she'd been banished. I figured she had to be pretty ticked off to see her top position in the family taken over by India, who was sitting contentedly on the couch with John.

There's a basic rule when it comes to problems between dogs, and it goes like this: Anytime there's a problem, no matter who starts it or who attacks whom, it's *always* the fault of the subordinate dog. When there's a skirmish beginning or one dog is threatening the other, you always correct the subordinate dog first. Notice that I said correct, not punish. You just want to stop what the dog is doing. You can take the subordinate dog and tell him to lie down in the corner. Then you must go back and correct the dominant dog so that he doesn't take advantage of the situation. He can be put in another corner. Remember, both dogs also have a hier-archical relationship with you: Your role is to be dominant to both of them.

This has to be done carefully, without the added stimulation that punishing or yelling would bring to the situation. The more of that you do, the more likely it is that the dog will bite or become fearful. The way you go about resolving these relationship prob-lems is to try to re-establish the original, or at least the current, status among the dogs—although in some cases you may need to reverse the status and start over. We talked it over for a few min-utes, and the Frankels agreed that Dixie needed to be the lead dog and India had to go back to being second banana.

"I guess India's the one who should be out on the sun porch," John said. We looked through the glass as Dixie lay down glumly, her eyes glued to John and Cindy. I nodded.

"I feel so sorry for India," said Cindy.

I understood the feeling, but it wasn't the way to be thinking right now. They needed to understand the pecking order if things weren't going to get worse.

The Frankels agreed to re-establish Dixie in the leadership role. That meant giving her the best resources—for example, food, treats, or attention from people—first. India would be kept in her subordinate role by receiving things second, and even then not in Dixie's presence, at least not for a while.

People often think it's mean to treat one dog better than the other. The idea isn't to withhold food and other resources entirely from the second dog but just to give them second. Dogs don't live in a democracy, where every dog is potentially equal. In fact, de-spite the myths, neither do dogs try to get to the top level of the hierarchy. Most of them are perfectly happy being subordinate and will never try to climb the ladder at all.

Dogs get along best when they occupy stable roles, regardless of whether one is superior to another. These roles are worked out by the dogs themselves, under the influence of such things as ge-netics and personality. It is not necessarily the bigger dog or the older dog who becomes the dominant force in the household. I have seen many instances of a dog ruling the roost for years, only to have a new puppy come on the scene and take over in short order. After all, puppies are only small for a few months, and it's not size that counts in any event.

Owners can foster harmony by making each dog feel good in his own role. You are not punishing the dog in the subordinate role. You are enabling him to do things in a particular way that will feel good and won't have him competing with the one in the dominant role.

You have to be aware of what dogs consider important and how they view each other's roles. *You can't sleep on the foot of the bed—that's mine. You can't have access to the pillow on the couch—that's mine, too. But you can do anything else you want, even eat first, as long as I have these two comfortable places to lie down.*

That's the curious thing about dominant and subordinate roles. They're often defined in terms of particular resources. Just because a dog is dominant in relation to soft resting places doesn't mean that he's dominant in relation to things that taste good. It's up to the owner to give the top dog those things that matter to him when you're trying to reinforce his dominant role.

For the first few weeks of the Frankels' program, they kept their dogs separate as much as possible. They kept them in separate quarters, took separate routes during walks, and used different doors to go in and out. They also kept the dogs away from the scenes of their earlier crimes in order to prevent territorial disputes. During this time, the dogs were learning to be calm rather than aggressive. Eventually, the Frankels would bring the dogs together, help them be friends again, and be prepared to separate them if they started showing signs of aggression.

The last I heard, the Frankels' program worked well. Although they never walked the dogs together on the split lead again, they were able to restore the tradition of snack time, with rawhide chews for everyone. Cindy gave me one last call.

"Guess what, John," she said.

"What?"

"India's finally laughing again!"

"Okay," I laughed, giving in. "This time, I believe you."

NOT EVERY ISSUE THAT ARISES in multiple-pet households is a matter of dominance or submission. Sometimes, adding another pet to the family simply creates a logistical problem that no one anticipated. This is what happened to the chairman of the psychology department at Mercer University in Macon, where I teach.

Frank Dane is a respected professional in social psychology. He's also my boss, so I was a little nervous when he bent over my desk one day and quietly asked if I would drop by the house and help him and his wife, Linda, resolve "a little cat-and-dog issue." Naturally, I said sure, and a few days later I went by after work to see what was up.

I'd anticipated that there was probably a problem in the relationship between the pets. As it turned out, what they had was really more of a behavioral problem—one that was wrapped up in some logistical complications. I didn't know this at first, though, because Frank and Linda were a bit embarrassed to talk about it.

"I've heard just about everything, Frank," I said, trying to put them at ease. Privately, I was wondering just what these rascals had been up to.

Frank and Linda looked at each other. While I waited, I stroked the cat, a calico named Tootsie. Frank cleared his throat.

"Have they been fighting?" I prompted, trying to get the ball rolling. Linda had told me earlier that Tootsie was a recent arrival in the family, following the death of her owner in the Midwest. Frank and Linda hadn't hesitated to adopt Tootsie, but I would have told them, had they asked, that sometimes these impulsive decisions to take on more animals—no matter how noble the cause—end up as big mistakes. Managing two pets or more is exponentially more difficult than managing one, as I presumed they'd found out.

I already knew that they'd owned their dog, an eight-year-old black Lab named Rufus, for about four years. He was the kind of well-behaved dog who seemed eternally grateful to his family for rescuing him from a shelter. But I wouldn't have been surprised if the sudden appearance of Tootsie had set off a round of battles for superiority. Generally, the cat wins, even when he's the newcomer.

"It's not about fighting," Linda said. "They get along fine." Sure enough, Rufus was sitting calmly at Frank's feet, gazing mildly at the cat.

"Rufus is eating out of Tootsie's box," Frank explained.

I broke into a smile. "Oh, it's the old 'poo-poo breath syndrome.' "

"There is such a thing?" asked Linda.

"I told you, I've seen everything," I said. "So Rufus is getting into the cat litter. That's not so unusual."

Frank and Linda looked relieved. When I pressed them for more details, they told me their story. When they first brought Tootsie back from the airport, they set up her litter box in the laundry room, and everything was fine for a week or two. That changed when they sprayed Tootsie for fleas—unfortunately, also in the laundry room. Tootsie totally freaked out and wouldn't go in there again, even to use her box. Little cat accidents started to appear around the house. So they moved Tootsie's litter box to the bathroom.

While Rufus never had occasion to go to the laundry room, he did occasionally wander into the bathroom, and he quickly discovered a new taste sensation. No one's really sure why dogs occasionally develop a taste for cat droppings. It's possibly because the tidbits contain undigested particles of cat food, which most dogs love. Personally, I suspect that some dogs are too timid to approach cats directly and instead satisfy their innate olfactory urges by dining at the litter box. Who knows? In any event, what's perfectly acceptable for dogs isn't acceptable to their owners. Frank and Linda were in the habit of encouraging wet, sloppy dog kisses, and it didn't take them long to notice that Rufus's breath had changed for the worse.

"We've moved that litter box all over the house, but the dog won't stay out of it," Frank said. "I can't be standing by all day to clean it out every time the cat goes." I was certainly seeing a new side of Frank, whom I usually encountered in a more scholarly setting. I hid a smile, thinking of him lurking around the litter box trying to beat Rufus to the punch.

"What would you suggest we do?" Linda asked.

I suggested starting with a tour of the house. Frank and Linda showed me the different places they had put the box, none of which had deterred Rufus. Then we searched out all the remaining spots that they hadn't tried, and they told me why they wouldn't work. Finally, we found ourselves in the library on the bottom level of their tri-level home, where the litter box currently sat.

"This is the best spot so far, but we can't keep Rufus out all the time," Linda said. I saw that there wasn't a place to install a cat door, which is often the easiest solution, so I told them that they would need to put a second box in the bathroom downstairs. This would be a backup location for the cat to use temporarily while we figured out a way to keep Rufus out of the main litter box.

Frank and Linda weren't enthusiastic about putting the litter box in their bathroom, but I explained that it was a perfectly reasonable location and about the only one they hadn't ruled out. I suggested that they leave the box in the bathtub with the curtain pushed to the middle. This would give Tootsie some privacy as well as an escape route, which cats need in order to feel comfortable. I also suggested that they buy a special doorjamb that would allow the door to be opened only a few inches, just wide enough for the cat to get in but not wide enough for the dog. Then I began thinking of ways that would allow them to keep the box in the library, keep the dog out, and let the cat in. It was a tall order.

I suggested that they get a new litter box, one with a totally different shape, color, and style. I didn't want Rufus to see the new box and be reminded of his previous dining pleasures. After looking around the library some more, I recommended that they put the box in the corner, with some big houseplants in front of it for privacy. Further, I told them to put a strip of sticky tape on the floor a few feet in front of the plants and a row of marbles on top of the tape. I knew from experience that dogs don't like stepping on marbles, especially when they start rolling around underfoot. In addition, this setup would act as a signal. If Frank and Linda saw that the marbles had rolled off the tape, they would know that Rufus had been trespassing. We watched as Tootsie stepped daintily over the marbles without disturbing them. When Frank and Linda looked at me, I explained that there is nothing dainty about a black Lab and that the booby trap would work.

Frank had heard or read somewhere that adding monosodium glutamate (MSG) to a cat's food will cause the stools to taste bad. I had a hard time imagining that they tasted good without the MSG, but Frank wanted to give it a try. He also wanted to pour Tabasco sauce on the stools, so if Rufus took a bite he'd get an unpleasant surprise. It seemed to me that it would be easier just to remove them from the box than to season them like a burrito, but what could I say? He was my boss.

A few days later, Frank dropped by my office again and told me the tactics had worked very well. Rufus broke through the booby trap once or twice, but his breath was definitely improving. Not wanting to take any chances, Frank also added a high-tech solution. I had casually mentioned that he could set up a motion detector, using lasers, around the litter box. Frank loved the idea. He went to an electronics store and picked out an expensive security system complete with an alarm. One blast from the alarm was enough to send Rufus running back upstairs. By this time, I'm sure the dog was beginning to think that boring old dog biscuits were starting to look pretty good.

Within a week, Frank didn't need the security system anymore. Rufus had begun backing away when he saw the tape on the floor because he associated it with the alarm. Within two weeks, the problem had disappeared. Rufus went back to dog food. Tootsie had two boxes and no fleas. And I went back to mundane meetings with my boss, secure that his little cat-and-dog issue had been resolved to his satisfaction and that I could plan on keeping my job.

CONSIDERING RUFUS'S CULINARY adventures, it's a good thing Frank didn't own a dog like Spike, a doberman–Lab-mix who was having a turf battle with his buddy, Tramp, a German shepherd–Lab-mix. Spike was what we call a leash fighter. He hated submitting passively to a leash. He would grab the leash in his mouth and hold onto it as if to say, *If we're going for a walk, I'm going to hold the leash!*

Spike's owners, Marcia and Sam Tucker, followed their trainer's advice and put some bitter apple on the leash. Bitter apple is a pet repellent that is said to taste horrible to dogs. But, Spike loved it and licked up every bit. The Tuckers' trainer then recommended sprinkling the leash with Tabasco. Spike liked that even better. With all the extra seasoning, he was less likely than ever to let go of his leash—but that was the least of the Tuckers' troubles.

As I mentioned earlier, dogs living together need to know their respective places in the household. In most families, the dogs sort out their roles fairly quickly. That relationship pretty much dictates their behavior in most other respects down the line.

Most of the time, Tramp and Spike were the best of friends. When they were in the house, they played together and lay around together. They didn't compete over toys or food. Spike was king. He set the rules. Tramp deferred to him without question. But in the yard, Tramp would take over and become the boss while Spike meekly followed his lead.

Here was a situation in which the dogs were in stable roles, even though the roles reversed, depending on where they were. Unfortunately, problems occurred at Checkpoint Charlie— the sliding glass door that led from the dining room to the patio. Here the dogs' roles were in transition, and the doorway had become a virtual battleground whenever the dogs were going in or out.

"When I open the door," Marcia told me, "Spike starts going out, but Tramp forces his way past him so he can go out first. Then Tramp turns around and starts barking and growling at Spike, who is still standing in the doorway."

"Does that stop Spike?"

"For a minute, but then he tries to slink out and Tramp nails him."

"Spike has never liked going out," Sam remarked. "When he was young, I used to have to carry him out. And he'd always run back in right away or open the door with his nose."

The doorway turf war had been going on for about six months, ever since Spike looked through the glass door and spied a squirrel on the deck. He tore after it and went right through the glass door. "He had to spend three days at the vet's," Marcia said. "When he came home, Tramp had changed the rules."

"Meaning that he wouldn't let Spike out the door anymore?"

"Right."

It sounded to me as though during Spike's absence, Tramp had decided, *You left and I really missed you, but don't come back. If you do come back, there are some new rules now.*

"Want to see what this confrontation looks like?" Sam offered. I didn't really want to take him up on it. I always try to avoid soliciting aggression in dogs, especially if the owners might put themselves at risk for getting bitten. But the dogs had to go out anyway, and I reluctantly agreed to watch their interaction and see if I could learn anything.

The problem occurred just as the Tuckers had described. The one part they hadn't told me, but which I could see for myself, was that along with Tramp's display of aggressive signals were a couple of unmistakable play-bows. When dogs bend their front ends way down and put their rears up the air, it's a sign of play. Was Tramp actually soliciting play from Spike instead of wanting to hurt or challenge him? Possibly, it was a little of both.

The problem, I figured, was that Spike just wasn't a player. Although he seemed attached to Tramp in his own way, staying near him during the day, he'd never really liked other dogs and wasn't all that eager to interact. So, whatever Tramp's intentions, Spike wasn't playing along, and what may have begun as play-fighting quickly turned into real fighting.

This didn't strike me as a particularly complicated problem. I recommended that the Tuckers simply let the dogs out at different times or let them use different doors. Even though this approach wouldn't solve the underlying issues, it would certainly solve the problem. People sometimes get too wrapped up in the issues and don't think logically about all the options. That's when people go to counselors and dog owners hire animal psychologists.

As I suspected, letting the dogs out at different times and through different doors made a big difference. I also recommended that the Tuckers get in the habit of feeding the inside dog some treats and playing with him while the other one was outside. This would keep the inside dog from wanting to follow the other one to the door, where a confrontation was inevitable. It also would serve to put the inside dog in a good mood so he'd be less likely to pick a fight during the going-out scenario. In addition, I suggested that they try to give each dog a lot more exercise. Tired dogs are a lot less likely to be aggressive dogs.

As it turned out, the extra exercise bore some unexpected fruit. I found out several weeks later, during a follow-up phone call, that on the course of his longer walks, Tramp found a girlfriend, a nice standard poodle, several blocks away. The two dogs would play and romp to their heart's content while their owners chatted away. Tramp became much less interested in fighting with Spike as the weeks went by.

"Thanks for your help," Sam said. "We're finally back to normal."

"I think you should thank that poodle, too," I said. "It's great that Tramp turned out to be a lover, not a fighter."

ZORRO, AN EXUBERANT TWO-YEAR-OLD German shepherd, was also a lover. He just about loved his companion, a nine-year-old cat named Ginger, to pieces—quite literally. At least, that's what Ginger seemed to be afraid of. She went to great lengths to avoid Zorro's overly affectionate romping and occasional chases around the house. In fact, Ginger was so freaked out that she was almost a prisoner in her own home.

This situation was more or less the flip side of the multiple-pet scenario in which various pets don't get along. When an exuberantly friendly type is paired with a smaller, peace-and-privacy-seeking pet, there's going to be a lot of stress and chaos for everyone. You can't change the pets' personalities. All you can do is help them interact in such a way that the victim can escape, regroup, or claim her own space when she needs to.

"I can't get Ginger to come downstairs anymore," said Michelle Baron when we met. "And the situation keeps getting worse."

As we spoke, I saw Zorro panting at the bottom of the stairs. At the top of the stairs, I saw a cute orange cat staring down at our little group. "Zorro is very patient," said Michelle. "He's willing to stand there until she tries to come down. It could be half an hour or more. And he does it several times a day."

"Has Zorro ever caught Ginger or hurt her?" I asked. The cat's aversion to the friendly dog would be easier to understand if she had met some kind of misfortune at his paws.

"Oh, no," Michelle said. "He just likes to chase her around and maybe lick her. But she doesn't want any part of it. In fact, she's raked his nose with her claws a few times."

"But that doesn't stop him from trying to make friends, right?"

"You got it," she said, smiling for the first time. "He won't give up."

I asked Michelle to describe the cat's daily routine.

She gestured upstairs. "That's her routine."

"What do you mean?"

"I mean, she just sits upstairs most of the time. I have to bring her food and water, and I keep her litter box up there in the bathroom. She simply will not come down unless Zorro is outside or behind the baby gate in the kitchen—and he whines if I put him there."

Wow. This was worse than I realized.

"Does the cat ever go outside?"

"Ginger has always loved to go out," she said. "But sometimes, Zorro chases her when they're outside, too. Actually, he goes after any cat he can find. That's his hobby."

"So now she doesn't go outside at all?"

"She'll go if she can sneak past him down the stairs. . . . Here she comes."

I watched as Ginger stealthily crept down the first few stairs. Zorro was absorbed in giving me an introductory sniff, so Ginger probably thought this was her best shot.

When she was about halfway down, Zorro looked up. *Aha!* he seemed to be thinking. He stuck his head through the slats in the banister and gave a friendly woof.

Ginger raced back up the stairs.

"This goes on all day," Michelle said. "She never makes it outside." She gestured toward a dining room window that was wide open, even though the air conditioning was on.

"I keep it open all the time, just in case," she said.

I watched as Ginger made several more attempts to come downstairs. She was a bit too slow and a bit too timid—an unfortunate combination, given the obstacles in her way.

Zorro didn't seem to be having such a ball, either. On Ginger's second attempt, he slipped and slid around the hardwood floor. He couldn't get any traction at all. When German shepherds try to move quickly on hardwood floors, they invariably end up taking a tumble.

After talking for an hour, I was as ready as Michelle to see an end to all this. But these things are never solved right away. As a matter of fact, it took several months of working with both pets to get them past their unusual impasse.

Zorro clearly had to do his part. He needed to learn to sit and stay on command and to be patient enough to allow Ginger to come close without giving chase. I showed Michelle how to keep Zorro on a short leash during their training exercises, and she worked with him regularly. I also advised her to give Zorro a time-out by putting him in a separate room when he misbehaved. He soon learned that chasing Ginger in the house earned him a few minutes in solitary.

It was important that we not do anything to discourage Zorro's playful nature. I asked Michelle to take him out regularly and throw a ball or Frisbee around. This would help him learn that, when he wanted to play, Michelle was the one to turn to, not the cat.

To make it easier for Ginger to come downstairs, Michelle taped brown paper across the banister. When Zorro couldn't see the cat coming down, he was much less likely to give chase. Ginger, in turn, couldn't see Zorro, which meant that she was less likely to turn tail and run. Ginger soon learned to scoot down the stairs and out the window or over the baby gate before Zorro had time to react.

Now that Zorro wasn't in a state of perpetual excitement, he was much easier to be around. Ginger gradually worked up the courage to come close and check him out. It didn't look like they were ever going to be the bosom buddies that Zorro had envisioned, Michelle told me later, but Ginger did end up tolerating him pretty well. And for a lot of cat-and-dog combinations, tolerance is about as good as it's going to get.

Living with more than one pet, whether they're dogs, cats, goldfish, or gerbils, can be a trial. But I figure that in this rough-and-tumble world, we need all the animal friends we can find. In most cases, there's no real reason for pets to end up in the dog-house because of the way they act together. They can learn to live together in peace.

So, all things being equal, I encourage multiple-pet house-holds—if you have the resources to set things up with the pets' best interests rather than your convenience in mind, and if you have the patience to cope when the place becomes a zoo. And, as the owner of three dogs and a cat, I can guarantee you that it will.

But when the whole gang is piled on the bed at night, every-thing falls into place. I wouldn't change it for the world.

Chapter Twelve

The Dog Who Devoured the House

DOLORES AND TIM FITZGERALD HAD recently bought a home and moved in with their infant daughter, two bearded collies, and a lot of high hopes. The fact that the house needed redecorating and a bit of structural work didn't faze this energetic young couple. They were going to do the remodeling with new Sheetrock, wallpaper, and paint as they went along. It might take a few months, but everything would be perfect when they were done . . . or so they thought.

Six months later, the three of us were sitting in the master bedroom, inspecting the wreckage. I could see why Dolores had sounded a little panicked when she called to set up a consultation.

The room looked as though someone had come in swinging a pickax. "Misty is eating the whole house," Dolores said miserably. "Chunk by chunk," Tim added.

I looked down at the dogs. Misty sat pleasantly at our feet, looking as innocent as the day she was born. Rusty gazed off into space and sighed, then lowered his bearded chin to his paws. They looked calm enough to me, but something was certainly setting them off.

"What exactly has she eaten?" I asked.

"Everything," Tim said. "Sheetrock, plaster, wallpaper, wood-work, you name it."

I took out my pencil and made a few notes. "Start at the beginning," I suggested.

Misty had started her career as a demolition expert soon after they moved into the house, Tim explained. After the first few episodes, they took Misty to their vet, who suggested that she might have a nutritional deficiency. After running some tests, he discovered Misty was slightly low on calcium and gave her some supplements. This isn't as strange as it sounds, since dogs who are low in certain nutrients will occasionally develop strange tastes—for dirt, Sheetrock, or other inedible objects. In this case, however, the supplements didn't help. So their vet recommended that they give me a call.

"Why do you think she's doing this?" Dolores asked.

I had a couple ideas. There was a very good chance that Misty simply hadn't adjusted well to the move. That, combined with the new baby in the house, might have shaken her confidence and made her anxious and insecure. Dogs who are anxious will some-times deal with their emotional turmoil by destroying everything in sight.

"Let's go back to the beginning, before the move," I said. "I want to get the whole picture before I draw any conclusions."

I knew I was going to have to probe the family's history, going back at least six to eight months, before I could piece this puzzle together. I also knew I was going to have to come up with a workable solution fairly quickly. Misty was clearly suffering from some kind of anxiety, and ingesting construction materials couldn't be good for her. It was important for her mental and physical health to find out what was going on. Besides, the Fitzgeralds were eager to get back to their renovating, and all this damage was costing them a bundle.

Somewhat to my surprise, Tim and Dolores revealed that things hadn't been perfect even before the move. In their previous apartment, they told me, Misty had occasionally chewed on shoes or the carpet. The chewing also predated the arrival of little Erin. So much for my "big changes" theory.

While we talked, I explained to the Fitzgeralds that it was not really necessary to know exactly what triggered Misty's misbehavior in the first place. I've found that deep background questions are most useful for eliminating suspected sources of problems. For instance, if Rover never bit anyone until his 10th birthday, it's a pretty sure bet that he doesn't have a temperament problem. But that doesn't tell us what he does have. As long as Rover can't explain what's wrong, and the owners aren't able to observe him 24 hours a day, we have to be content with educated guesses to answer the "why" part of the equation.

What concerns me most is usually the "how." How to stop the misbehavior and provide the dog with a healthier, socially acceptable alternative.

Despite those earlier problems, Tim said, Misty's destructive bent didn't really surface until the time of the move, and it had continued off and on for the past five months. The damage nearly always occurred at night, he added. They'd never actually caught the guilty party in the act.

"Did you know Misty was the culprit right away?" I asked.

"There wasn't much doubt," Tim said, reaching down to rub Misty's head. "We'd see her in the morning with all these little pieces of white stuff stuck in her beard. When we saw what happened to the Sheetrock, it wasn't hard to put two and two together. Right, Misty?"

Misty looked up and smiled happily. She didn't look like a home-wrecker to me. If anything, she seemed surprisingly content. "I can guess that you haven't physically punished her for wrecking the house?"

"No," Tim said. "We don't spank the baby for throwing her toys around or spitting up on her clothes, so why punish Misty?"

"We figure dogs will be dogs," Dolores added, "but we sure want her to stop it."

This was a pretty lenient attitude considering the condition of the house. I don't think many owners would have been quite so understanding. More than once, I've seen people go nuts over a chewed-up sock.

"Well, dogs will be dogs, but you have a right to expect your pets to leave your house alone," I commented. "It's good that you haven't complicated things by punishing her, but this can't be allowed to continue."

I had a few reasons for being grateful that the Fitzgeralds hadn't gone after Misty with a rolled-up newspaper. Since the incidents all took place at night, hours before the damage was discovered by the human members of the family, Misty would have had no idea why she was being punished. Unless you actually catch them in the act, dogs have a hard time linking punishment with a particular crime. Scolding or whacking them with a paper after the fact will certainly scare them, but they won't have the foggiest idea why you're doing it.

I've also found that any kind of physical or verbal punishment will increase a dog's stress level, and I was sure that Misty's destructive habits were directly related to her inability to handle stress very well in the first place. One or two smacks and she might have started in on the furniture and appliances.

The easiest solution, I explained, would be to confine Misty at night. Admittedly, this wouldn't get to the root of the problem, whatever that was, but it would interrupt the pattern of destruction and give Misty a chance to reorder her priorities, from chewing to sleeping.

The best way to confine her would be to use a crate. Most people have an automatic aversion to crates because to human eyes they seem like jails. And even some dogs see it that way. But many dogs naturally gravitate to small, enclosed places because they make them feel safe and secure, not to mention warm. Most dogs won't have a problem with crates, especially when they're introduced to them early on and as long as the crate is used as a comfortable getaway and not a place of punishment.

Misty hadn't been crated before, however, so this posed a possible dilemma. On the one hand, she hadn't built up any unpleasant associations about cages. On the other hand, it isn't always easy to introduce an adult dog to a crate if she hasn't encountered one as a puppy. But I wanted to give it a try.

It was obvious that Tim and Dolores weren't thrilled with the idea. "It doesn't seem like a nice thing to do to a dog," Dolores said. But when I broached the subject again, they reluctantly agreed to discuss it, which they proceeded to do.

"We already tried putting her in the basement," Dolores said.

Tim rolled his eyes. "Don't remind me."

At my questioning look, Dolores explained that Misty had no problem staying in the basement. She passed the time by gnawing the Sheetrock off the walls.

"Okay, let's go for the kennel, then," Tim said.

"Good. We'll try it with the door open at first and see if she stays in there all night," I suggested. "I guess you'll know by the state of the wallpaper in the morning." Tim gave me a look. "Rusty can sleep right outside the crate to keep Misty company," I added.

To sweeten the deal for Misty, I suggested that they entice her into the crate with a dog treat and some favorite toys. It would also be helpful to put the crate in a place where Misty felt comfortable. "Where does she like to sleep?" I asked.

"She usually goes to sleep on our bed," Dolores said.

"Does she like to lie anywhere else in the room, maybe during the day?"

"She likes to lie under the window when it's sunny," Dolores explained.

"Okay, so let's try it there," I said, writing the location on my diagnostic sheet.

Then I gave them some specific suggestions for getting Misty used to the crate. It would be helpful, I told them, if they'd just let the crate sit around for a day or two with the door closed. This would allow Misty to get used to its presence without actually going inside. After that, they could put a treat inside at bedtime and coax her in. Using coercion was out of the question because then she'd see the crate as threatening instead of safe.

"It may take a few days for her to go in," I told them as I prepared to leave. "If that's the case, try to be patient and go at her speed. We want this to be a good experience for Misty."

Tim called me a week later, and I could tell right away from the tone of his voice that things had gone well. "We've had Misty in the crate from the first day," Tim said happily. "She went right in and stayed there all night. I think she went out a couple of times, though, because there were new paint chips on the floor. When can we close that kennel door?"

"Better wait a week or so," I suggested. "You don't want her to feel trapped. And remember, this nighttime feeding frenzy is a pretty well established habit by now. She needs some time to get used to not doing that anymore."

Tim called back two weeks later. "Guess what, John? No more white chips in Misty's beard. I think we are over the hump." And they were.

Luckily, I never had to go to the next step, which would have been to follow their veterinarian's advice and put the dog on some kind of anti-anxiety medication. Even though we never really found out the "why" of this problem, the "how" fell right into place. As the new paint and wallpaper went up, so did the spirits of this once-again happy family.

A DESTRUCTIVE CANINE ISN'T THE type of thing most people anticipate when they're planning a move, but that's how it often is with behavioral problems. I've dealt with hundreds of cases over the years in which seemingly inconsequential events—moving to a new house, for example, or putting a dog in a kennel for a few days—triggered weeks or months of serious misbehavior.

For dogs, even little surprises can be upsetting. Any change in their routine may be sufficiently upsetting that they'll begin acting out in various ways. Every dog reacts to surprises differently, of course. This is governed by all sorts of things, from the dog's genetic makeup, which influences his ability to handle everyday life, to the influence of other stressors in his life. Two dogs experiencing the same surprise will have totally different reactions. That's part of what makes dogs so interesting.

I remember a three-year-old German shepherd named Rebel who started a five-day stay at a boarding kennel as a mild-mannered Dr. Jekyll and came home a raving Mr. Hyde. "The kennel people swore that nothing happened there to upset her," said Rebel's owner, Millie Brown, when we met to discuss her newfound problems. "But I don't believe them."

"You never really know," I said. "Does the place have a good reputation?"

"Oh, yes," she said. "But, I've never used them before—or any other kennel for that matter."

"Just going away could have upset your dog," I told her. "Does she normally have any separation anxiety?"

"Not really," Millie said. "I go to work every day and she's fine. Used to be fine," she corrected herself. "There was never any damage or barking or anything."

"How did she used to greet you?" I wanted to know if Rebel typically gave her an over-the-top, prolonged greeting when she came home, which is often a telltale sign of separation anxiety.

"Well that hasn't changed. She usually gets up, comes over and says hello, and then wanders off," said Millie. That answered that question.

"Any guess as to what may have happened at the kennel, Millie?"

"I believe they put a muzzle on her," Millie said. "But of course, they say they didn't. When Rebel came home, she had little sores on her mouth."

"Well, we will probably never know the truth, so let's just go on," I said.

It took about an hour for Millie to tell me all the terrible things Rebel had started doing in the previous three weeks. Here was one client I wouldn't have switched places with. She had put up with a lot.

Before going to the kennel, Millie explained, Rebel had been a quiet, obedient dog. The week after she got back, Rebel tore apart the trash cans in the kitchen and bathroom, spreading the contents throughout the apartment. Then she defecated on top of the trash. This happened three times in one day, Millie said, until she wised up and hid the trash cans.

Rebel didn't stop there. She went into Millie's bedroom at night—this was in January, when it gets pretty cold even in Atlanta—and pulled the comforter, blanket, and sheet from Millie's side of the bed. She repeated this bizarre routine two nights in a row. The next night Millie shut the dog out of the bedroom for the first time in Rebel's life.

I didn't know quite what to make of it. The damage occurred whether or not Millie was home, so I didn't think it was separation anxiety. Millie was convinced that Rebel was getting back at her for leaving her in the kennel, but I had problems with that as well. The scientific part of me knows very well that dogs don't really think that way. But I couldn't entirely disagree with her revenge theory, since the nonscientific part of me wanted to say, "Makes sense." Debating the reasons, however, wouldn't bring us closer to a solution. Rebel clearly needed to re-establish a more suitable routine, preferably one in which she was rewarded for good behavior.

The easiest place to begin was by removing temptation. Millie had already done this by stashing the trash cans. I recommended that she replace them with containers that were harder to get into and to continue keeping them out of Rebel's reach.

I noticed that Rebel tended to follow Millie around the house quite a bit, which is common in dogs who are nervous about being left alone. I suggested that she praise Rebel when the dog lay down some distance away. This would help Rebel get the idea that good things come to she who waits.

It was also important that Millie give Rebel more exercise, followed by a treat when she came back in. A tired, not-so-hungry dog is a content dog, I explained. And a content dog is less likely to go looking for trouble. Finally, I suggested that she and Rebel practice basic obedience commands, like "Sit" or "Stay." This would get Rebel back in the habit of trying to fulfill her owner's expectations, and then getting little rewards when she did well. After all, Rebel had received precious few bits of praise lately.

Just in case anything outside was stimulating the dog—Millie thought kids might be tapping on the windows to tease her—we closed the blinds. I asked Millie to leave a television or radio on while she was at work in order to mask any street noises, which could be contributing to Rebel's mischief-making.

And I made sure that Millie understood that she wasn't to punish the dog anymore—she had done a lot of yelling in the past three weeks, she admitted—because it would only lead to more anxiety. The idea was to create a very structured routine that would help Rebel feel more comfortable and give her more opportunities for praise.

As it turned out, this simple program worked like a charm. There was only one more bout of misbehavior the following week, and none at all after that. The last time Millie called, she explained that while Rebel may have found revenge to be sweet, she apparently found reconciliation even sweeter.

"By the way," she added, "I'm going away for Easter week."

"Oh, boy," I said. "Well, I have two words for you."

"Dog sitter," we said in unison.

FOR SOME DOGS, GOING TO A KENNEL is like being shipped to another continent. The first time especially, they don't know what to expect, and the disruption to their routine can be traumatic. But un-welcome surprises come in small packages as well. I'm thinking of simple things, like going to the veterinarian or the groomer. While most dogs breeze through these events without any problems at all, others fall to pieces—usually as soon as they get home.

This is what happened with Clover, an Irish wolfhound who had his dewclaws removed at seven months of age. After the op-eration—and for the rest of his life—Clover went berserk when anyone tried to touch his paws. He was suspicious of strangers and literally panicked when his owners took him to the vet.

I met Clover about 15 years ago and spent quite a bit of time trying to find solutions. I even suggested that the family take al-ternate routes to the vet's office so Clover at least would arrive in a calm state of mind. But Clover was an observant dog. If he recog-nized so much as a grocery store or a park along the way, he'd im-mediately go bananas. Today, of course, a number of vets use mo-bile vans to make house calls, but those weren't commonly used at the time.

Getting groomed, for some dogs, is no less traumatic than going to the vet. I'm thinking of a three-year-old cocker spaniel named Pooch. During a routine haircut, Pooch got nicked on the ear, and he never forgot it. His owners, Jerry and June Berkey, gave up trying to have him professionally groomed because he'd go bal-listic as soon as he saw where they were going. They decided to groom him at home, but the damage had already been done. The sight of the grooming area in their basement would launch Pooch into a frenzy of barking and biting. In fact, anything that re-minded him of grooming, even a brush touching his coat, would trigger a reaction.

"Pooch used to love being brushed," June explained when she called to talk about the problem. Cocker spaniels need grooming every two to three weeks to maintain their proper appearance, and Pooch was starting to look pretty scruffy. The only way to groom him anymore, June said, was to give him a strong tranquilizer pre-scribed by their vet. Even then, it was a gamble that Pooch would be calm enough to go through with it. Sometimes, they gambled wrong and were bitten anyway, despite all of their precautions.

Dogs with intense anxiety usually have a whole series of cues—sights, sounds, or smells—that cause their anxiety levels to gradually climb. For Pooch, these cues included the sight of a brush, walking down the basement stairs, and the sound of the clippers. Each cue would ratchet up the poor little dog's anxiety a notch. By the time he'd experienced several cues, he was almost a basket case.

I thought his reactions—biting, growling, and snapping—were pretty extreme, especially since they could be triggered by nothing worse than a nice brushing. But then I discovered another fact that made everything fall into place.

They'd just learned that Pooch had a skin allergy, June explained, which made him uncomfortable when people touched him. I put down my pencil for a moment. It didn't seem likely that the skin condition alone was uncomfortable enough to trigger Pooch's intense reactions, but it almost certainly made his fears worse. So I knew we had to deal with that before we'd be able to make any real progress.

Fortunately, their veterinarian had a lot of experience treating allergies, and he was able to relieve most of the irritation in just a few weeks. Once that was taken care of, I worked with the Berkeys to help desensitize Pooch to the horrors of grooming.

For starters, I asked the Berkeys to think of a place in the house that could be Pooch's special room—a place that Pooch wouldn't associate with fear or discomfort. The laundry room would be perfect, June decided. Pooch never had cause to go down there, and there was plenty of room to set up their grooming supplies.

Before they even thought about grooming Pooch or setting up their supplies, I explained that they should periodically take him to the laundry room and lavish him with treats, affection, and gentle strokes. I wanted Pooch to think, *This is a good place where I feel great, instead of a place where I get hurt. I like it here.*

Once Pooch clearly understood that the laundry room was a great place to be, I said, they should slip down there one day and leave one of the instruments of torture, such as a pair of scissors, on the floor and put a treat on top.

It didn't take Pooch long on his next visit downstairs to notice the scissors or the treat. He wasn't thrilled with this new development at first, but he definitely wanted the treat. So after a few false starts, he went over and snapped it up—and, of course, nothing happened. The Berkeys repeated this exercise several times, using different grooming tools. Pooch gradually learned that there was nothing to fear. Quite the contrary. Grooming tools, he discovered, often brought tasty rewards.

It was time to move to the next step. Once a day or so, I told the Berkeys, they should pick up the electric shears and, without turning them on, give Pooch a quick touch, then set them down and give him some praise. They were to do the same thing with the brush and scissors. It took a few weeks, but once again, Pooch was discovering that nothing bad was going to happen.

The final step, of course, was to actually begin grooming Pooch, not all at once, but maybe a few snips at a time. As he got more and more comfortable, I explained, they'd be able to groom him for longer periods. And eventually, that's exactly what happened. Within a month, they were giving Pooch full-fledged groomings and getting grateful looks instead of bites for their efforts.

MEDICAL PROCEDURES AND INANIMATE objects like scissors aren't the only things that can make life a bit too interesting for our unsuspecting canine friends. New people can be even more upsetting, especially little people. That's what a young border collie named Nell discovered when she started hanging out with her owners, Lila Bench and her boyfriend, Brad, in one of Atlanta's pleasant parks.

I met Lila and Brad in their cheaply furnished, tiny apartment. It wasn't a great place, except that it had a million-dollar view overlooking Piedmont Park. Lila was clearly devoted to Nell and her two cats, but just as clearly, she was very upset. Life had been going great, she explained, until fate intervened.

Nell was a playful dog who got along well with people and other pets. She trotted to work with Lila three days a week, keeping her company throughout the day. At night, Nell slept outside the bedroom door. She'd only come into the bedroom in the morning when it was time to wake her owners up. Then Lila or Brad—or both of them—would take Nell for a run before work. At night, they'd head to the park again for a game of Frisbee. If dogs think of Heaven, I thought, it probably looks a lot like this.

Enter a four-year-old child with a plastic sword. Lila was nearly crying as she told me what happened next.

"The little boy started hitting Nell with the sword, and he wouldn't stop when I told him to. By the time his mother caught up with him—she had been at the ice cream stand—Nell was really scared and cowering."

"That's a shame," I said. "Did she recover quickly?"

"Not really," Lila said. "She stood there sort of shaking for quite a while, and then we just went home because we were both upset."

This incident might not have been significant had not another one followed on its heels. This time the problem came in the form of an even younger child, a toddler marching through the park with a big carrot in each hand and, once again, some rather inattentive parents.

"Nell was just romping around and she saw this cute child with the carrots," Lila recalled. "Before I knew what was happening, Nell ran over and grabbed one of the carrots out of the kid's hand and nipped her right on the face. The child started wailing and her parents came running over. That's when I sort of lost it."

I couldn't imagine this gentle young woman losing it, but Brad quickly confirmed her story. "She went berserk," he said.

Lila had immediately tackled Nell and pinned her to the

ground. "She struggled to get up, but I wouldn't let her move a muscle," Lila said.

"Was the child hurt?" I asked.

"Not really," said Brad. "Her parents swept her off pretty quickly, though. They didn't hang around to discuss it or anything."

"So what happened with Nell?" I asked.

"Well, I must have kept her on the ground for about 10 minutes," Lila said. "She wanted to get up, but I wouldn't let her. I couldn't believe she had bitten that baby for no reason."

"I guarantee she had a reason," I said, trying to make her feel better. "Not a socially acceptable reason, but one that made sense to her."

"Why would she do that?"

"I really don't know," I said. "It is strange that this would happen out of the blue. She's never attacked anyone else, right?"

"No!" said Lila quickly.

"That's not quite true," Brad said. "What about that time she wouldn't let the maintenance man in? And she growled at your niece, and we had to shut her in the bedroom."

"You're right," Lila said in a small voice. "I forgot about those. But she didn't bite anyone."

"Let's get back to the park," I said. "What else happened?"

"After about 10 minutes, a dog friend of Nell's came up to us. I was calming down, so I let Nell up. But instead of playing, she tucked her tail and ran off."

"Uh-oh."

"I chased her all through the park," Lila said.

Finally, she caught Nell and brought her home. That should have been the end of it, but after that Nell was a changed dog. Whenever they passed a child, Lila said, Nell would lunge as though she wanted to bite. It had gotten to the point that she and Brad were afraid to take her out anymore.

"Nell probably associates the pain and trauma of the punishment—you holding her down—with the little girl," I reasoned. "Even though you punished her, it was the child she was focusing on."

Lila responded by hanging her head. "She could be afraid of you now, too," Brad said, trying to give a little comfort. He wasn't too far off, actually. She was lucky.

At any rate, the couple had decided that Nell would have to be under their control when they were outside the apartment, but the leash itself was a problem. Nell wasn't used to it and didn't like it one bit. And that's where I came in.

Here was this great dog with some aggressive tendencies who just happened to meet up with the wrong people. Now she was more reactive than ever. I agreed that Nell would have to be leashed in the future. To keep her under control while she got used to the idea of being leashed, I suggested they try the Gentle Leader, a device that I've mentioned previously.

This gives owners a big advantage. Even a dog the size of a border collie can be pretty powerful if she is determined to lunge or pull her owner along. With the Gentle Leader, however, she'll quickly learn that pulling or lunging won't accomplish anything, and she might as well walk quietly. At the same time, of course, the system helps keep other people safe.

This was only a defensive measure. To really resolve the problem, we needed something more. And it just so happened that the key to helping Nell dropped right into Lila's lap.

Someone had given Lila a doll. It was three feet tall, about the same size as the kids who had started Nell on her life of crime. Rather than wait to see how the dog would do with real kids, which would have been too dangerous, Lila and I agreed that we would try to fool Nell with the doll. I knew from experience that this was possible, and it was preferable to putting someone at risk.

I thought that with a little practice we might be able to teach Nell to act entirely different when she was near a child. Here's what we did. I set the doll outside the apartment with a dog treat concealed in its hand. Then I told Lila to come out of the apartment with Nell. As they approached the doll, Nell's expression quickly became ominous. She seemed to be thinking, *Hey, kid, get away from my door—I eat shrimps like you for breakfast.*

As they got a little closer, however, Nell's expression changed. *Oh, my gosh, what kind of kid is this?* she seemed to be thinking. *And what is that nice smell?* She walked right up to the doll and nosed the treat from its hand. Any idea she may have entertained about launching an attack was forgotten as she crunched and swallowed the treat.

Before I left, I told Brad and Lila to keep practicing with the doll. They should move it from one place to another, I said. I also recommended that Brad stand near the doll and move it around a little when Nell approached. They used this ploy for about a week, and, believe it or not, Nell always behaved as though the doll were a real child—a child she no longer wanted to attack.

By this time, I was confident that Nell would do pretty well with children in the park. She still had to be restrained, of course, but the real danger seemed to have passed. I recommended that Lila and Brad not allow strangers to come right up and pet Nell since there was no way to be sure that she wouldn't react. What they could do, however, was hand strangers, especially children, dog treats and ask them to toss them a few feet in front of Nell. Most everyone liked doing this, so soon Nell was getting more than her share of treats, along with some extra positive attention.

On top of this, I recommended that Lila and Brad come up with a list of Nell's happy words, like "Outside," that they could use to lighten Nell's mood if she ever showed a flash of bad temper. It turned out to be a rather lengthy list because in spite of her troubles, lots of things made this dog smile.

Nell didn't change overnight, but after about 10 weeks, Lila said, they were no longer worried about how Nell would do with children. They did save the Gentle Leader, which they used when Lila's niece came to visit. After all, why tempt fate again?

ONE OF THE BIGGEST SHOCKS FOR a dog—and one that often causes conflicts deep in the canine heart—is the arrival of a new baby. The dog understands right away that this tiny, squalling bundle of joy is part of the human clan and, by extension, part of the dog's family. He also understands that all of a sudden the baby is getting an awful lot of attention and he's getting hardly any at all. As you might expect, this can cause a lot of problems.

I was a bit surprised when I answered the phone one day and heard Luke Stillman on the line. I had first met Luke and his wife, Barbara, several years before when their Gordon setter, McGee, suffered from a worrisome case of separation anxiety. It had been a fairly simple case, and McGee got over it fairly quickly. I hadn't expected to hear from them again.

Luke and Barbara were getting ready to have their first baby, Luke explained. He was hoping that I might be able to drop by and answer some questions that had them concerned.

"McGee doesn't seem to like kids very much," Luke said when we got together a week later. "And Barbara is worrying herself sick about it."

I've been asked more than once to help prepare dogs for their owners' blessed events. I wish more people would think ahead this way before mixing together babies and dogs, because there are enough adjustments to worry about when the baby comes home. The pets often find themselves lost in the shuffle, which can create behavioral problems on top of behavioral problems.

"I want McGee to like the baby, and I don't want him to feel left out of things," Barbara said. "I don't want to have to shut him in a room just because we're worried."

"There's no reason you should have to," I said, greeting the dog with a few pats. "But you mentioned that he doesn't seem to like kids. Why do you say that?" I had suddenly remembered that McGee once lived across the street from an elementary school. If there is one experience that can turn dogs against kids, what with the inevitable teasing through the fence, this had to be it.

"We tried him out with a baby and a preschooler recently," Barbara began.

My eyebrows went up. "Really?" I asked. Talk about human guinea pigs.

"Yeah, the preschooler was here visiting, and McGee didn't do all that great. He was okay as long as Jordan was sitting down or not moving . . ."

"What did he do the rest of the time?" I broke in.

"Well, he actually snapped at Jordan once when he was running around."

"Okay," I said. Understandable, but not good. "And what about the baby?" I was almost afraid to ask.

"Well," said Luke, "that was pretty interesting. Barbara was holding him while she sat on the couch. McGee climbed right up on the couch and practically climbed on top of them."

Barbara stroked McGee, who was lying happily by her side. "Poor McGee," she said. "Not too jealous, are you?"

The story I'd just heard was worrisome. McGee was obviously very attached to Barbara, and he was just as obviously showing signs of jealousy. Throw in a new baby and there was clearly the potential for problems. Still, I didn't think it would be too hard to change McGee's behavior. The key, I knew, was exposure: I wanted to get McGee totally accustomed to the sights, sounds, and smells of babies before a real one came into the house. By that time, he'd consider it old hat. No surprises.

For starters, I asked the Stillmans to borrow their neighbor's baby again and tape-record all those baby sounds—the gurgling, screaming, crying, yelling, laughing, and anything else that came out of his mouth. Then, once a day or so, they should get McGee settled down very comfortably. They were to play the tape at a very low volume, stroking him all the time. What dog could have a problem with that? Not McGee.

Next, I asked them to finish equipping the nursery if they hadn't done it already. I didn't want McGee to wake up one day and suddenly notice that Barbara's home office was missing and all this new stuff had taken its place. Once the nursery was equipped, I said, they should encourage McGee to go in and look around. In fact, they should encourage him to sleep there if he wanted to.

After this, I recommended that they get one of those dolls that cry when you press a switch. The idea was to give McGee a glimpse of the sights and sounds of a real baby. I also suggested that they borrow a soiled diaper from the neighbors. (I figured this was one loan they wouldn't have to repay.) Dogs experience the world largely through their sense of smell. When the baby finally came, this would be one more area where McGee would be fore-warned. Again, no surprises.

As part of an ongoing program, I said, they should display or use the various pieces of baby gear at different times and in dif-ferent places. Each time McGee was exposed to the objects, they should ask him to sit quietly and praise and pet him when he did. McGee ate all this up, they told me during one of our follow-up phone calls. He was curious about all the goings-on, but he seemed comfortable with everything so far.

What McGee was learning was that all these baby smells, sights, and sounds were perfectly safe. He was also getting the mes-sage that the baby was a person whom he should treat like other people. This was to ensure that he didn't mentally label the baby as potential prey—a rare occurrence, but one that is possible. I gave the Stillmans one or two tips about not ever leaving the baby and McGee alone in the same room—the same advice I would give regarding any infant or toddler and any dog.

I encouraged them to relieve the dog of any protection re-sponsibilities he may have been encouraged to take on. People often think that it is a good idea to train their dogs to be watch-dogs for the children. But this can be a dangerous game, since dogs aren't always discriminating about whom they bite. I asked them not to reward the dog for barking or growling at strangers, rushing to the window when he heard a sound, or stationing himself be-tween family members and visitors. This type of behavior was to be ignored or corrected. Behavior that was calm and quiet was to be encouraged and rewarded.

The Stillmans were the perfect clients, willing to try and do anything to protect their baby as well as their dog. After our initial visit and a few follow-up calls, I didn't hear from them for a while and I assumed everything had gone fine.

Several weeks later, Luke called. They had had a little girl, he told me. Her name was Jillian and she'd been home for just a week.

Luke had turned into the proverbial proud papa, and he couldn't stop talking about the baby. I let him go on for a few minutes, but all the time I was wondering about McGee. Maybe he'd been forgotten after all.

"And McGee is doing great," Luke said. "He just loves the baby, so there aren't any problems at all."

I finally exhaled. One week down, only five to six years to go. I gave Luke my congratulations and told him not to throw away my phone number—just in case.

WHEN PEOPLE THINK OF EVENTS THAT can throw a dog's emotions into a tailspin, they usually imagine things like abuse, teasing, or simply neglect. And in fact, these types of "surprises" often result in rather serious behavioral problems. But it's important to remember that dogs, unlike humans, don't understand everything that's going on around them. They don't know, for example, that they're going to a kennel because you won't be home to feed them. All they know is that one day they're home getting their ears scratched, and the next day they're in this strange place all alone, and they don't have the slightest idea why. For this reason, even small changes in a dog's life can feel like very big events.

In today's combined families, dogs have to cope with more "strangers"—new step-parents, roommates, and significant others—than ever before. This leads to confusion as the dogs try to figure out who these new people are and, more important, why they're getting all the attention. For pets as well as people, jealousy can be a dangerous emotion, as Ross Cutler was discovering.

I've known Ross for quite a few years, ever since I helped his dog, a beautiful Akita named Cheyenne, get through some rather tough times when they moved to Ross's new home in Atlanta. Now there was another problem. Ross's significant other, Maxwell

Hawkins, had moved in three weeks before, and Cheyenne was making their life miserable.

"Never mind offering me unconditional love and all that stuff," Max said when we met. "I'd settle for having this dog let me say good morning without biting the heck out of me."

"That doesn't seem like much," I agreed.

Max had been a regular visitor to the house for a long time before he moved in, and Cheyenne never seemed to mind. But once he moved in with all his belongings, Cheyenne went on the warpath. She would stand, sit, or lie between the two men every chance she got.

Even as Ross and Max were describing the problem, I noticed Cheyenne edging her way over from the fireplace. She quietly positioned herself directly in front of Ross—her way of letting us all know, in no uncertain terms, that Ross belonged to her and no one else.

Ross had gotten Cheyenne when she was a puppy four years before, and he'd always lavished her with attention. I also knew that Ross tended to encourage Cheyenne's natural protectiveness, so the current situation wasn't all that surprising. At the same time, I couldn't blame Max for being worried. Cheyenne looked pretty serious, and Akitas are never a breed to mess with.

If Cheyenne had done nothing more than stand guard or push her way between the two men, the situation wouldn't have been so serious. But I learned that Cheyenne had bitten Max twice. On more than one occasion, she growled when he tried to come into the bedroom at night. This was putting a strain on the couple's relationship, to say the least. I asked what had triggered the biting.

"Last week I was playing catch with Cheyenne, and she wouldn't give up the tennis ball," Max said. "That's when she bit me. I didn't realize she was so possessive."

Actually, this behavior fit right into what they had been describing. Dogs can get extremely emotional about their toys, and it's not surprising that an old tennis ball served as a flash point in a turf war between a dog and what she perceived as a human interloper. In much the same way, Cheyenne obviously considered Ross part of her "stuff," too.

"Max, why don't you pick out some new toys for Cheyenne?" I said. "That might help you begin a relationship of your own." I told him about a relatively new toy called a Buster Cube, which holds dog treats inside hidden compartments. As the dog shoves the toy around and pushes it with his nose or paws, bits of food will occasionally fall out. Some dogs will play with these toys for hours.

"Just leave the tug-of-war stuff at the store," I added.

"Don't worry," Max said.

I also suggested that Max take some real responsibility for the dog. Besides playing with her, he should feed her some of the time. It would also be good to take her for walks—with Ross at first and later by himself.

"What should I be doing?" Ross asked. "Or not doing?"

"You should be taking the responsibility of protecting you away from Cheyenne," I said. "And you should be praising anything she does that is compliant to you and to Max."

With these suggestions, the two were able to gradually bring Cheyenne around to accept Max as a perfectly acceptable new person in her main man's house. The key was for Max, the "intruder," to create some real ownership of Cheyenne. Once that was done, Cheyenne could reciprocate and claim some ownership of her new buddy.

NO MATTER HOW MUCH WE TRY TO change the ways in which dogs fit into our lifestyles, in the end it's always the dog who chooses how he's initially going to behave. We can take it, leave it, or take steps to change it.

I continually marvel at the sheer number of things that can go wrong with our canine friends. No matter how much we protect and pamper them, every day they confront confusing and stressful environments that their ancestors never had to cope with. It's up to us, their owners, to help them make the adjustments.

My hat is off to those owners—like most of those I've mentioned in this book—who feel that their dogs deserve full and happy lives and are willing to do whatever it takes to resolve any problems that happen to crop up. We know in our hearts that our devoted dogs would do the same for us if they could. That's what best friends are all about.

Suggested Reading

My clients occasionally ask me to recommend books that deal with their dogs' specific problems such as house-soiling, biting, phobias, or destructive behavior. Sometimes they just want to know more about dog behavior or dog training, especially training that will teach them how to get their dogs to do what they want them to in a humane yet effective way.

Some of the books I recommend are the same ones used by professionals in their work as applied animal behaviorists, and all of them are wonderful resources for understanding dogs more fully. In the list below are some of my favorites, along with a few comments about each.

Askew, Henry. *Treatment of Behaviour Problems in Dogs and Cats: A Guide for the Small Animal Veterinarian.* Oxford: Blackwell Science, 1996.

> A clearly presented guide for the small animal veterinarian and educated dog owner. It deals with pets in the family, understanding dog behavior and behavioral problems, and general treatment principles.

Dodman, Nicholas H. *Psychopharmacology of Animal Behavior Disorders.* Oxford: Blackwell Science, 1997.

> Organized by behavioral problems, this book addresses the use of drugs and how they work in the treatment of behavioral disorders.

Houpt, Katherine A. *The Veterinary Clinics of North America Small Animal Practice, Progress in Companion Animal Behavior,* vol. 27, no. 3. Philadelphia: W. B. Saunders Co., 1998.

> Includes fascinating chapters on topics such as puppy socialization classes, dog communication, and the assessment and treatment of barking.

Landsberg, Gary M., Hunthausen, Wayne, and Ackermann, Lowell, eds. *Handbook of Behavior Problems of the Dog and Cat.* London: Butterworth-Heinemann, 1997.

> A clearly written how-to book that addresses common behavioral problems.

Overall, Karen L. *Clinical Small Animal Behavior*. St. Louis: Mosby, 1997.

The chapter, "Normal Canine Behavior," is a scholarly review of the scientific literature on behavior—it's my favorite chapter in the book. The book as a whole is most appropriate for the professional animal behaviorist.

Reid, P.J. *Excel-erated Learning: Explaining in Plain English How Dogs Learn and How Best to Teach Them*. Oakland, Calif.: James and Kenneth Publishers, 1996.

This is a very readable book on the use of learning theory and its application to training and the treatment of common behavioral problems in dogs. Trainers particularly will regard this as a valuable resource.

Serpell, James, ed. *The Domestic Dog: Its Evolution, Behaviour and Interactions with People*. New York: Cambridge University Press, 1996.

This book takes a scholarly approach. Especially interesting are chapters on social and communicative behaviors and canine aggression—a must for grad students.

Voith, Victoria L. and Borchelt, Peter L., eds. *Readings in Companion Animal Behavior*. Trenton, N.J.: Veterinary Learning Systems Co., 1996.

The chapters consist of summaries of important research—for example, development of canine behavior and dog bites to people—as well as straightforward, easy-to-follow chapters on topics such as teaching sit and stay, punishment, fears and phobias, and separation anxiety. This book is found on most of my colleagues' bookshelves.

To obtain a list of applied animal behaviorists certified by the Animal Behavior Society or for information about careers in animal behavior, you can write:

Animal Behavior Society
2611 East 10th Street, Office 170
Indiana University
Bloomington, IN 47408-2603
Web site: www.cisab.indiana.edu/ABS

Index

B

M

N

O